高等学校英语专业系列教材
Textbook Series for Tertiary English Majors

高等学校英语专业系列教材 求知 STEM
Textbook Series for Tertiary English Majors

总 主 编 石 坚

副总主编 黄国文 陈建平 张绍杰 蒋洪新

编委单位（排名不分先后）

广东外语外贸大学	华南农业大学
广西大学	陕西师范大学
云南大学	武汉大学
中山大学	贵州大学
中南大学	贵州师范大学
四川大学	重庆大学
东北师范大学	重庆邮电大学
西安外国语大学	湖南师范大学
西安交通大学	......
华中师范大学	

高等学校英语专业系列教材
Textbook Series for Tertiary English Majors

STEM | 求知

总 主 编：石 坚
副总主编：黄国文 陈建平 张绍杰 蒋洪新

国际组织与国际公务员培养

E

International Organizations:
Shaping Multilateralism through the International Civil Service

主 编 葛静静

重庆大学出版社

图书在版编目（CIP）数据

国际组织与国际公务员培养：英文／葛静静主编
. -- 重庆：重庆大学出版社，2025.6
求知高等学校英语专业系列教材
ISBN 978-7-5689-3929-4

Ⅰ.①国… Ⅱ.①葛… Ⅲ.①国际组织—英语—高等
学校—教材②国际组织—公务员制度—英语—高等学校—
教材 Ⅳ.①D813

中国国家版本馆CIP数据核字（2023）第095138号

国际组织与国际公务员培养

葛静静　主　编

责任编辑：杨　琪　　版式设计：孙　婷
责任校对：刘志刚　　责任印制：赵　晟

*

重庆大学出版社出版发行

出版人：陈晓阳

社址：重庆市沙坪坝区大学城西路21号

邮编：401331

电话：（023）88617190　88617185（中小学）

传真：（023）88617186　88617166

网址：http://www.cqup.com.cn

邮箱：fxk@cqup.com.cn（营销中心）

全国新华书店经销

重庆天旭印务有限责任公司印刷

*

开本：787mm×1092mm　1/16　印张：18　字数：471千
2025年6月第1版　　2025年6月第1次印刷
ISBN 978-7-5689-3929-4　　定价：60.00元

总　序

　　进入 21 世纪，高等教育呈现快速扩展的趋势。我国高等教育从外延式发展过渡到内涵式发展后，"质量"已成为教育改革与发展的关键词。由国务院颁布的《国家中长期教育改革和发展规划纲要（2010 年—2020 年）》（以下简称《纲要》）明确要求狠抓本科教育人才培养存在的主要问题，厘清高等教育人才培养目标、理念、社会需求，制订本科教学培养模式、教学内容和方法、质量保障与评估机制，切实提高人才培养的质量。我国英语专业在过去的数十年中经过几代人的努力，取得了显著的成绩和长足的发展。特别是近年来随着经济社会的快速发展和对外交流活动的增多，"一带一路"倡议的提出和"讲好中国故事"的需要，英语专业的学科地位也随之大大提升，目前规模发展得十分庞大。英语专业虽然经历了一个"跨越式""超常规"的发展历程，但规模化发展带来的培养质量下滑、专业建设和人才需求出现矛盾、毕业生就业面临巨大挑战等严峻的现实表明，英语专业的教育、教学与育人又到了一个不得不改的关键时刻。

　　《纲要》在强调狠抓培养质量的同时，也提出了培养"具有国际视野、通晓国际规则、能够参与国际事务和国际竞争"人才的战略方针。基于这样的战略需求，外语专业教学指导委员会明确提出了人才"多元培养，分类卓越"的理念。基于这样的理念，《普通高等学校本科专业类教学质量国家标准》（外国语言文学类）（以下简称《国标》）对英语专业本科的现有课程设置提出新的改革思路：英语专业课程体系包括公共课程、专业核心课程、专业方向课程、实践环节和毕业论文（设计）五个部分；逐步压缩英语技能课程，用"内容依托式"课程替代传统的英语技能课程，系统建设语言学、文学、文化、国别研究等方面的专业课程。

　　自 2001 年开始，在重庆大学出版社的大力支持下，我们成立了由华中、华南、西南、西北以及东北地区的知名专家、学者和教学一线教师组成的"求知高等学校英语专业系列教材"编写组，以《高等学校英语专业英语教学大纲》为依据，将社会的需求与培养外语人才的全面发展紧密结合，注重英语作为一个专业的学科系统性和科学性，注重英语教学和习得的方法与规律，培养学生能力和育人并举，突出特色和系列教材的内在逻辑关系，反映了当时教学改革的新理念并具有前瞻性，建立了与英语专业课程配套的新教材体系。"求知高等学校英语专业系列教材"经历了十余年教学实践的锤炼，通过不断的修订来契合教学的发展变化，在教材的整体性和开放性、学生基本技能和实际应用能力的培养、学生的人文素质和跨文化意识的培养这三方面上有所突破。通过这套系列教材的开发建设工作，我们一直在探讨新的教学理念、模式，探索英语专业人才培养的新路子。今天，我们以《国标》为依据，回顾我们过去十多年在教学改革上所做的努力，我们欣慰地看到我们的方向是契合英语专业学科定位和发展的。随着《国标》指导思想的明确，为了适应英语专业学科课程设置的进一步调整，我们对"求知高等学校英语专业系列教材"进行了新一轮的建设工作。

全新的系列教材力求在以下方面有所创新：

第一， 围绕听、说、读、写、译五种能力的培养来构建教材体系。在教材内容的总体设置上，颠覆以往"以课程定教材"的观念，不再让教材受制于刻板的课程设置体系，而是引入课程大纲（Program）理念，根据《国标》中对学生的能力要求，针对某方面的具体能力编写对应的系列教材。读写和听说系列不再按照难度区分混合编排题材，而是依据文体或专业性质的自然划分，分门别类地专册呈现，便于教师在教学中根据实际需要搭配组合使用。例如，阅读教材分为小说类、散文类、新闻类等；口语教材分为基本表述、演讲、辩论等专题成册。

第二，将五种能力的提升融入人文素养的综合提升之中。坚持英语专业教育的人文本位，强调文化熏陶。在跨学科新专业不断涌现的背景下，盲目追求为每种新专业都专门编写一套教材，费时费力。最佳的做法是坚持英语专业核心教材的人文性，培养学生优秀的语言文化素养，并在此基础上依照专业要求填补相关知识上的空缺，形成新的教材配比模式和体系。

第三，以"3E"作为衡量教材质量的标准。教材的编写上，体现参与（Engaging）、赋能（Enabling）、启迪（Enlightening）的"3E"功能，强调教材的人文性与语言文化综合能力的培养，淡化技能解说。

第四，加入"微课""翻转课堂"等元素，便于课堂互动的开展。创新板块、活动的设计，相对减少灌输式的授课（lecture），增加学生参与的研讨（seminar）。

我们希望通过对这套系列教材的全新修订和建设，落实《国标》精神，继续推动高等学校英语专业教学改革，为提高英语专业人才的培养质量探索新的实践方法，为英语专业的学生拓展求知的新空间。

"求知高等学校英语专业系列教材"编委会

Foreword

By Neville Cant[1]

For the majority of uninformed people, including myself, we view International Organisations (IOs), in their broadest terms, as being very bureaucratic, money needy and achieving little to help mankind to live in peace with each other and our environment—even with the best of intentions. Moreover, there is a perception that joining their ranks requires personal connections rather than professional expertise. However, Jingjing's book challenges these misconceptions by exploring the evolution, purpose, and necessity of such organizations, with a particular focus on the United Nations (UN).

Jingjing humanizes the bureaucrats behind these institutions, shedding light on their varied roles and the critical contributions they make—often unnoticed by the public. She has put a human face to these hardworking individuals who actually make such a difference to the world in a way that makes permanent change for our betterment.

The most important part is that she has removed the mask, opened the pathway and door for the specialists of the future who wish to contribute to a positive world and provided advice that only comes from those who have gone before them. The

---

1 This foreword was kindly provided by Nev at my invitation as the editor. Below is a brief self-introduction from my dear friend Nev: "I'm a very average person who was fortunate enough to grow up on the land in Otago, New Zealand, with a balance for our environment. Like so many people in life, there are tragedies but also many good times, from helping people to grow their wealth, and then returning to farming both for health and sanity of the soul. After I had recently left the land, a whole new culture and life awaited me in Auckland where I shared many wonderful discussions with the editor. I am so grateful to her and friends for all I have through balance and having a place to restore my soul."

understanding of their high standards of integrity, dependence and willingness, gives potential applicants an excellent way forward making one wish he were forty years younger and restarting life.

She then finishes with some real people and examples of achievements, frustrations and their perseverance in extremely challenging situations where the reader can understand the commitment these servants make on our behalf.

This is a truly enlightening book that engages you from start to finish with so much in between.

It is a great privilege to have read and experienced a vital part of our society that many of us take for granted. I wish those many new recruits much success using this book with a lightened path to a bright future and the differences they will make for our world.

Preface

To be an international civil servant is the top dream job for millions of young people around the world.[1] Things are basically the same here in China. But why do international organizations exist? What is it like to work for an international organization such as the United Nations? And, how can a fresh graduate without work experience pitch an application to an international organization? The questions raised present intriguing leads for academic research.

This book tries to offer the perspectives of field workers with relevant expertise on these fundamental topics and is structured around these issues. In general, this book is broken up into two main parts. The first part contains a sketch of a theoretical framework for the study and analysis of international organizations. The second part includes feasible instructions for applying to international organizations. Details are provided as below.

Part I first provides an overview of the legal principles governing International Organizations (IOs). The term "international organization" is used here as "a cluster concept which does not depend on a set of fixed criteria" so as to avoid leaving out organizations that could have an impact on the global order.[2] International organizations come in many different forms, but one way to categorize them is by dividing them into Inter-Governmental Organizations (IGOs) and Non-Governmental Organizations

---

1   Wei Liu, "China Wants More Chinese to Work in International Organizations", *The Diplomat*, August 24th, 2018.

2   Angelo Golia and Anne Peters, "The Concept of International Organization", Max Planck Institute for Comparative Public Law & International Law (MPIL) Research Paper, No.2020-27, in: Jan Klabbers (ed.), *Cambridge Companion to International Organizations Law*, Cambridge: Cambridge University Press, 2022.

(NGOs). For illustration, some exemplary Inter-Governmental Organizations, are provided, like the UN, the ASEAN, and the EU. Examples of Non-Governmental Organizations won't be given due to space restrictions.

Three major theoretical perspectives on the role of international organizations in world politics are then covered—namely, realism, liberal institutionalism, and constructivism. Specifically, (*neo-*)realists maintain that international organizations are the means by which states achieve their self-interest, and, thus, contribute little to global peace and security; (*neo-*)liberals, on the other hand, believe that international organizations encourage cooperation by establishing a forum for member-states to pursue common interests, and that they constrain the behaviour of member-states through enforcing institutional norms and rules. In a similar vein, constructivists argue that international institutions would develop their own identities, and could precipitate member-states to coordinate even if their power-maximizing interests are not satisfied.[1]

The remainder of this part presents perspectives on the development of the modern international civil service, examines the changing roles of the international civil servants, and suggests potential directions for international administration (include, civil service recruitment, management, and training) so that readers can get a glimpse of how international organizations are staffed. See Chapter 3 and later in Chapter 4 for more details. It is crucial to understand that, the primary purpose of staff positions (such as those held by specialists of different kinds, administrative support staff, and personnel responsible for liaising with governments and with other international organizations, etc.) is to assist in implementing the objectives of the organization (i.e., the establishment of long- or medium-term plans).[2]

The relevant information and job-hunting advice can be found in **Part II** for all those interested in careers within the IGOs and NGOs. To emphasize, the aim here is not to give readers a complete picture of all international organization positions. Rather, it is

---

1 See e.g., Lisa Martin and Beth Simmons, "International Organizations and Institutions", in Walter Carlsnaes, Thomas Risse and Beth A. Simmons (eds.), *Handbook of International Relations*, Sage Publications, 2012, pp.326-351; Endalcachew Bayeh, "Theories on the Role of International Organizations in Maintaining Peace and Security", *International Journal of Multidisciplinary Research and Development*, v.1, n.7, 2014, p.347; Liesbet Hooghe, Tobias Lenz, and Gary Marks (eds.), *A Theory of International Organization*, Oxford Scholarship Online, 2019.

2 Norman A. Graham and Robert S. Jordan (eds.), *The International Civil Service: Changing Role and Concepts*, Pergamon Press, published in cooperation with UNIAR, 1980, p.28.

to widen their exposure to and access to professional prospects in international affairs by encouraging them to think "outside the box".

For this purpose, Chapter 5 summarizes the major college and career pathways by which students can acquire skill sets that are recognized and in demand, and that might prepare them for careers in international organizations. It also offers advice on how to network, write resumes, interview for jobs, and maintain an online presence. Cressey et. al (2014), for instance, recommended that, candidates should pay close attention to nationality restrictions when looking at employment openings. An outstanding illustration of this is the UN Young Professionals Program (YPP), whose examination, in the annual recruitment exercise, is exclusively open to nationals of participating countries—the list of which varies from year to year.[1]

Chapter 6 covers informative testimonies about what these jobs in international organizations are really like from both junior and senior professionals active in these fields. Miss Bi Fei, a current English teacher in the College Student Learning and Development Center of New Oriental Education and Technology Group, Mr. Christopher Crachiola, a former US Peace Corps volunteer instructor at Sichuan International Studies University (SISU), and Mr. Zhao Yao, an energy specialist at the World Bank Group, are just a few of the people who generously share their knowledge and experience. Through the aforementioned personal narratives and insights, it is anticipated that the readers will realize that their future can hold the career of their dreams, and that a world of opportunities awaits them as they become more open-minded and gain new perspectives on life.

1　Laura E. Cressey, Barrett J. Helmer and Jennifer E. Steffensen (eds.), *Careers in International Affairs* (9th edition), Georgetown University Press, 2014, p.109.

Table of Contents

Part II　Practice-Based Guideline

Part I

Theoretical Background

Chapter 1

An Introduction to International Organizations

We need support from many regional and sub-regional organizations. We need support from business communities, we need support from religious communities and local communities and even philanthropic organizations, first of all, to solidify our political will.

— Ban Ki-moon, former Secretary-General of the UN[1]

---

1   "Ban Calls on World Leaders to Emulate Mandela's Example to Bring Peace in 2014", *UN News: Global Perspective Human Stores*, December 16th, 2013.

Overview

Learning Objectives

a. To understand the different meanings associated with the term "international organization";

b. To describe the creation, design and effectiveness of international organizations as institutional forms, and make sense of their trajectories of change;

c. To review the main theories and academic perspectives applied to the study of international organizations, focusing on how the role of international organizations has been conceptualized across the different academic disciplines.

Main Contents

Against the backdrop of creating world interdependence, international organizations play an increasingly important role in tackling the world's biggest issues and are still carrying out important tasks—where they can. The purpose of this chapter is to advance the understanding of international organizations by viewing them in the milieu of world politics. For this end, this chapter provides an overview of the historical processes, basic set-ups, functions, and responsibilities of international organizations. It will then proceed to investigate the sources and nature of international institutions from theoretical perspectives. The theories discussed below include *neo*-realism, *neo*-liberal institutionalism, as well as constructivism—and its theory of institutions being a socially constructed concept determined by the sharing of ideas.[1] It will finally conclude with the idea that international organizations play a crucial role "as a stage for States to bring matters to the attention of the international community".[2]

---

1 Sophie Crockett, "The Role of International Organizations in World Politics", *E-International Relations*, February 7th, 2012.

2 Ibid.

Warm-up

Quick quiz: test your knowledge about the international organizations before you get started.

1. What was the first generally recognized international organization?

   A. The League of Nations.

   B. The World Trade Organization.

   C. The Organization of American States.

   D. The Central Commission for Navigation on the Rhine.

2. What global organization was founded in *The Treaty of Versailles* and sought to guarantee global peace through "collective security"?

   A. The United Nations.

   B. The League of Nations.

   C. The Freedom House.

   D. The World Trade Organization.

3. What two security organizations dominated the Cold War era?

   A. The Security Council and the North Atlantic Treaty Organization.

   B. The North Atlantic Treaty Organization and the Comintern.

   C. The North Atlantic Treaty Organization and the Warsaw Pact.

   D. The Anti Comintern Axis Organization and the League of Nations.

4. What organization is made up of mostly former British colonies?

   A. The Commonwealth of Nations.

   B. The League of Nations.

   C. The Organization for African Unity.

   D. The North Atlantic Treaty Organization.

5. What characterizes Geneva as an international city?

   A. The fact that different languages are spoken there.

   B. The fact that there is an international airport.

   C. The presence of a large number of important international organizations.

   D. Because many nice people live in Geneva.

6. How many countries are members of the United Nations?

   A. 187.

   B. 190.

C. 193.

D. 201.

7. Which of the following UN organs has the authority to issue binding resolutions on all member states?

A. The General Assembly.

B. The Security Council.

C. The International Court of Justice.

D. The Economic and Social Council.

8. Which world organization uses commonly the letters UNESCO instead of its whole name?

A. The UN Education, Science and Culture Organization.

B. The UN Educational, Scientific and Cultural Organization.

C. The UN Educational, Social, and Central Organization.

D. The UN Educational, Sociology and Cult Organization.

9. Which of the following institutions cannot be considered as international organizations?

A. The United Nations.

B. The World Health Organization.

C. The Government of Norway.

D. The World Food Programme.

10. What large international organization had its humble beginnings with the European Coal and Steel Community (ECSC)?

A. The European Organization for Nuclear Research (CERN).

B. The European Atomic Energy Community (Euratom).

C. The European Union (EU).

D. The Western European Union (WEU).

Section 1

The Basics about International Organizations

1.1　Concept Definition

An international organization is an organization with an international membership, scope, or presence.[1] It can be defined, following *The International Law Commission*, as an "organization established by a treaty or other instrument governed by international law and possessing its own international legal personality".[2] International organizations usually have states as members, but often other entities can also apply for membership. The two main types of international organizations are Inter-Governmental Organizations (IGOs) and international Non-Governmental Organizations (NGOs).

Inter-Governmental Organizations (IGOs), also known as Multi-Governmental Organizations: the type of organization most closely associated with the term "international organization". These are organizations that are made up primarily of sovereign states (referred to as member states), and whose members are held together by treaty or other inter-governmental agreement, to carry out projects and plans in common interest. Notable examples include the United Nations (UN), the European Union (EU), the International Labour Organization (ILO) and the International Monetary Fund (IMF).

The Yearbook of International Organizations, which aims to identify and list all "international organizations", according to a broad range of criteria,[3] defines such bodies as:

　　a. being based on a formal instrument of agreement between the governments of member states;

　　b. including three or more nation states as parties to the agreement;

　　c. possessing a permanent secretariat performing ongoing tasks.

1　Frederi P. Miller, Agnes F. Vandome, John McBrewster, *International Organization*, Alphascript Publishing, 2010, p.1.

2　Louis de Gouyon Matignon, "The Differences between International and Supranational Organizations", in *Space Legal Issues*, July 17th, 2019.

3　*The Yearbook of International Organizations* includes detailed information on 74,000 international organizations from 300 countries and territories, 42,000 of which are active organization. *The Yearbook* is a trusted tool for studies and research in all subjects of civil society activities, including Political Science, Law, International Studies, International Relations, Sociology, Demography and Peace Studies. See more in the official website of Union of International Associations.

Armstrong et al. (2016) identified three essential conditions for an international governmental organization to exist: first, independent political communities; second, rules agreed among such communities that purport to regulate their relations with each other; and third, a formal structure to implement and enforce the rules.[1] It is significant that, without the first, a regulatory structure would be essentially imperial or hegemonial, even if it were not actually part of a single polity; without the second, orderly relations, where they existed, would be a random consequence of informal interaction among sovereign entities; and, without the third, rule enforcement would depend on diplomacy and statecraft rather than at least some element of management by a standing body created for that purpose.[2]

A **Non-Governmental Organization (NGO)** is a single association or a federation of various organizations without governmental or state ties and not belonging to or associated with a government. The view of the Economic and Social Council of the United Nations concerning NGOs is implicit in its *Resolution 288 (X)* of 27 February 1950: "Any international organization which is not established by inter-governmental agreement shall be considered as a non-governmental organization for the purpose of these arrangements."[3]

A more specific definition given by the World Bank is: "private organizations that pursue activities to relieve suffering, promote the interests of the poor, protect the environment, provide basic social services, or undertake community development".[4] The World Bank typically interacts with two categories of NGOs:

a. Operational NGOs—whose primary purposes are to design and implement development-related projects and provide assistance to less developed regions and/or to disaster-stricken communities, and;

b. Advocacy NGOs—whose primary purpose is to defend or promote a specific cause, and to influence the policies and practices of governmental agencies and other bodies.[5]

---

1 David Armstrong, Lorna Lloyd, John Redmond, "The Rise of the International Organization", in *International Organization in World Politics*, part of *The Making of the Twentieth Century*, London: Red Globe Press, 2004, pp.1-15.

2 Ibid.

3 *Yearbook of International Organizations 2020-2021*, Brussels: Union of International Associations (UIA), 2020, p.9.

4 The World Bank: *Operational Directive (OD) No. 14.70*, August 1989.

5 "NGOs and the Bank", Incorporating FY95 Progress Report on Cooperation between the World Bank and NGOs, Poverty and Social Policy Department, June 1996.

The differences between these types of NGOs should not be viewed as rigid, however. A growing number of NGOs engage in both operational and advocacy activities, and some advocacy groups, while not directly involved in designing and implementing projects, focus on specific project-related concerns.

Compared with Inter-Governmental Organizations, Non-Governmental Organizations have the following characteristics:

a. NGOs vary widely in size, capabilities, and development focus.[1] They are typically value-based organizations which depend, in whole or in part, on charitable donations and voluntary service. Although the NGO sector has become increasingly professional over the last two decades, principles of altruism and voluntarism remain key defining characteristics.[2]

b. The membership of non-governmental organizations is unofficial and diverse.[3] Non-Governmental Organizations' easy informality and open-access attitudes may be best reflected in their inclusive membership and flexible institutional set-up.

c. The missions of Non-Governmental Organizations are broad and professional. The work organized by Non-Governmental Organizations include, but not limited to, areas like poverty reduction, human rights protection, cultural exchanges, peace education, etc. Most Non-Governmental Organizations are often concerned with only one specialized area that is often neglected or not managed by governments. With their extensive professional advantages, NGOs are therefore highly specialized in addressing these specific issues.[4]

1.2　Historical Development

The evolution of the modern nation-state and the consequent development of an

---

1　The World Bank, *Report No. 18399: NGOs in Bank-supported Projects: An OED Review*, Sector and Thematic Evaluations Group, Operations Evaluation Department, September 14th, 1998, p.1.

2　"IGO-NGO Cooperation: World Bank-NGO Cooperation", Source from the website of the Duke University Libraries, accessed June 8th, 2021.

3　于永达：《国际组织》，北京：清华大学出版社，2011，第13页。

4　See e.g., Eric Werker and Faisal Z. Ahmed, "What Do Nongovernmental Organizations Do?", *The Journal of Economic Perspectives*, v.22, n.2, 2008, pp.73-92; Nicola Banks, "The Role and Contributions of Development NGOs to Development Cooperation: What Do We Know?", in Sachin Chaturvedi et. al (eds.), *The Palgrave Handbook of Development Cooperation for Achieving the 2030 Agenda*, Palgrave Macmillan, 2021, pp.671-688.

international order founded upon a growing number of independent and sovereign territorial units inevitably gave rise to questions of international cooperation. Diplomatic representation became more widespread as the system expanded and political and economic relationships multiplied. It soon became apparent, however, that diplomatic contacts in themselves were unable to cope completely with the complexities of the international system and the concept of the international conference evolved as a form of extended diplomacy. Such gatherings dealt with problems that concerned more than two or three states and, in many cases, resulted in an international treaty or formal peace.

The first major instance of this occurred with *The Peace of Westphalia*[1] in 1648, which ended the Thirty Years' War of central Europe and formally established the modern secular nation-state arrangement of European politics.[2] The French wars of Louis XIV were similarly brought to an end by an international agreement of interested powers, and a century later the Napoleonic Wars terminated with the Congress of Vienna in 1815. This latter conference can be taken as a significant turning-point, for it marked the first systematic attempt to regulate international affairs by means of regular international conferences. The Congress system lasted, in various guises, for practically a century and institutionalized not only the balance of power approach to politics, but also a semi-formal international order.

Following the French Revolution and the Napoleonic Wars, leaders of the major European powers met periodically, in a system of consultation known as the Concert of Europe, to attempt to preserve the status quo and to protect their governments from internal rebellion. Later in the 19th century, various international organizations, such as the International Telegraph Union (1865; now the International Telecommunication Union), the Universal Postal Union (1874) were established to provide specialized services and to perform specific tasks.

---

1 *The Peace of Westphalia* was the collective name for two peace treaties signed between May and October 1648 in the Westphalian cities of Osnabruck and Munster.

2 Thirty Years' War (1618-1648), in European history, was a series of wars fought by various nations for various reasons, including religious, dynastic, territorial, and commercial rivalries. Its destructive campaigns and battles occurred over most of Europe, and, when it ended with *The Treaty of Westphalia* in 1648, the map of Europe had been irrevocably changed.

Featured History[1]

The Concert of Europe was a particular expression of an international system founded on balance. It was established in Vienna in 1815, and collapsed a century later with the beginning of the Great War. It had characteristics that distinguished it from the order that arose from *The Peace of Westphalia* in the seventeenth century, and *The Treaty of Utrecht* in the eighteenth century, even if fundamentally the principles behind it pertained to the balance of power.

The system instituted a certain multilateralism that was expressed through congresses and conferences, and was based on the values of a shared civilization. It established a set of principles, rules and practices that helped to maintain balance between the major powers after the Napoleonic Wars, and to spare Europe from another broad conflict. From the 1860s, it reached its limits in Prussia's rise in power, the implementation of constraining alliances in times of peace, and the profound changes of an increasingly globalized diplomacy.

In 1899 and 1907 European and non-European states met to develop rules to regulate armaments and the conduct of war. These conferences produced the Hague Conventions, which included agreements on the peaceful settlement of war, the treatment of prisoners of war, and the rights of neutral states. These various meetings and agreements served as precursors to the international organizations of the 20th century, such as the League of Nations (1919) and the United Nations (1945).

The nineteenth century also witnessed a considerable growth in international non-governmental associations, such as the International Committee of the Red Cross (founded in 1863) and the International Law Association (founded in 1873).[2] These private international unions demonstrated a wide-ranging community of interest on specific topics, and an awareness that cooperation had to be international to be effective. Such unions created the machinery for regular meetings and many established permanent

---

1   Source from: Stanislas Jeannesson, "The Concert of Europe", *Encyclopédie d'histoire numérique de l'Europe*, published online on June 22nd, 2020.

2   Chapter 22: International Organisations", in Malcolm N. Shaw, *International Law* (9th edition), University of Cambridge, 2021, pp.982-1018.

secretariats.[1] The work done by these organizations was, and remains, of considerable value in influencing governmental activities and stimulating world action.

During one of the bloodiest periods in European history, the idea of the League of Nations was introduced by U.S. President Woodrow Wilson. Unfortunately, the League ultimately failed in its primary purpose of preventing war. However, in the aftermath of the Second World War, the desire for an organized approach to global peace was rekindled, leading to new efforts for international cooperation. As early as August 1941, American president Roosevelt and British Prime Minister Churchill had conceded *The Atlantic Charter*, a declaration of principles which would serve as the basis, first, for a declaration of the wartime allies, and later, after the State Department had overcome President Roosevelt's initial reluctance to commit himself to the creation of a post-War organization, for *The Charter of the United Nations*.

Also, during the War, in 1944, the future of economic cooperation was mapped in Bretton Woods, where agreement was reached on the need to cooperate on monetary and trade issues, eventually leading to the creation of the International Monetary Fund and the General Agreement on Tariffs and Trade, among others.

The resurrection of the largest battlefield of the Second World War, Europe, also came accompanied by the rise of a number of organizations. To channel the American Marshall aid, a relatively small number of European states started a unique experiment when, in 1951, they created the supranational European Coal and Steel Community, some years later followed by the European Economic Community and the European Community for Atomic Energy, all three of which have now been subsumed into the European Union.

Moreover, elsewhere too organizations have mushroomed. On the American continent, the early Pan-American Conference was recreated so as to become the Organization of American States. In addition, there are more localized organizations such as CARICOM[2] and MERCOSUR[3]. In Africa, the wave of independence of the

---

1　Chapter 22: International Organisations", in Malcolm N. Shaw, *International Law* (9th edition), University of Cambridge, 2021, pp.982-1018..

2　The Caribbean Community (CARICOM) is the oldest surviving integration movement in the developing world. It is a grouping of twenty countries: fifteen Member States and five Associate Members. For more information, see the official website of the CARICOM.

3　The Southern Common Market (MERCOSUR for its Spanish initials) is a regional integration process, initially established by Argentina, Brazil, Paraguay and Uruguay, and subsequently joined by Venezuela and Bolivia—the latter still complying with the accession procedure. For more information, see the official website of the MERCOSUR.

1950s and early 1960s made possible the establishment of the Organization of African Unity[1] in 1963, with later such regional organizations as ECCAS (in central Africa) and ECOWAS (western Africa) being added. In Asia, some states assembled in ASEAN[2], for their security, Australia and New Zealand joined the US in ANZUS. A relaxed form of cooperation in the Pacific Rim area, moreover, is channeled through the Asia-Pacific Economic Co-operation (APEC)[3].

In short, the development of international organizations has been, in the main, a response to the evident need arising from international intercourse rather than to the philosophical or ideological appeal of the notion of world government.[4] The many international organizations created within the past centuries have themselves become a force within the world community. They have modified the patterns of world politics significantly; and they have slowly begun to acquire the status of world institutions serving the needs of a commonwealth greater than the sum of the nations that compose it.[5]

1.3   Organizational Structure

An organizational structure defines how activities such as task allocation, coordination, and supervision are directed toward the achievement of organizational aims. Organizational structure affects organizational action and provides the

---

1   The Organization of African Unity (OAU) was an inter-governmental organization established on May 25th, 1963 in Ethiopia, with 32 signatory governments. It was disbanded and replaced by the African Union (AU) on July 9th, 2002. Some of the key aims of the OAU were to encourage political and economic integration among member states, and to eradicate colonialism and neo-colonialism from the African continent. For more information, see the official website of the African Union.

2   The Association of Southeast Asian Nations, or ASEAN, was established on August 8th, 1967 in Bangkok, Thailand, with the signing of the ASEAN Declaration (Bangkok Declaration) by the Founding Fathers of ASEAN, namely Indonesia, Malaysia, Philippines, Singapore and Thailand. Brunei Darussalam then joined on January 7th, 1984, Vietnam on July 28th, 1995, Lao PDR and Myanmar on July 23rd, 1997, and Cambodia on April 30th, 1999, making up what is today the ten Member States of ASEAN. For more information, see the official website of the ASEAN.

3   The Asia-Pacific Economic Cooperation (APEC) is an intergovernmental forum established in 1989 to leverage the growing interdependence of the Asia Pacific. APEC's 21 members aims to create greater prosperity for the people of the region by promoting balanced, inclusive, sustainable, innovative and secure growth and by accelerating regional economic integration. For more information, see the official website of the APEC.

4   Mizanie Abate, Alemayehu Tilahun, "The Historical Development of International Organizations", *Abyssinia Law*, April 8th, 2012.

5   Charles Easton Rothwell, "International Organization and World Politics", *International Organization*, v.3, n.4, 1949, p.605.

foundation on which standard operating procedures and routines rest.[1] The larger the organization, the greater the dependence and interdependence between its components of its organization and outside organizations, the media, and the public. Thus, large organizations are composed of multiple layers and branches, each with specific assigned functions.[2]

1.3.1　Inter-Governmental Organizations

Each of these organizations has its own internal structure[3], and generally, is comprised of deliberative and policy-making bodies, executive and judicial bodies, administrative and regulatory bodies, etc. Sometimes specialized and ancillary institutions appear in a number of international organizations whose proper functioning guarantees the orderly functioning of the international organizations to which they belong.

(1) The Policy-Making Mechanism

The policy-making mechanism of international organizations, as the core of the international organizations, has a direct impact on the efficiency and effectiveness of decision-making in international organizations. They generally exist in the form of "General Assembly", "Congress", and their members are composed of representatives of various members of international organizations.

The functions of the decision-making bodies of international organizations are as follows: the formulation of policies, the review of budgets, the admission of new members, the election of executive heads, the election of members of executive organs and the implementation of their reports, the formulation and revision of charters, the making of recommendations or decisions on related matters, and the implementation of internal oversight. It should be noted that resolutions made by such bodies may change depending on the nature of the resolution. The resolutions made by them are also

---

1　The organizational structure determines which individuals get to participate in which decision-making processes, and thus to what extent their views shape the organization's actions. It can also be considered as the viewing glass or perspective through which individuals see their organization and its environment.

2　Often, divisions of responsibility within organizations are assigned titles, such as upper, middle, and lower management, and have functions similar to those of coordination and control entities. In many ways, the processes used in leading, controlling, and decision-making basically are the same.

3　An Inter-Governmental Organization usually has a formal, permanent structure that uses various organs and/or bodies to accomplish its tasks.

generally constructive, supervisory, and not binding in nature.

Taking the Shanghai Cooperation Organization (SCO)[1] as an example, its deliberative and decision-making body is the Council of Heads of State of Member States. The Council of Heads of State of Member States is generally responsible for studying and defining strategies, priority areas and basic directions for multilateral cooperation within the SCO framework, through important documents of the SCO. The Council of Heads of State is held annually and is normally held alternately by Member States in alphabetical order of country names. The countries that hold regular meetings are the states that chair the organization.[2]

(2) The Executive Bodies

International organizations generally also have executive bodies used to implement resolutions of the deliberative and policy-making bodies of international organizations, generally in the form of "executive boards", "councils" and "executive committees". Its functions are primarily to implement the relevant decisions of the highest organs of power, to deal with matters within the management of the organization, to make recommendations, plans and programmes of work and to put them into practice.[3] The membership of the body is generally composed of representatives of a small number of Member States elected by the deliberative and policy-making bodies.

In addition, it may be distributed in accordance with the principle of geographical equity or elected in accordance with other specific criteria and may also be delegated by Member States on a fixed basis. It is important to note that, unlike the deliberative and policy-making bodies, resolutions made by the executive bodies of international organizations within the scope of their functions are somewhat binding. The implementing agencies could also participate actively in the decision-making process of the General Assembly, address matters within the jurisdiction of the organization, make recommendations, plans, work programmes and implement them.

1　The Shanghai Cooperation Organization (SCO) is a Eurasian political, economic, international security and defence organization established by China and Russia in 2001.

2　郑启荣主编《国际组织》，北京：高等教育出版社，2017，第98页。

3　梁西：《梁著国际组织法》第6版，杨泽伟修订，武汉：武汉大学出版社，2011，第32页。

In the case of the International Monetary Fund[1], its executive body, known as the Executive Board, has 24 executive directors (and 24 alternates) who are responsible for the Fund's general operations, and for this purpose they exercise the powers delegated to them by the Board of Governors, as well as those powers conferred on them by *The Articles of Agreement*[2]. They "function in continuous session" at the Fund's headquarters and meet as often as business may require, usually several times a week. The Board normally makes decisions based on consensus, but sometimes formal votes are taken. The votes of each member equal the sum of its basic votes (equally distributed among all members) and quota-based votes. Therefore, a member's quota determines its voting power.[3]

(3) The Judicial Bodies

In some international organizations, there are also judicial bodies, which are generally exclusively responsible for hearing legal issues. When international disputes arise, the judiciary is also responsible for resolving them by legal means. These judicial bodies usually have special statutes that provide for the jurisdiction of the courts, the application of the law and judicial proceedings.[4] Judges in these judicial bodies are selected through a series of strict procedures and have the right to exercise their functions in full independence and cannot represent any authority.

The International Court of Justice in the Hague, the Netherlands, is one of the six major organs of the United Nations and the principal judicial organ of the United Nations. It has two main jurisdictions: the need for it to adjudicate disputes voluntarily submitted to Member States in accordance with the exercise of their sovereignty, and the question of legal issues that the United Nations General Assembly and the Security Council can consult with international law. The International Court of Justice

---

1　The International Monetary Fund (IMF) is a major financial agency of the United Nations, and an international financial institution funded by 190 member countries, with headquarters in Washington, D.C.

2　*The Articles of Agreement of the International Monetary Fund* were adopted at the United Nations Monetary and Financial Conference (Bretton Woods, New Hampshire) on July 22nd, 1944. As the charter of the organization, the Articles lay out the Fund's purposes, which include the promotion of "international monetary cooperation through a permanent institution which provides the machinery for consultation and collaboration on international monetary problems". Source from the website of the International Monetary Fund, "About the IMF/Articles of Agreement", accessed on July 1st, 2022.

3　Source from the website of the International Monetary Fund, "About the IMF/Governance Structure", see also the website of Encyclopedia of the Nations "United Nations Agencies/The International Monetary Fund (IMF)-Structure".

4　郑启荣主编《国际组织》，北京：高等教育出版社，2017，第 101 页。

is composed of 15 judges. When electing judges, candidates for judges are eligible for election only if they receive an overwhelming majority of votes in favour of the United Nations Security Council and the General Assembly, respectively, for a term of 9 years each. The President of the International Court of Justice is also elected by all judges by secret ballot for a term of 3 years each.[1]

(4) The Administrative and Regulatory Bodies

The administrative and regulatory bodies in international organizations are mostly referred to as the secretariat, which generally provide administrative and management services to other agencies, implement policies and planning programmes developed by other agencies, and have a variety of functions, such as finance, conference services, research, etc. The supreme officer of such a body would normally be referred to as the Secretary-General or the Officer-in-Chief, elected by the General Assembly to perform the functions prescribed by the organization during his term of office and to represent the organization externally. The main task of the agency and its head is to deal with the daily administration and management of international organizations, to coordinate the activities of the permanent organs of the organization and to provide them with a variety of services.[2]

The UN Charter describes the Secretary-General as the "Chief Administrative Officer" of the organization, who shall act in the capacity and perform "functions as are entrusted" to him or her by the General Assembly, Security Council, Economic and Social Council and other United Nations organs.[3] *The Charter* also empowers the Secretary-General to bring to the attention of the Security Council any matter that threatens international peace and security:

- To propose issues to be discussed by the General Assembly or any other organ of the United Nations;
- To bring to the attention of the Security Council any problem which the

---

1   Source from the website of the International Court of Justice, "The Court/The Court".

2   The United Nations Secretariat in New York is a typical example. It is the administrative and regulatory body of the United Nations, serves other United Nations bodies and is responsible for the daily affairs of the United Nations and for the implementation of programmes and policies developed by other organs. The Supreme Officer is the Secretary-General of the joint unit for a term of 5 years and may be re-elected. The UN Secretary-General is recommended by the UN Security Council. 参考梁西：《梁著国际组织法》第 6 版，杨泽伟修订，武汉：武汉大学出版社，2011，第 32 页。

3   Source from the website of the United Nations Secretary General, "Home/About/The Role of the Secretary-General", accessed on June 10th, 2021.

Secretary-General feels may threaten world peace;

- To act as a "referee" in disputes between Member States;

- To offer his or her "good offices".

Fact Check[1]

Does the Secretary-General act alone?

No. The Secretary-General would fail if he or she did not take careful account of the concerns of Member States. Any course of action, whether it concerns sending peacekeeping troops to war-torn areas or helping a country rebuild after a war or a natural disaster, must be set by the Member States. But the Secretary-General must also uphold the values and moral authority of the United Nations, and speak and act for peace, even at the risk, from time to time, of challenging or disagreeing with those same Member States.

(5) Specialized and Subsidiary Bodies

In some cases, specialized and subsidiary bodies (subgroups) will also be established within international organizations in accordance with a number of provisions and realities. Most of these bodies are technical, advisory committees that discuss and study technical issues within the functions of the principal organs, submit reports, recommendations or drafts, and assist and complement the work of the principal organs.[2] Usually, such bodies are composed of Member States, but because of the different scope of functions of the various international organizations, they may also consist of some Member States or be composed of government representatives or individual experts. It can be temporary or permanent; it can be regional, and it can be worldwide. The complex and flexible form of specialized and auxiliary institutions of international organizations, which are responsible for a large number of concrete practical tasks, is a very important part of maintaining the functioning of international organizations.

For example, the European Union (EU) is comprised of a number of institutions

---

1 Source from: *Everything You Always Wanted to Know about the United Nations*, New York: Department of Public Information, United Nations, 2010, p.22.

2 郑启荣主编《国际组织》，北京：高等教育出版社，2017，第 103 页。

with the European Council at the top. Another 3 of the institutions that are key to the decision procedures, and the passage of legislation are the Council of the EU[1], the European Parliament, and the European Commission. Related to the United Nations are 15 specialized agencies that coordinate their work with the UN but are separate, autonomous organizations. They work in areas as diverse as health, agriculture, telecommunications, and weather. In addition, there are 24 programmes, funds, and other bodies with responsibilities in specific fields. [2]

1.3.2   Non-Governmental Organizations

Although not all the NGOs have been catalogued, in 2004, the Union of International Associations indicated that there are >40,000 NGOs worldwide[3]. These NGOs range in size, and each has its own, specific administrative structure and norms regarding coordination with other agencies, financial resources, sustainability, willingness to have their activities evaluated, relations with donors, etc.[4] Some are very large with substantial administrative components such as Save the Children, and the International Medical Corps (IMC).[5]

Take Greenpeace as an example. The Greenpeace organization consists of Greenpeace International (Stitching Greenpeace Council) in Amsterdam, Netherlands, and Greenpeace offices (independent National and Regional Greenpeace organizations, NROs) around the world.[6] A key principle of Greenpeace's global operating model is that NROs in accordance with the Framework and agreed programme priorities develop and independently carry out their campaign projects. They may do so by themselves or in groups ("clusters").

---

1   The European Council and the Council of the European Union should not be confused with the Council of Europe. The latter is not a EU body. It is concerned primarily with human rights issues, democracy, and rule of law. It was founded in 1949 and in 2011, had 47 member states. The European Union was founded in 1961, and as of 2011, had 27 member states.

2   See more in *Everything You Always Wanted to Know about the United Nations*, New York: Department of Public Information, United Nations, 2010, p.7.

3   Sally Leverty, "NGOs, the UN and APA", source from the website of American Psychological Association, " Home/ Office of International Affairs/APA at the United Nations", accessed on December 26th, 2024.

4   Ibid.

5   "7. Administrative Structures", *Scandinavian Journal of Public Health*, v.42, n.14, 2014, pp.76-81.

6   Bonizella Biagini and Ambuj Sagar, "Nongovernmental Organizations (NGOs) and Energy", in Cutler J. Cleveland (editor-in-chief), *Encyclopedia of Energy*, Elsevier Science, 2004.

Greenpeace International's role is to coordinate NROs so that high-level strategy is adhered to, and that learnings from project evaluations benefit the whole network. The NROs are responsible for implementing and carrying out campaigns that fall under the long-term global campaign programme. Each NRO consists of one or more separate legal entities and has its own board in a supervisory role. These boards are usually elected by a voting membership of volunteers and activists, who are firmly rooted within the local environmental communities. This reflects Greenpeace's aim to work together, since environmental issues and their solutions do not stick to national borders.[1]

As above, the wide variety and complexity of working on different themes, at different levels, or targeting different audiences, make it extremely difficult to create a generic outline of an organizational structure. Even so, a typical NGO's organizational structure might be illustrated in Figure 1.

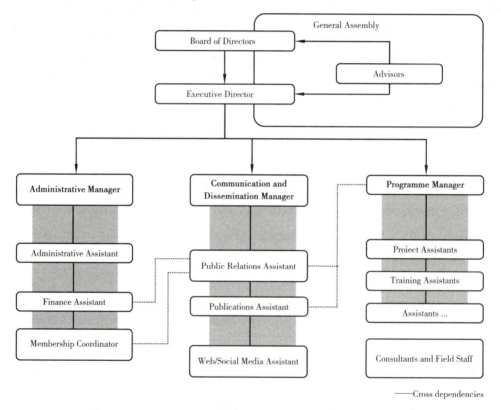

Figure 1   The Typical Organizational Structure of an NGO[2]

---

1   Sources from the official website of the Greenpeace International, "Greenpeace/#About Us/Our Structure".

2   This figure is copied from Hari Srinivas, "Organizational Structure of an NGO", *GDRC Research Output E-104*, Kobe, Japan: Global Development Research Center.

In general, the top management of an NGO consists of three entities—the Board of Directors, the General Assembly, and the Executive Director.

a. At the top is the Board of Directors of the NGO. An NGO Board is a legal requirement in most countries in order to get it officially registered with the local authorities. Depending on the type of NGO, a Board may be responsible for a number of tasks, for example hiring and supervising the Executive Director, develop and approve budgets, etc. Board members will also be expected to champion the NGO's cause, and represent the NGO to the larger community. Often, the Board is the first contact that an NGO's target audience have, and in some cases, it is the first contact where people's concerns are actually heard—due to the high standing of Board members in the community.

Within the board set-up itself, an NGO board selects and appoints chairpersons for the Board, and also participates on committees and working groups of the NGO.[1] It also sets operational guidelines, work plans and budgets for the NGO and policy and programme support.

b. Next comes the Executive Director, who may also be called by other names such as Coordinator, Chief Operating Officer, or CEO. He or she is responsible for the overall direction in which the NGO moves, and the responsibility for managing the day-to-day activities of the NGO. The Executive Director is also member of the Board—usually its Executive Secretary. He or she reports to the Board. The Board of Directors and the Executive Director may be assisted by advisors. These advisors are optional, but are useful to create a good image of the NGO, and enhance its "brand name" besides providing specialist advice for the NGO.

c. The highest body that guides and advises the overall development and progress of the NGO is the General Assembly. While day-to-day decision-making and management are handled by the Board, the Executive Director, and the staff members, the General Assembly plays a crucial role in setting the broader strategic direction for the organization. A General Assembly may or may not be required by law (and not all NGOs have a General Assembly), but such a body helps in

---

1   Ali Mostashari, "An Introduction to Non-Governmental Organizations (NGO) Management", *Iranian Studies Group at MI*, June 2005.

creating a good transparent image for the NGO, in building trust with its partners and stakeholders, and in public relations and fund-raising activities. The General Assembly usually meets annually or biannually, and is held sequential to a Board Meeting. Depending on the NGO's by-laws, members of the General Assembly can also participate in the meetings by proxy, usually deferring to the Executive Director to cast their vote when needed.

Section 2
The International Organizations in World Politics

2.1　International Organizations and Globalization

The term "globalization" first entered the English lexicon through *The Webster's Dictionary* in the year of 1961.[1] "30 years later it became part of the daily language as an obsessive word"[2]. In Dinu et. al (2003), the concept was understood as "the process of functioning of the global economy, which, in the global society, has become able to create global decision structures meant to solve global problems"[3].

Indeed, "globalization " can be seen as a means or system of acceptance and adherence to global problems of mankind, that need combined efforts to be solved.[4] It calls for multilateral cooperation and collective action on a range of non-economic issues that occur in almost all countries concerning technical, social economic, political and ecological mutual elements.[5] To increase cooperation and mutual accountability, several political and economic institutions were hence founded, including: the United Nations (UN), the

---

1　Meera Warrier and Uwe Wunderlich, "Globalization: The World and the Debates", *Aston Publications Explorer*, p.4.

2　Dorina Tănăsescu, Felicia Dumitru, Georgiana Dincă, "The Role of the International Organisms in the Globalization Process", in Hector Cuadra-Montiel (ed.), *Globalization—Approaches to Diversity*, Open access peer-reviewed Edited Volume, Intech Open Book Series, 2012, p.79.

3　Marin Dinu, Cristian Socol, Marius Marinaș, Cosmin Mosora, Globalizare și integrare economică: culegere de teste-grilă și studii de caz, Bucure   ti: Editura Economică, 2003.

4　Dorina Tănăsescu, Felicia Dumitru, Georgiana Dincă, "The Role of the International Organisms in the Globalization Process", in Hector Cuadra-Montiel (ed.), *Globalization—Approaches to Diversity*, Open access peer-reviewed Edited Volume, Intech Open Book Series, 2012.

5　IMF Staff, "Globalization: A Brief Overview", *International Monetary Fund Issues Brief*, May 2008, p.1.

International Monetary Fund (IMF), the World Bank (WB), the General Agreement on Tariffs and Trade (GATT).

Quick Quiz

Not everyone welcomes this image of the global village. To some it seems like an image of *post-colonial dominance* of the world by the West. They prefer to see the world in terms of their own family or their own nation. They may say, "we do not want to live in a village that someone else makes for us and controls." They worry that the global economy will have everyone resemble the families of the world that have the most economic and political power. They do not want to be second-class citizens in this village, and they do not want to give up their own treasured ways of life.

Others worry that conflict will increase as time and distance shrink. From news reports, everyone can see that religious, ethnic, economic, and political differences continue to divide people. They rightly ask, "How can I and my family members get along with members of the other family who seem so different from us?" They see troubles in other families and wonder why they can't solve their problems. Above all, every family wants to protect itself. No one wants the problem of another family to spread to their family.

Questions

Why do some people not welcome the image of the global village? What are some of the challenges of living in a global village? And how to deal with those challenges?

Today, although some critics argue that these institutions have come to be a domesticating force for weaker nations,[1] most still feel international organizations are acting as healthy members of the global community, maintaining open political processes and adhering to internationally accepted legal norms. In general, the active roles of international organizations in the process of globalization can be summarized as follows:

a. First, international organizations are the creators of global legal principles, rules

---

1 See e.g., Joseph M. Grieco, "Anarchy and the Limits of Cooperation: A Realist Critique of the Newest Liberal Institutionalism", *International Organization*, v.42, n.3, 1988, pp.485-507; John J. Mearsheimer, "The False Promise of International Institutions", *International Security*, v.19, n.3, 1994-95, pp.5-49.

and systems. Most international cooperation is based on international law, and the establishment of international conventions also provides institutional guarantees for cooperation among States. International organizations had assumed the task of codification of international law and the establishment of international conventions, and in practice, international organizations stepped into the shoes of formulating global legal tenents, regulations, and architectures.

This can be well demonstrated by the role played by international organizations in the international economic sphere. Under the background of economic globalization, the increasing degree of liberalization of the circulation of goods, services, capital, technology and people on a global scale has made economic ties between countries increasingly close. This requires existing international economic organizations, such as the World Trade Organization and the International Monetary Fund, to adapt to the new situation, formulate new rules for the management of related economic activities, balance the rights and obligations of Member States while coordinating the distribution of benefits among Member States, so that the global economy will develop smoothly.

b. Second, international organizations implement and supervise the global rules in the global arena. Due to the limitations of the traditional international system, the international community has so far not had a judicial body that enforces international legal rules and has jurisdiction over all States. This will, to some extent, make international cooperation more difficult, so it is necessary to establish a set of exclusive monitoring enforcement and punishment mechanisms in various Inter-Governmental Organizations to promote, in a certain sense, the implementation of global rules.

Take the World Trade Organization and the International Monetary Fund as examples. The Trade Policy Review Mechanism (TPRM) established by the World Trade Organization aims to examine the implementation of multilateral trade agreements by countries. Such an inspection mechanism, although not mandatory, has also been a good way to improve the World Trade Organization's ability to monitor trade rules and regulations. The International Monetary Fund has also contributed to the growth of the world economy by monitoring currency exchange rates and the trade situation of countries to provide corresponding technical and financial assistance.

c. Thirdly, international organizations regulate the process of globalization to some extent. As the product and embodiment of multilateral cooperation among states, international organizations do not become world governments above sovereign states. However, out of the need for international cooperation, international organizations are increasingly gaining the power of the transfer of Member States, thus enabling them to exercise the governmental administrative functions of the international community.

Consider the role played by the United Nations in global environmental governance. The first United Nations Conference on the Human Environment[1], held in Stockholm in 1972, succeeded in evoking the international community's focus on environmental protection. Since its entry into the 21st century, the United Nations Environment Programme has strengthened its cooperation with institutions such as the World Meteorological Organization and the International Maritime Organization by organizing and adopting dozens of important international environmental agreements on the governance of the atmosphere, oceans, endangered species, Antarctica and toxic waste.

d. Last but not least, international organizations have also become dispute settlers in the process of globalization. The development of the process of globalization has promoted international economic exchanges, but the friction and disputes brought about by exchanges have increasingly become an unavoidable problem for the international community. In response to such a situation, international organizations have developed a series of dispute settlement mechanisms. This dispute settlement mechanism enables small and vulnerable developing Member States to effectively safeguard their legitimate rights and interests in the friction arising from their dealings with developed Member States, and is conducive to creating a stable and peaceful environment for the development of globalization.

In the light of the foregoing, international organizations provide the legal principles, rules and systems necessary for the development of globalization, regulating

---

1   The United Nations Conference on the Human Environment (also known as the Stockholm Conference) was an international conference convened under United Nations auspices held in Stockholm, Sweden from June 5th-16th, 1972. It was the UN's first major conference on international environmental issues, and marked a turning point in the development of international environmental politics. Source from: the website of the United Nations "Conferences/Environment and Sustainable Development/Stockholm 1972", accessed on June 26th, 2021.

and constraining globalization, which is likely to be laissez-faire. At the same time, international organizations have properly addressed the problems that have arisen in the process of globalization as a means of promoting the healthy and balanced development of globalization. In general, international organizations are an integral part of the globalization process.

2.2 International Organizations and Global Governance

Global governance and the international organizations that form its backbone are worth studying because the most pressing issues in world politics today—poverty, international terrorism, the proliferation of weapons of mass destruction, disease, regional conflict, economic stability, climate change, and many others—cannot be solved without multilateral cooperation.[1]

The dominant trends of this era—particularly increased economic globalization and an emerging global civil society—also suggest that the rules of world politics are now generated through the interaction of international governmental organizations, non-governmental organizations, norms, regimes, international law, and even private-public governance structures. Increasingly, the functions of governance—defining standards of behavior, allocating resources, monitoring compliance with rules, adjudicating disputes, enforcement measures—occur at a global level to deal with common security concerns and transnational issues.[2]

Do You Know[3]

Taking a global view reveals some interesting facts about issues that transcend national boundaries and cannot be resolved by any one country acting alone:

- that hunger and malnutrition are the number one health risk worldwide?
- that unclear water and poor sanitation are the leading causes of child mortality?

---

1 Brian Frederking and Paul F. Diehl(eds.), *The Politics of Global Governance: International Organizations in an Interdependent World* (5th edition), Lynne Rienner Publishers, 2015, p.1.

2 Joseph S. Nye and John D. Donahue, *Governance in a Globalizing World*, Washington, DC: Brookings Institution, 2000.

3 Source from: The website of the United Nations, "The Essential UN/Fast Facts", accessed on September 10th, 2020.

- that in 1946, the UN established six official languages (Arabic, Chinese, English, French, Russian and Spanish) for its meetings and distributed documentation?
- that the UN is an Oscar winner with its short film, "First Steps", being awarded Best Documentary Short Subject in 1947?
- that in just one day, April 22nd, 2016, a record number of 174 nations signed *The Paris Agreement*, a global pact facilitated by the UN, through which members agreed to tackle climate change?

The academic field of international organizations began to study how IOs were part of larger patterns of world politics, particularly regarding conflict and peacekeeping and has more explicitly theorized "global governance", bringing about greater prospects for expanding the roles, functions, and powers of international organizations in global governance.[1] For them, the United Nations acts as a "linchpin institution" at the center of these multi-actor interactive networks concerned with the "trans-spatial" management and non-coercive resolution of global issues beyond the capacity of individual states to resolve.[2]

Most of the IGOs considered to this point conform to a particular pattern or template. They have been formed by sovereign states to provide cooperative solutions to various international problems but without transforming or even significantly affecting the foundation stone of the contemporary international system, namely the fact that the sovereign state itself is the sole location and source of legitimate political authority: the principle of non-intervention in a state's internal affairs. The main exception to this model is the European Union, whose members have pooled a limited measure of sovereign power in the common institutions of the Union, but even in that case, states retain the capacity to withdraw from the Union should they choose to do so, leaving

---

1　Inis L. Claude, *Swords into Plowshares* (New York: Random House, 1959); Ernst B. Haas, "Types of Collective Security: An Examination of Operational Concepts," *American Political Science Review* 49 (March 1955): 40-62; Karl W. Deutsch et al., *Political Community and the North Atlantic Area* (Princeton: Princeton University Press, 1957).

2　See e.g., James N. Rosenau, *Along the Domestic-Foreign Frontier: Exploring Governance in a Turbulent World* (Cambridge: Cambridge University Press, 1997); Anne-Marie Slaughter, *A New World Order* (Princeton: Princeton University Press, 2004); Michael Barnett and Raymond Duvall, eds., *Power in Global Governance* (New York: Cambridge University Press, 2005).

ultimate authority in the hands of the states.[1]

The prohibition of intervention "is a corollary of every state's right to sovereignty, territorial integrity and political independence". It is closely linked to the concept of domestic affairs, what the French tend to call *domaine réservé*; and also, to the international legal limits on a State's jurisdiction to prescribe and to enforce.[2] Famed Swiss legal philosopher Emmerich de Vattel was arguably the first jurist to articulate the non-intervention principle in his treatise *The Law of Nations*, published in 1758. The willingness of states to abide by the principle, however, has waxed and waned since that time, depending on the political agenda and national interests involved. For example, with the rise of the Iron Curtain and the Cold War, the Soviets adamantly opposed any outside intervention or influence to destabilize the political and economic order in the newly formed Soviet republics, a stance that was enforced most visibly by the erection of the Berlin Wall. Similarly, post-World War II colonial powers relied on the duty of non-intervention to prevent outside interference with efforts to control colonial liberation movements, while pro-liberation groups argued that intervention was justified.

In contemporary times, the non-intervention principle received official United Nations recognition when the General Assembly adopted *The Declaration on the Inadmissibility of Intervention and Interference in the Domestic Affairs of States* in 1965. The International Court of Justice also weighed in on the interpretation of the non-intervention principle in the Nicaragua case brought by Nicaragua against the United States, which arose based on allegations of American support for contra rebels. As explained in the summary of the 1986 judgment:

> *The principle of non-intervention involves the right of every sovereign State to conduct its affairs without outside interference.... As to the content of the principle in customary law, the Court defines the constitutive elements which appear relevant in this case: a prohibited intervention must be one bearing on matters in which each State is permitted, by the principle of State*

---

1 See e.g., David Armstrong, Lorna Lloyd, John Redmond, "Towards Global Governance?", in *International Organization in World Politics*, part of the *Making of the Twentieth Century* book series, London: Red Globe Press, 2004, pp.231-250.

2 Christian on Tue, "The Principle of Non-intervention in Contemporary International Law", Association of Accredited Public Policy Advocates to the European Union, May 2nd, 2019.

sovereignty, to decide freely (for example the choice of a political, economic, social and cultural system, and formulation of foreign policy). Intervention is wrongful when it uses, in regard to such choices, methods of coercion, particularly force, either in the direct form of military action or in the indirect form of support for subversive activities in another state.

Featured History[1]

The Republic of Nicaragua v. The United States of America (1986) was a case where the International Court of Justice held that the U.S. had violated international law by supporting the Contras in their rebellion against the Sandinistas and by mining Nicaragua's harbors.

On 27 June 1986, the Court delivered its judgment on the merits. The findings included a rejection of the justification of collective self-defence advanced by the United States concerning the military or paramilitary activities in or against Nicaragua, and a statement that the United States had violated the obligations imposed by customary international law "not to use force against another State", "not to intervene in its affairs", "not to violate its sovereignty", and "not to interrupt peaceful maritime commerce". The Court also found that the United States had violated certain obligations "under Article XIX of *The Treaty of Friendship, Commerce and Navigation between the Parties* signed at Managua on 21 January 1956", and that it had committed acts such to deprive that treaty of its object and purpose.

It decided that the United States was under a duty immediately to cease and to refrain from all acts constituting breaches of its legal obligations, and that it must make reparation for all injury caused to Nicaragua by the breaches of obligations under customary international law and *The 1956 Treaty*, the amount of that reparation to be fixed in subsequent proceedings if the Parties were unable to reach agreement.

More recently, in 2005, the International Court of Justice reiterated the principle of non-intervention in its judgment against Uganda for supporting rebel forces in the

---

1　Source from: The website of the International Court of Justice, "Military and Paramilitary Activities in and against Nicaragua" (Nicaragua v. United States of America)/Overview of the Case, accessed on July 10th, 2021.

Democratic Republic of the Congo. As the Court stated in paragraph 164 of its judgment, and quoting the Nicaragua case, the principle of non-intervention prohibits a State "to intervene, directly or indirectly, with or without armed force, in support of an internal opposition in another State".

While the traditional understanding of the non-intervention principle limited the sovereign power of individual states, it has been extended to also restrict the power of the United Nations when engaging in collective action. Article 2(7) of *The UN Charter* expressly provides that other than Security Council actions authorized under Chapter VII of *The Charter*, "[n]othing contained in the present Charter shall authorize the United Nations to intervene in matters which are essentially within the domestic jurisdiction of any state..." Similarly, multinational corporations and other private entities could arguably violate the non-intervention principle by using their substantial economic influence to coerce sovereign governments into adopting any number of legal, political or economic policies. Such liability, however, would necessarily involve attributing the coercive behavior to the home state of the organization.[1]

2.3 International Organizations and Civil Society

Over the past two decades, a combination of social movement activists, academics, and developing countries have mounted a formidable critique of international organizations like the World Trade Organization. Allegedly, such organizations sacrificed domestic concern for social and economic inequalities and environmental protection to the false regulatory imperatives of the global market.[2] The critique has been accompanied by a call for greater involvement, within international organizations, of "civil society", to decide on foreign aid, regulatory pre-requisites for free trade, measures necessary to protect the environment, and other, pressing issues of global governance.[3]

---

1   Carolyn A. Dubay, "A Refresher on the Principle of Non-intervention", published by the International Judicial Academy, with assistance from the American Society of International Law, in *International Judicial Monitor*, Spring 2014 Issue.

2   Francesca E. Bignami, "Civil Society and International Organizations: A Liberal Framework for Global Governance", *Duke Law Scholarship Repository*, 2007, pp.1-2.

3   Miles Kahler, "Global Governance Redefined", in Andrew Sobel (ed.), *Challenges of Globalization: Immigration, Social Welfare, Global Governance* (1st edition), 2009.

According to the World Bank, "civil society" refers to "the wide array of non-governmental and not-for-profit organizations that have a presence in public life, expressing the interests and values of their members or others, based on ethical, cultural, political, scientific, religious or philanthropic considerations."[1] Civil Society Organizations (CSOs) thus can cover social movements, volunteer organizations, mass-based membership organizations, Non-Governmental Organizations (NGOs), labour unions, community groups, indigenous groups, charitable organizations, faith-based organizations, professional associations, and foundations, that are exercising their civil liberties and participating in public life.[2]

Civil society actors are often also referred to as the "third sector" of society, distinct from the government and commercial for-profit actors. When mobilized, civil society actors are able to play multiple roles. They are an important source of information for both citizens and government; they fulfill important duties of checks and balances in democracies; they monitor government policies and actions, and curb the broad powers exercised by national ministers, international bureaucrats, and multinational corporations;[3] they provide both immediate relief and longer-term transformative change—by defending shared interests, purposes, and values; advocating the wishes of the people and public's rights (including but not limited to health, environment and economic rights); providing solidarity mechanisms and enhancing participation of communities in the provision of services and in policy decision-making...[4] In a healthy civic space, these functions entail upholding the human dignity of marginalized groups and highlighting gaps left by governments.

In the last 30 years, and especially after the end of the Cold War, the presence of civil society actors in international affairs has become increasingly relevant. It is now widely recognized that global or transnational civil society actors have been significant international actors as advocates for policy solutions, service providers, knowledge

---

1   The website of the World Bank, "Who We Are/Partners/Civil Society/Overview".

2   The website of UNDP, "Our Partners/Civil Socity Organizations/UNDP and Civil Socety".

3   Ben Davis, "What Do You Mean by Civil Society?", *Mvorganizing.org, Knowledge Bank: Quick Advice for Everyone*, June 1st, 2021.

4   Adluri Subramanyam Raju(ed.), *Human Security in South Asia: Concept, Environment and Development*, New York: Routledge, 2020.

brokers, or simply watchdogs over human rights compliance by governments and private actors.[1] At the international level, civil society action is predominantly focused on building a new conceptual and political framework within which the democratic accountability of decision-making processes, within global governance arrangements, can be legitimately demanded.[2]

A number of international organizations have also supported the inclusion of civil society actors within international decision-making. The UN, for example, has actively promoted cooperation with civil society in global governance, especially in relation to the world summits which have provided a forum for global civil encounters to occur. More accurately, civil society can join in the work of the UN in one of two ways:

a. Consultative status with the Economic and Social Council (ECOSOC). It provides Non-Governmental Organizations with access to not only ECOSOC, but also to its many subsidiary bodies, to the various human rights mechanisms of the United Nations, ad-hoc processes on small arms, as well as special events organized by the President of the General Assembly.[3] As of April 2021, 5,593 NGOs enjoyed active consultative status with ECOSOC.

b. Association with the UN Department of Global Communications (DGC, formerly DPI). The Civil Society Unit of the Outreach Division in the DGC is mandated to link the Organization with CSOs that are associated with the DGC and to support the department's efforts to disseminate information on the priority issues on its agenda, including sustainable development, creating a safer and more secure world, helping countries in transition, empowering women and young people, and addressing poverty, among others. Over 1,500 CSOs with strong information programmes on issues of concern to the United Nations are currently in formal association with the DGC, giving the United Nations valuable links to people and communities around the world.[4]

---

1   Raffaele Marchetti, "The Role of Civil Society in Global Governance", Report on the joint seminar organized by the EUISS, *The European Commission/DG Research*, and UNU-CRIS, Brussels, October 1st, 2010.

2   Ibid.

3   "BCIU Awarded UN ECOSOC Consultative Status", source from the website of Business Council for Interntaional Understadning, June 20th, 2023.

4   Source from the website of the United Nations, "The UN and Civil Society/Join Us in Building a Better World".

Section 3

The Leading Theories about International Organizations

The different international relations theories approach international organizations from their own set assumptions about how the international system works, and the role of international organizations within their respective positions. Based on how they view the world, international organizations serve a specific role in international affairs. So, for example, for a theory that advocates power and security, international organizations may be seen as functioning a particular way given this behavioral characteristic, whereas someone else who views the international relations theory as something different, could also in turn have a different perception of international organizations.

3.1　A Realist's Vision

For the realist scholars whose views prevailed from the 1940s to the 1960s, international organizations, as by-products of the European Westphalian anarchical state-based system of international relations, had neither identity, structural, and functional autonomy nor the capacity to influence the statist environment from which they sprang.[1] Realists emphasized the importance of state sovereignty, military power, and national interests in world politics and thus were less likely to expect states to delegate important powers to international organizations.

This is not to say that they don't matter, but rather, that international organizations might not be achieving what some hope that they do. As Pease (2012) explained, "International organizations can also play an intervening role in great power calculations", something in line with the state-interest argument.[2] Realists counter that international organizations are merely a projection of self-interested states who devise them to maintain or increase their own relative share of power in the anarchical system. Differently put, these organizations are used by the hegemony and great powers to further their interests in the international system. Other non-great-power

---

1　Jacques F. Fomerand, "Evolution of International Organization as Institutional Forms and Historical Processes since 1945", *Oxford Research Encyclopedias*, updated on December 13th, 2023.

2　Kelly-Kate S. Pease, *International Organizations: Perspectives on Global Governance*, London: Pearson Education, 2012.

states may also use international organizations to attain goals and to have a voice within the existing system.[1]

Realists often point to major wars in the past as an example of failed attempts of international organizations. These international organizations came out of conflict, created to stop additional wars from breaking out. Yet, this is not what has happened. Rather, international organizations such as the League of Nations, and also the United Nations were unable to stop conflict from taking place.

Read This[2]

"Concert", "League" or "United Nations" [...] IGOs come into existence because states, especially powerful ones, share common interests which they have elected to pursue in multilateral settings which they control. In their operation, IGOs are instruments of national policies, arenas, effector of great power agreements or legitimizers of dominant state policies. Their independent role is negligible and marginal. They can have no purposes of their own.

Realists argued that order could only be established by the enlightened use of diplomacy and force. It was the traditional route of alliances and the balance of power, not some potentially transformative international organizations, that would maintain order. More recently, focused on the structure of the international political system, realists emphasized that international organizations are essentially creatures and servants of their principals. However, there are also arguments that international organizations can matter in some matters:

a. Firstly, international organizations provide a mechanism for great-power collusion. Great powers usually benefit from the existing order and have an interest in maintaining it. After all, the fact that they are great powers suggests that they are doing well under existing rules and institutions. International organizations may not be useful if great-power interests collide, but do permit great powers to control other states in international systems;

---

1   Donald J. Puchala, "World Hegemony and the United Nations", *International Studies Review*, v.7, n.4, 2005, pp.571-584.

2   Iris L. Claude Jr., *The Changing United Nations*, Third Printing, Random House, January 1968.

b. Secondly, international organizations are useful for making minor adjustments within the existing order, while the basic underlying principles and norms remain uncompromised. An enduring international order must be flexible to account for changes in national interests and for rising and declining states;

c. Thirdly, international organizations can be agents of international socialization. International organizations legitimize the existing order, thereby gaining the acceptance of the status quo by those who are dominated;

d. Fourthly, international institutions are the "brass ring" so to speak: the right to create and control them is precisely what the most powerful states have fought for in history's most destructive wars.

Now, after almost a century of IGO practice, the prevailing view is that international organizations do enjoy a significant though still conditional and fluctuating degree of independence. "Liberal-institutionalist" and "constructivist" critiques of realism have shaped the contours of this paradigm change.

3.2　An Idealist's Vision

Since the 1970s, a growing field of theory which places international organizations rather than states as the primary referent in theories of world politics has emerged. The heterogeneous group of "liberal-institutionalists" offers a wide variety of prognoses about the factors accounting for the expanding scope of international organizations' "actorness".

For "liberal-institutionalists", international organizations represent a firm challenge to the realist position which posits state power as the primary referent in world politics. They argue that international organizations are central to our understanding of international relations and their effects cannot be divorced from the actions of states which operate underneath international organizations' rules and norms.[1]

For a liberal-institutionalist who advocates the possibility of cooperation in international relations, international organizations are quintessential, as they not only allow a physical platform and space for state cooperation, but within the international organizations' charter is often a set of requirements that states and non-state actors have

---

[1]   Robert O. Keohane, "International Institutions: Two Approaches", *International Studies Quarterly*, v.32, n.4, December 1988, p.383.

regarding this cooperation in international affairs. International organizations are not formed for calculated interests of one state (solely for their own power),[1] but rather, these organizations are created because of their need with regards to international issues. Thus, for a state, they have a lot of positive incentives to join an international organization.

Arguing that IGOs' primary function is to act as facilitators of interstate cooperation, liberal-institutionalists have explored the types of constellations of interests that are most likely to lead to the emergence of IGOs and to contribute to their success. Some have underlined the fact that the effectiveness of IGOs does not necessarily hinge on the continued existence of a hegemon, as argued by realists. Others have shown how the "regimes" into which IGOs are embedded reduce uncertainty about the preferences and behaviors of concerned state as well as non-state actors, thus providing a structured and predictable environment that generates expectations of further cooperation as well as reduced transaction costs.

An offshoot of this argument is the "public good" approach, which emphasizes that IGOs are more effective than markets in the provision of such "global conditions" as peace, health, environmental stability, foreign aid, and poverty elimination. Yet another line of reasoning is the idea that IGOs can help states develop shared values and norms and resolve collective action problems in the maintenance of peace and security and the promotion of sustainable development. Furthermore, they challenge the idea that the international system is all about the need for military power.

Thus, for liberals, international organizations are avenues for diplomacy, cooperation, and international peace. They often point to various achievements on human rights, environmental policies, among other issues such as economic cooperation and interdependence to illustrate the positive role of international organizations in international affairs. In fact, not only do international organizations allow actors to come together to solve issues, but their presence more specifically helps to circumvent the "collective action problem" issue, where, by working together, much more can be accomplished than if each state or actor works individually.

Liberalists argue that the more interdependent countries become with one another, the more of a need there will be for international organizations to help in the sharing of

---

1 There is not a need for a hegemon to exist for an international organization to continue functioning.

information, and with regards to coordination and cooperation efforts.

And unlike realists' views of international law, "[f]or liberals, the rule of law is the foundation of society and international law is the foundation of global society". International law is a key element in the evolution of international human rights, international environmental issues, as well as other themes such as just war theory—with the formation of international courts such as the International Court of Justice (ICJ) and the International Criminal Court (ICC).

It also emphasized the role of Non-Governmental Organizations in influencing the beliefs, norms, rules, and procedures of evolving regimes. Realists incorporated this approach with "hegemonic stability theory", arguing that any stability brought about by regimes is associated with a concentration or preponderance of power in one state. That "hegemon" achieved multilateral cooperation, according to this approach, through a combination of coercive threats and positive rewards.[1]

Think This

The collective economic and political dominance of the victorious Western liberal democracies in the immediate post-war period accounted for a near-hegemony in the international system. Against this backdrop, the allied nations constructed international organizations to marshal peace. Indeed, the five principal allies during the Second World War were founder members of the United Nations, the United Kingdom, the United States, France, Soviet Union and China forming the all-powerful permanent Security Council. The three Western allies (the United Kingdom, the United States and France) were also founders of NATO and the Soviet Union founded the Warsaw Pact.

In fact, it is important to recognize that the globally significant international organizations of today did not simply emerge, but were constructed by a small number of powerful states in the period after the Second World War. This raises several interesting questions in relation to the title question:

1　See e.g., Robert O. Keohane, *After Hegemony: Cooperation and Discord in the World Political Economy*, Princeton: Princeton University Press, 1984, pp.57-60; Robert Gilpin, *US Power and the Multinational Corporation*, New York: Basic, 1975.

a. Are international organizations persistent because they are founded by successful states and if so, do founding states retain power by means of international organizations?

b. Do states form international organizations in order to be governed by them, as institutionalists suggest, or do states form institutions in order to control or influence the international environment in the pursuit of power and the promotion of national interest, as realists might suggest?

3.3　A Constructivist's Vision

Constructivism is seen as one of the newer, yet also highly influential international relations theories. Constructivism suggests that international relations, and within that international organizations, are in and of themselves not necessarily pessimistic and towards issues such as power and security, nor are they innately positive and cooperative in their nature. But rather, relationships and institutions are viewed a certain way depending on the actors. As Hurd (2014) explained, "actors behave toward the world around them in ways that are shaped by the ideas that they hold about the world, and that these ideas are generated by past interactions".[1] Therefore, while the past helps form how actors interact, this is not permanent; interactions, as well as negative or positive perceptions, are not infinite, but can be altered.

Constructivists have questioned the realist ideas that international structures and states' interests—especially their sovereignty—are given, contending instead that they are constructed through social practice, socialization, and the interaction of a multiplicity of actors.[2] National interests are shaped by multilateral institutions to such an extent that for some observers of the European Union, this process of value internalization has in fact anchored the Union in the core interests of national governments. In this context, states are prominent, but other actively involved actors include Non-Governmental Organizations, advocacy networks and social movements, and issue-specific transnational expert

---

1　Ian Hurd, *International Organizations: Politics, Law, Practice*, Cambridge: Cambridge University Press, 2014.

2　Sarina Theys, "Introducing Constructivism in Iternational Relations Theory", *E-International Relations*, February 23rd, 2018.

networks, among others.

Numerous case studies document the constructivists' insights. Audie Klotz (1995) explained how the sanctions regime adopted against the apartheid regime in South Africa developed out of the emergence of a global norm of racial equality that led states to redefine their interests. In her pioneering work *National Interests in International Society* (1996), Finnemore highlighted the role of UNESCO, the Red Cross, and the World Bank in reconstituting states' interests and the perception of international problems.[1]

In the same vein, Peter Katzenstein (1996) underlined the importance of the cultural institutional context of policy and the constructed identity of states, governments, and other political actors as determinants of national security policy.[2] Socialization processes have been identified in particular institutions of the European Union. The large-scale, multi-year, multi-volume, multi-million-dollar United Nations Intellectual History Project maps out the origins and evolution of key ideas and concepts about international economic and social development that were hatched though United Nations institutions.

Further insights into the mechanisms through which IGOs acquire "actorness" can be found in studies embedded in the sociology of law and revolving around the "principal agent" notion. "Contracts," "agency slack," "shirking," "autonomy," "discretion," "agency losses," and "reflexive" or "adaptive" learning contribute to the emergence of IGOs as "managers," "enforcers," and "authorities". These propositions have been applied to the European Union, the World Bank, and environmental institutions.

In a similar vein, the deepening autonomy of IGOs has been explained through the template of "constitutionalism"; that is, the interaction of a constituent with normative and organizational principles, the institutional setting, the conditions of membership, the exercise of political power, and the interface between centers of power. On a parallel track and drawing from the commonplace observation that organizations tend to acquire a life of their own, Barnett and Finnemore (1999) made the compelling argument that IGOs may deviate from and expand their original mandates in ways dictated not

---

1   Martha Finnemore, *National Interests in International Society* (1st edition), New York: Cornell University Press, 1996.

2   Peter J. Katzenstein, *Cultural Norms and National Security Policy and Military in Postwar Japan*, Series of Cornell Studies in Political Economy, New York: Cornell University Press, 1996.

by states but by the "constitutive" nature of bureaucracies and their culture.[1] Even "technical" or "functional" agencies are not immune, as the case of the World Health Organization[2] shows when it embraced the broad mandate of the attainment by all the people of the highest possible level of health. In some cases, these transformations may in fact lead to internal dysfunctions and "pathologies", ranging from fraud to corruption and managerial failures to "turf wars".[3]

Another interesting factor to note is the portrayal of the Secretary-General (SG) within the United Nations. The SG's initial role of entrepreneurship and chief of all administrative matters within the organization was a political decision, as nations did not want to transmit the notion of a global governance to the world community. However, it has been extremely debated amongst scholars and internationalists that the changing roles and duties of the "head" of the UN has signified a symbolic change for the international system. This was observed especially during the Kofi Annan years, when the Secretary General's duties expanded to unforeseeable dimensions, largely opposed by the United States.[4] It is claimed that the Secretary General is the world's prime example of responsibility without power, which is not always understood. The fact that he has no sovereign rights, duties or resources could signify that he has become a reflection of the organization itself.

The license granted to the Secretary-General by Member States is for mediation, rallying of nations, and generating awareness of pressing issues, which can be further extended to many of the acting organs of the organization. The increase in the Secretary-General's powers is a matter of grave concern among the major power players of the UN, and this essentially shows that States are not, in fact, moving towards a "global

---

1 Michael N. Barnett and Martha Finnemore, "The Politics, Power, and Pathologies of International Organizations", *International Organization*, v.53, n.4, 1999, pp.699-732.

2 The World Health Organization leads and champions global efforts to achieve better health for all. WHO's primary role is to direct international health within the United Nations' system and to lead partners in global health responses. From emerging epidemics such as COVID-19 and Zika to the persistent threat of communicable diseases including HIV, malaria and tuberculosis and chronic diseases such as diabetes, heart disease and cancer, WHO brings together 194 countries and work on the frontlines in 150+ locations to confront the biggest health challenges of our time and measurably advance the well-being of the world's people. See more on the website of the World Health Organization.

3 Jacques F. Fomerand, "The Evolution of International Organizations as Institutional Forms and Historical Processes since 1945: Quis custodiet ipsos custodies?" *Oxford Research Encyclopedia, International Studies*, March 2010, pp.2-4.

4 Marion Traub-Werner, "Free Trade: A Governmentality Approach", *Environment and Planning A: Economy and Space*, 2007, p.197.

government" and that the role of the United Nations as an international institution is to promote dialogue and discussions in a multilateral framework and not to intervene in sovereign territory. An example of this was in the Secretary-General's *Millennium Report* （Annan, 2000) where he ensured States that the Secretariat was fully accountable to them and the founding principles of the United Nations as "an Organization dedicated to the interests of its Member States and of their peoples" would be preserved.[1] In light of this, the role of the United Nations is to serve as a facilitator for cooperative action between Member States and non-state actors.

Tasks

Activity 1　Reading Comprehension

Read the following questions first and try to find the correct answers from the passage.

Friends of the Earth (FOE) campaigns on a range of problems including rainforests, the countryside, water and air pollution and energy. Friends of the Earth International Secretariat P.O.Box 19199 1000 G.D. Amsterdam　**Friends of the Earth** The Netherlands	Greenpeace uses peaceful but direct action to defend the environment. It campaigns to protect rainforests and sea animals，stop global warming and end pollution of air, land and seas. It also opposes nuclear power. Greenpeace International Keizergracht 176　**GREENPEACE** 1016 DW Amsterdam The Netherlands
BirdLife International is an organization which works to save endangered birds all over the world. BirdLife International Wellbrook Court Girton Road Cambridge CB3 ONA England　**BirdLife INTERNATIONAL**	WWF—World Wide Fund For Nature is the world's largest private international organization for the protection of nature and endangered species. Information Officer WWF International Avenue du Mont-Blanc 1196 Gland Switzerland　**WWF**

1. If you want to learn more about the organizations, you can_____.

　A. call them　　　　　　　　　　　　B. write them a letter

1　Kofi Annan, *We the Peoples—The Role of the United Nations in the 21st Century*, Millennium Report of the Secretary-General, 2000, p.73.

C. visit them   D. send them an e-mail

2. BirdLife International is an organization trying to _____.

   A. reduce pollution   B. defend rainforests

   C. protect ocean animals   D. save endangered birds

3. If you oppose nuclear power, you can join_____.

   A. Friends of the Earth   B. World Wide Fund for Nature

   C. Greenpeace   D. BirdLife International

4. What can we learn about WWF?

   A. It helps to protect nature and save endangered animals.

   B. It is the world's largest international organization.

   C. It works for private companies and rich people.

   D. It is a private organization in the United States.

5. Which is the best title for the passage?

   A. Environmental Protection Organizations.   B. Global Traffic Problems.

   C. Endangered Animals.   D. Natural Beauty.

Activity 2 General Knowledge Test

1. Is globalization a good or bad process? Why?

2. What are the Millennium Development Goals (MDGs)? Can you define sustainable development?

3. How many principal organs does the United Nations have, and what are they?

4. Try to name at least two Secretaries-General of the United Nations.

5. How many members does the Security Council have?

6. Where is the International Court of Justice located?

7. Which country was the last Trust Territory to achieve self-government thanks to the Trusteeship Council?

8. What does UNICEF stand for?

9. How would you define poverty?

10. True or False: China has more votes at the General Assembly than Monaco because its population is larger.

Activity 3 | Short-Answer Questions [1]

UN peacekeeping is far from perfect, and much can be done to improve the performance of missions on the ground. But we also can't expect peacekeeping alone to solve the kinds of intractable conflicts that have arisen today, at least not with the mandates, resources, and time frames usually proposed by the Security Council.

It is unrealistic to suggest that a UN peacekeeping operation will deliver on its state-building mandate in countries like the Central African Republic anytime soon. And, as scholars have suggested, changes in these kinds of settings happen in fits and starts, with relapses, failings, and setbacks. There is no straight line from conflict to peace.

The UN, at best, may play a small role in facilitating national-level changes. But it can make a difference. Recent studies have shown UN peacekeeping can help reduce overall conflict rates, protect hundreds of thousands of civilians from slaughter, warn the world of impending violence, and even gradually tip the scales in favour of peace. While not the kind of national transformation envisioned in some of today's peacekeeping mandates, these studies show the tangible impact the UN can have on people's lives.

On the anniversary of UN peacekeeping, these accomplishments are worth celebrating (and indeed worth tracking more systematically). A new realism would build on these successes and recognise that UN peacekeeping can and does deliver well beyond the tasks of ceasefire monitoring 70 years ago, even if it is unlikely to resolve today's most intractable conflicts.

◀ • Questions

1. Discuss with your group partner what are the main assumptions of liberalism and what roles should the international organizations play in liberalists' vision.
2. Do you agree with the above-mentioned opinion that UN peacekeeping still needs realism?

Activity 4 | Buzz Discussion

NOTE: *This session is designed to give participants time to think about the world they live in, realize the complexities and paradoxes of the world, and think about the role of education in guiding younger generations on how to live in a rapidly changing world*

---

1   Excerpts from Adam Day, "Realism Should Guide the Next Generation of UN Peacekeeping", *Our World* by the United Nations University, June 6th, 2019.

full of challenges.

Think about the news articles that you have read in papers or through any other forms of media recently.

List three issues that deal with local or global challenges and write them on a sticky note:

a._____

b._____

c._____

Ex: Increasing number of migrants and conflicts in communities;

Ecological destruction: flooding, deforestation, rising sea level, etc.;

High rate of youth unemployment.

Put the note on a whiteboard or wall for everyone to see.

Share with the group about what you think/feel about the issues, your personal experiences related to the issues, and what you noticed were common characteristics among the issues.

Think about how to address the issues facing your local communities and the global community and how local issues (or issues that may be considered "local") are related to global issues and how these affect each other.

EX: rising conflicts between refugees and community members in a local community—how is this related to global conflicts of armed forces and crisis?

Activity 5 | Short Essay Writing

Lall (2017) made an important point about IO performance by arguing that "the primary obstacle to effective institutional performance is not deviant behavior by IO officials—as conventional "rogue-agency" analyses suggest—but the propensity of states to use IOs to promote narrow national interests rather than broader organizational objectives"[1]. In your opinion, do international organizations do what they are meant to do? What determines the implementation by IOs? And, how to raise the effectiveness of international organizations?

Pick up one subject/case on international organizations and write a short essay. Essays should include theories of IOs, missions, history, geography, actions, and efficiency or inefficiency of the IOs and ways of solving the problems of one IO.

---

1 Ranjit Lall, "Beyond Institutional Design: Explaining the Performance of International Organizations", *International Organization*, v.71, 2017, p.245.

Chapter 2

Selected Examples of International Organizations

In facing challenges of the scale that lie before us, all peoples and nations should focus on what we have in common: our shared desire to live freely and securely, in health, with hope and with opportunity. Those are the interests and aspirations of the American people, and they are shared by billions around the world.

—Susan E. Rice, former US Ambassador to the UN[1]

---

1 Previously, Ambassador Rice served President Barack Obama as National Security Advisor and U.S. Permanent Representative to the United Nations (2009-2013). In a world of 21st Century threats that pay no heed to borders, Ambassador Rice helped rebuild an effective basis for international cooperation that strengthened the United States' ability to achieve its foreign policy objectives and made the American people safer.

Overview

Learning Objectives

a. To examine different range of international Inter-Governmental Organizations, using the UN, ASEAN and EU as representative examples;

b. To better understand the roles and structures of various organizations.

Main Contents

International organizations typically play a role in setting the international agenda, mediating political negotiations, providing a platform for political initiatives, and acting as catalysts for coalition-formation.[1] International organizations also define the salient issues and decide which issues can be grouped together, and thus help governmental priority determination or other governmental arrangements.[2] The effectiveness of international Inter-Governmental Organizations in fostering economic, political and social cooperation and integration will be further illustrated in this chapter through the use of some notable examples. Examples include the United Nations, especially the Department of Peace Operations (DPO), the Association of Southeast Asian Nations (ASEAN), and the European Union (EU).

Warm-up

Is Regional the New Global?[3]

There are over 80 regional organizations globally, addressing issues from trade and security cooperation to trans-border water management and migration. Their rising number notwithstanding, it is the growing mandate and ambition of regional organizations, which is becoming a key feature of international relations.

---

1 OECD, *The Contribution of International Organisations to a Rule-Based International System*, April 10th, 2019, available at: https://www.oecd.org/gov/regulatory-policy/IO-Rule-Based%20System.pdf

2 Kenneth W. Abbott and Duncan Snidal, "Why States Act through Formal International Organizations", *The Journal of Conflict Resolution*, v.42, n.1, 1998, pp.3-32.

3 Source from: Miroslav Dusek and Victor Willi, "Is Regional the New Global?", World Economic Forum, October 23rd, 2012.

In the current global context, regional organizations are fast becoming the "vehicles of choice" for countries to address pressing challenges, which require international cooperation. This development seems to be a reaction to the continuous gaps in global governance and also to the rather incremental evolution of the Breton Woods Institutions. The latter are still to fully reflect key global trends such as the re-balancing between Global North and South, the significance of emerging markets and the overall multi-polar nature of the world's power architecture.

The key question is how the potential of these organizations can be maximized to improve the state of the world's regions while at the same time acting as catalysts for enhanced global cooperation. There are three main areas to be covered:

a. The first one relates to the identity of regional organizations. We will address the mandate and purpose of regional organizations in the 21st century, given the evolving global environment and the various transformations shaping regions from within.

b. The second set of questions relates to regional responses to human security. Although some of these organizations are working in different areas to reduce the multiple dangers to human security, the results are mixed when it comes to armed conflicts. Why have regional initiatives not been more successful in the prevention and management of armed conflicts, and how can regional organizations contribute more effectively to guarantee human security?

c. Finally, trade will feature prominently on the agenda. Specifically, we will ask decision-makers to think about how regional trade integration mechanisms, for example in the areas of customs, border administration, procedures and tariffs, can be utilized and adapted to offer a roadmap for the re-invigoration of a global trade regime.

◀ • Questions

1. "Is regional the new global"? What do you make of the statement?

2. According to this article, what are the main areas to be covered when it comes to regional organizations? Do you have anything to add?

3. The task of global governance has become even more daunting, as traditional security threats are intertwined with non-traditional ones and new global challenges keep emerging. Based on your personal understanding, what roles have regional organizations played in helping the global issues management?

Section 1

Universal Organization—The United Nations

Universal organizations are also known as "open" organizations. Membership of such an organization is not restricted to any region but is open to all States from all over the world as long as its membership requirements are met. The United Nations is a typical global organization, currently made up of 193 member states. This category also includes the specialized agencies of the UN: Universal Postal Union (UPU), Interpol, World Trade Organization (WTO), World Customs Organization (WCO), International Monetary Fund (IMF) and World Bank, to name a few.

Founded in 1945, the United Nations is the single largest IGO in the world. The UN's main goal is to keep peace. And peacekeeping has been hailed as one of the UN's essential functions to assist host countries in navigating the difficult path from conflict to peace.[1]

Even though peacekeeping is not explicitly stipulated in *The United Nations Charter*, it has become one of the principal tools used by the United Nations Security Council.[2] The legal basis for such action is found in Chapters VI, VII and VIII of *The Charter.* While Chapter VI deals with the "Pacific Settlement of Disputes", Chapter VII contains provisions related to "Action with Respect to the Peace, Breaches of the Peace and Acts of Aggression". Chapter VIII of *The Charter* also provides for the involvement of regional arrangements and agencies in the maintenance of international peace and security, provided such activities are consistent with the purposes and principles outlined in Chapter I of *The Charter.*[3]

---

1 United Nations, *United Nations Peacekeeping Operations: Principles and Guidelines*, New York: Department of Peacekeeping Operations & Department of Field Support, 2008, p.7.

2 Ibid., p.13.

3 Source from the website of the United Nations Peacekeeping, "Home/What is peacekeeping/Forming a new operation/Mandates and the legal basis for peacekeeping", accessed on June 12th, 2022.

1.1   What Is Peacekeeping?

Peacekeeping is a technique designed to preserve peace, however fragile, where fighting has been halted, and to assist in implementing agreements achieved by the peacemakers. Over the years, peacekeeping has evolved from a primarily military model of observing cease-fires and the separation of forces after inter-state wars, to incorporate a complex model of many elements—military, police and civilian—working together to help lay the foundations for sustainable peace.[1]

Peacekeeping has unique strengths, including legitimacy, burden sharing, and an ability to deploy and sustain troops and police from around the globe, integrating them with civilian peacekeepers to advance multidimensional mandates. Peacekeeping operations fulfill the role of neutral third party: they help create and maintain ceasefires and form a buffer zone between warring groups. They also provide a wide range of services, such as electoral assistance, training for local police forces, humanitarian action and help in clearing deadly landmines.[2]

Keep in Mind[3]

Although the focus here is on peacekeeping, it is important to understand how it relates to and differs from conflict prevention, peacemaking, peace enforcement and peacebuilding.

Conflict prevention involves the application of structural or diplomatic measures to keep intra-state or inter-state tensions and disputes from escalating into violent conflict. Ideally, it should build on structured early warning, information gathering and a careful analysis of the factors driving the conflict. Conflict prevention activities may include the use of the Secretary General's "good offices," preventive deployment or confidence-building measures.

---

1   United Nations, *United Nations Peacekeeping Operations: Principles and Guidelines*, New York: Department of Peacekeeping Operations & Department of Field Support, 2008, pp.17-18.

2   Source from the website of United Nations Peacekeeping, "Home/What is peacekeeping", accessed on April 23rd, 2023.

3   Source from: *United Nations, United Nations Peacekeeping Operations: Principles and Guidelines,* New York: Department of Peacekeeping Operations & Department of Field Support, 2008, pp.17-18.

Peacemaking generally includes measures to address conflicts in progress and usually involves diplomatic action to bring hostile parties to a negotiated agreement. The United Nations Secretary-General, upon the request of the Security Council or the General Assembly or at his/her own initiative, may exercise his or her "good offices" to facilitate the resolution of the conflict. Peacemaking efforts may also be undertaken by unofficial and non-governmental groups, or by a prominent personality working independently.

Peace enforcement involves the application, with the authorization of the Security Council, of a range of coercive measures, including the use of military force. Such actions are authorized to restore international peace and security in situations where the Security Council has determined the existence of a threat to the peace, breach of the peace or act of aggression. The Security Council may utilize, where appropriate, regional organizations and agencies for enforcement action under its authority.

Peacebuilding is a complex, long-term process of creating the necessary conditions for sustainable peace. It works by addressing the deep-rooted, structural causes of violent conflict in a comprehensive manner. Peacebuilding measures address core issues that affect the functioning of society and the State and seek to enhance the capacity of the State to carry out its core functions effectively and legitimately.

Peacekeeping has always been highly dynamic and over the past seven decades, has evolved into one of the main tools used by the international community to manage complex crises that pose a threat to international peace and security.[1] Beyond simply monitoring cease-fires, today's multidimensional peacekeeping operations are called upon to facilitate the political process through the promotion of national dialogue and reconciliation, protect civilians, assist in the disarmament, demobilization, and reintegration of former combatants; support the organization of elections, protect

---

1 Source from: *United Nations, United Nations Peacekeeping Operations: Principles and Guidelines,* New York: Department of Peacekeeping Operations & Department of Field Support, 2008, pp.17-18.

and promote human rights, and assist in restoring the rule of law.[1]

While most peacekeepers are serving military or police, 14 per cent are civilians who perform a wide range of functions, from serving as the civilian leadership of the mission to working in the areas of political and civil affairs, human rights, elections, strategic communications, IT, logistics, transport, and administration and more.[2] Women peacekeepers today also play a more significant role and are essential to enhancing the effectiveness of peacekeeping missions. They serve as police officers, troops, pilots, military observers, and in other uniformed and civilian posts, including management.[3]

1.2   What Does Peacekeeping Entail?

United Nations Peacekeeping began in 1948 when the Security Council authorized the deployment of UN military observers to the Middle East to monitor *The Armistice Agreement* between Israel and its Arab neighbours.[4] Since then, more than 1 million men and women have served under the UN flag in more than 70 UN peacekeeping operations.[5]

Over the years, the United Nations and its system (specialized agencies, funds and programmes) have helped prevent many conflicts from flaring up into full-scale wars and also negotiated the peaceful settlement of conflicts, and on many occasions, helped defuse hostilities by conducting successful peacekeeping operations in dozens of countries, including Cambodia, El Salvador, Guatemala, Mozambique, Namibia and Tajikistan.[6]

UN peacekeeping has also made a real difference in other places with recently

---

1   Source from the website of the United Nations Peacekeeping, "Home/What is peacekeeping", accessed on August 2nd, 2021.

2   Source from the website of the United Nations Peacekeeping, "Home/What is peacekeeping/Our peacekeepers/ UN Peacekeeping: 70 Years of Service & Sacrifice", accessed on April 25th, 2023.

3   Ibid.

4   The mission's role was to monitor the Armistice Agreement between Israel and its Arab neighbors—an operation which became known as the United Nations Truce Supervision Organization (UNTSO). See more from the website of the United Nations Peacekeeping, "Home/What is peacekeeping/Our history", accessed on August 2nd, 2021.

5   Spencer Feingold, "Who are the Blue Helmets? UN Peacekeeping, Explained", *World Economic Forum*, September 21st, 2022.

6   United Nations Department of Public Information, *Everything You Wanted to Know about the United Nations,* New York: United Nations Publishing Section, 2010.

completed or on-going operations, such as the UN Mission in the Central African Republic and Chad (MINURCAT), UN Organization Stabilization Mission in the Democratic Republic of Congo (MONUSCO), UN Operation in Burundi (ONUB), UN Mission in Sierra Leone (UNAMSIL), UN Mission in Ethiopia and Eritrea (UNMEE), and UN Mission in the Sudan (UNMIS).[1] By providing basic security guarantees and responding to crises, these UN operations have supported political transitions and helped buttress fragile new state institutions. They have helped countries to close the chapter of conflict and open a path to normal development, even if major peace-building challenges remain.[2]

Featured History[3]

The United Nations Mission in Liberia (UNMIL) was deployed in 2003 to help restore peace and security in the country. After nearly 15 years in Liberia, the UN peacekeeping mission there successfully completed its mandate on 30 March, 2018, having disarmed more than 100,000 combatants, secured about 21,000 weapons, enabled about one million refugees and displaced persons to return home and assisted in the holding of three peaceful presidential and legislative elections.

During UNMIL's nearly 15-year mandate, dozens of countries from around the world deployed troops and police. Significant contributions were made by African nations such as Nigeria, Ghana and Ethiopia; Asian countries including Pakistan, Bangladesh, India and China; and European countries such as Ukraine, Sweden and Ireland. Peacekeepers from the United States also played an important role. The UN's secretary-general António Guterres in a statement issued in early April, 2018 expressed his "respect to the memory of 202 peacekeepers who lost their lives" in Liberia.

---

1 Source from the website of the United Nations Peacekeeping, "Home/What is peacekeeping/Our history", accessed on August 2nd, 2021.

2 Source from the website of the United Nations Peacekeeping, "Home/What is peacekeeping/Our successes", accessed on April 23rd, 2023.

3 Source from the website of the United Nations Peacekeeping, "United Nations Peacekeeping Mission in Liberia completes its mandate", accessed on March 22nd, 2019.

Operations are largely staffed by military personnel who are equipped in UN-blue colored helmets, earning the forces the "Blue Helmets" moniker.[1] Police personnel and other experts such as humanitarian specialists, legal advisors and economists are also often deployed.[2] The blue helmet, which has become the symbol of United Nations peacekeepers, is carried during all operations, and worn when there is danger. Peacekeepers dress in their respective national uniforms. Governments that volunteer personnel retain ultimate control over their own military forces serving under the United Nations flag.[3]

The UN's peacekeepers constitute the second-largest deployed military in the world. Today, a little more than 110,000 military, police and civilian staff currently serve in 12 peacekeeping missions deployed on three continents,[4] representing a decrease in both personnel and peacekeeping missions, because of peaceful transitions and the rebuilding of functioning states.

However, the reduction in personnel and peacekeeping missions in the intervening years by no means indicates that the challenges faced by the UN are diminishing. The emergence of new conflicts spreading beyond local and regional boundaries signals that the demand for field missions is expected to remain high and peacekeeping will continue to be one of the UN's most complex operational tasks. Moreover, the political complexity facing peacekeeping operations and the scope of their mandates, including on the civilian side, remain very broad. There are strong indications that certain specialized capabilities—including police—will be in especially high demand over the coming years.[5]

---

1   Spencer Feingold, "Who are the Blue Helmets? UN Peacekeeping, Explained", *World Economic Forum*, September 21st, 2022.

2   Ibid.

3   Source from the website of the United Nations Peacekeeping, "Home/What is peacekeeping/Our successes", accessed on August 2nd, 2021.

4   There are currently 12 peacekeeping operations led by the Department of Peace Operations, including: MINURSO (Western Sahara), MINUSCA (Central African Republic), MINUSMA (Mali), MONUSCO (D.R. of the Congo), UNDOF (Golan), UNFICYP (Cyprus), UNIFIL (Lebanon), UNISFA (Abyei), UNMIK (Kosovo), UNMISS (South Sudan), UNMOGIP (India and Pakistan), UNTSO (Middle East). Source from the website of the United Nations Peacekeeping, "Where we operate", accessed on October 10th, 2021.

5   Source from the website of the United Nations Peacekeeping, "Home/What is peacekeeping/Our history", accessed on October 10th, 2021.

1.3 How Peacekeeping Operations Are Formed?

Today's multidimensional peacekeeping operations will continue to facilitate the political process, protect civilians, assist in the disarmament, demobilization, and reintegration of former combatants; support the organization of elections, protect, and promote human rights, and assist in restoring the rule of law.[1] As they are tailored to specific conflicts, peacekeeping mandates can differ significantly. Additionally, the size of peacekeeping missions can vary from a force of tens of thousands or just a few hundred.[2]

The formation of a peacekeeping mission can be an onerous process.

First and foremost, peacekeepers can only be deployed with the consent of the warring parties. This can be extremely challenging to obtain when conflicts are raging as governments and political groups are often reluctant to have international actors interfere in their affairs.

Keep in Mind[3]

There are three basic principles that continue to set UN peacekeeping operations apart as a tool for maintaining international peace and security.

These three principles are inter-related and mutually reinforcing:

A. Consent of the Parties

UN peacekeeping operations are deployed with the consent of the main parties to the conflict. In the absence of such consent, a peacekeeping operation risks becoming a party to the conflict; and being drawn towards enforcement action, and away from its fundamental role of keeping the peace.

---

1 Source from the website of the United Nations Peacekeeping, "Home/What is peacekeeping/Our history", accessed on August 2nd, 2021.

2 Spencer Feingold, "Who are the Blue Helmets? UN Peacekeeping, Explained", *World Economic Forum*, September 21st, 2022.

3 Source from the website of the United Nations Peacekeeping, "Home/What is peacekeeping/Principles of peacekeeping".

B. Impartiality

Impartiality is crucial to maintaining the consent and cooperation of the main parties but should not be confused with neutrality or inactivity. United Nations peacekeepers should be impartial in their dealings with the parties to the conflict, but not neutral in the execution of their mandate.

C. Non-Use of Force Eexcept in Self-Defence and Defence of the Mandate

UN peacekeeping operations are not an enforcement tool. However, they may use force at the tactical level, with the authorization of the Security Council, if acting in self-defence and defence of the mandate. In certain volatile situations, the Security Council has given UN peacekeeping operations "robust" mandates authorizing them to "use all necessary means" to deter forceful attempts to disrupt the political process, protect civilians under imminent threat of physical attack, and/ or assist the national authorities in maintaining law and order.

UN peacekeeping operations must also be authorised by the Security Council, the UN's principal body for dealing with international peace and security. This requires a passing vote by the fifteen-member body without a single veto from one of the five permanent members: China, France, Russia, the United Kingdom, and the United States. This, too, can be challenging as creating consensus around conflict is often difficult.

If agreed upon, the Security Council creates a resolution that details a specific mandate for the operation and names senior leaders to lead the mission.

The General Assembly, the UN's main policymaking and representative organ, then determines the financing and staffing of the mission. The burden of peacekeeping operations is split between all UN member states, with some countries covering more of the cost while others provide more military and police personnel. As of 2022, Bangladesh, Nepal, India and Rwanda are the top personnel-contributing countries while the United States, China, Japan and Germany are the top financing countries.

Since the UN has no standing peacekeeping force, each peacekeeping operation is formed on an ad hoc basis. As former UN Secretary-General Kofi Annan once said, UN peacekeeping is "the only fire brigade in the world that has to wait for the fire to break out before it can acquire a fire engine."[1]

Read This[2]

2018 marked the 70th anniversary of the inception of the UN peacekeeping operation. The practice of 70 years has shown that the UN peacekeeping operation is a long-term cause and will continue to be an important means to maintain world peace and security. As a permanent member of the UN Security Council, China has been active in the participation of UN peacekeeping operations. More than 30,000 Chinese peacekeeping personnel have served in over 20 peacekeeping missions since 1990.

On September 28th, 2015, President Xi Jinping addressed the United Nations Leaders' Summit on Peacekeeping and announced a series of important measures that China would take to support the UN peacekeeping operations. The Chinese government has been actively fulfilling this solemn commitment. China has completed the registration of the 8,000-strong peacekeeping standby force and dispatched a helicopter squad to UNAMID (Darfur). In the future, China will play a more active and constructive role in UN peacekeeping operations.

Section 2

Regional Organization—The Association of Southeast Asian Nations

Regional organizations are "organizations created by States that share a common geographic or policy bond".[3] Some organizations incorporate international membership. However, their membership is characterized by

---

1 "Who Are the Blue Helmets? UN Peacekeeping, Explained", *World Economic Forum*, September 21st, 2022.

2 Jiang Zhenxi, "UN Peacekeeping Operatins and China's Participation in the Time of Great Changes", *U.N. Association of China*, accessed on April 23rd, 2023.

3 James E. Hickey Jr., "The Source of International Legal Personality in the 21st Century", *2 Hofstra L.& Pol'y Symp.*, 1997, p.8.

boundaries and demarcations characteristic to a defined and unique geography, such as continents, or geopolitics, such as economic blocks. Examples include the African Union (AU), the Organization of American States (OAS), the Caribbean Community (CARICOM), the Arab League, Association of Southeast Asian Nations (ASEAN). [1]

The Association of Southeast Asian Nations (more commonly known as ASEAN) is an inter-governmental organization aimed primarily at promoting economic growth and regional stability among its members. There are currently 10 member states: Indonesia, Malaysia, Philippines, Singapore, Thailand, Brunei, Laos, Myanmar, Cambodia, and Vietnam.[2]

2.1 Why Was ASEAN Set Up?

ASEAN was founded half a century ago in 1967 by the five Southeast Asian nations of Indonesia, Malaysia, Philippines, Singapore, and Thailand. This was during the polarized atmosphere of the Cold War, and the alliance aimed to promote stability in the region. Over time, the group expanded to include its current 10 members.

ASEAN aims to promote collaboration and cooperation among member states, as well as to advance the interests of the region, including economic and trade growth. It has negotiated a free trade agreement among member states and with other countries such as China, as well as eased travel in the region for citizens of member countries.

Regional cooperation was further extended with the creation of the ASEAN Plus Three forum in 1997, which included China, the Republic of Korea, and Japan. And then the East Asia Summit, which began taking place in 2005, has expanded to include India, Australia, New Zealand, Russia and the United States.

---

1 Other IGOs are referred to as "selective organizations" or "specialized organizations" because they base their membership on a common policy or certain criteria. The Organization of the Islamic Conference (OIC, formerly Organization of the Islamic Conference), for example, bases its membership on religious affiliation, while Organization of the Petroleum Exporting Countries (OPEC), on the other hand, is comprised only of countries that produce oil.

2 Source from the website of the World Economic Forum, "What is ASEAN?", May 9th, 2017, accessed on April 17th, 2023.

Read This[1]

ASEAN Plus Three (AZPT) consists of ten ASEAN Member States and the People's Republic of China, Japan, and the Republic of Korea. With ASEAN acting as the driving force, the APT Cooperation process began in December 1997, and has since developed into the primary tool for promoting East Asian Cooperation towards the long-term goal of building an "East Asian Community". The APT cooperation continues to be broadened and deepened in a wide range of areas, including political-security, trade and investment, finance, energy, tourism, agriculture and forestry, environment, education, health, culture, and arts, etc., among others. The APT has grown to become one of the most comprehensive frameworks for cooperation in the region. Additionally, the APT is in favour of putting the ASEAN Community Vision 2025 into action.

In 2015, it established the ASEAN Economic Community (AEC), a major milestone in the organization's regional economic integration agenda. The AEC envisions the bloc as a single market with free flow of goods, services, investments and skilled labour, and freer movement of capital across the region.

True to its original mission, the organization strives towards peace and stability in the region: members have signed a treaty pledging not to develop nuclear weapons, and most have agreed to a counter-terrorism pact, which includes sharing intelligence and easing the extradition process of terror suspects.

2.2   What Does ASEAN Do?

The Leaders envision ASEAN as a peaceful, stable, and resilient region within a global community of nations while still maintaining ASEAN centrality. ASEAN Community is seen as a community with enhanced capacity and capabilities to take advantage of opportunities and respond to challenges in an effective manner. The ASEAN Community was launched in 2015 and is supported by three community pillars: the political-security community, the economic community, and the socio-cultural

---

1　Source from the official website of ASEAN Plus Three, "Home/About APT/About ASEAN+3".

community.[1]

(1) Political-Security Community

The ASEAN Political-Security Community (APSC) aims to ensure regional peace and a just, democratic, and harmonious environment.

To build on what has been constructed over the years in the field of political and security cooperation, the ASEAN Leaders have agreed to establish the ASEAN Political-Security Community (APSC). The APSC shall aim to ensure that countries in the region live at peace with one another and with the world in a just, democratic and harmonious environment.

The members of the Community pledge to rely exclusively on peaceful processes in the settlement of intra-regional differences and regard their security as fundamentally linked to one another and bound by geographic location, common vision and objectives. It has the following components: political development; shaping and sharing of norms; conflict prevention; conflict resolution; post-conflict peace building; and implementing mechanisms.

(2) Economic Community

The ASEAN Economic Community (AEC) is the realization of the region's end goal of economic integration. It envisions ASEAN as a single market and product base, a highly competitive region, with equitable economic development, and fully integrated into the global economy.

The history of AEC can be traced back as far as 1992 when the ASEAN Leaders mandated the creation of the ASEAN Free Trade Area (AFTA). Since then, efforts were intensified to broaden the region's economic potentials. The adoption of ASEAN Vision 2020 by the Leaders in 1997 has further envisaged ASEAN as a highly competitive region with free flow of goods, services, investments, a freer flow of capital, equitable economic development and reduced poverty and socio-economic disparities.

In 1998, the Leaders adopted *The Hanoi Plan of Action (HPA)*. It chartered out a set of initiatives for economic integration to realize the ASEAN Vision 2020. Recognizing the need for an integrated region, the Leaders issued *The Declaration of ASEAN Concord II* in 2003 which set out the establishment of ASEAN Community (initially targeted by 2020 but was later accelerated to 2015). *The Declaration of ASEAN Concord II* comprises of three pillars including the AEC.

1　Source from the website of ASEAN, "Home/Our Communities", accessed on April 23rd, 2023.

(3) Socio-Cultural Community

The ASEAN Socio-Cultural Community is all about realising the full potential of ASEAN citizens. *The ASCC Blueprint 2025* was adopted by the ASEAN Leaders at the 27th ASEAN Summit on 22 November 2015 in Kuala Lumpur, Malaysia.

ACSS is working towards:

A committed, participative, and socially responsible community for the benefit of ASEAN people;

An inclusive community that promotes high quality of life, equitable access to opportunities for all, and promotes and protects human rights;

A sustainable community that promotes social development and environmental protection;

A resilient community with enhanced capacity and capability to adapt and respond to social and economic vulnerabilities, disasters, climate change, and other new challenges, and a dynamic and harmonious community that is aware and proud of its identity, culture, and heritage.

To achieve this, Member States are cooperating on a wide range of areas, including: Culture and Arts, Information and Media, Education, Youth, Sports, Social Welfare and Development, Gender, Rights of Women and Children, Rural Development and Poverty Eradication, Labour, Civil Service, Environment, Haze, Disaster Management and Humanitarian Assistance and Health.

Many of these issues, such as human capital development, social protection, pandemic response, humanitarian assistance, green jobs and circular economy, are cross-sectoral in nature. To manage both the cohesiveness of the pillar and cross-sectoral issues, two platforms have been developed: a. the ASCC Council, supported by the Senior Officials Meeting on the ASCC (SOCA), and b. the Coordinating Conference on the ASCC (SOC-COM).

2.3　How Do Members Cooperate?

ASEAN is headed by a chair—a position that rotates annually among member states—and is assisted by a secretariat based in Jakarta, Indonesia. It is an intergovernmental organization where important decisions are usually reached through consultation and consensus guided by the principles of non-interference in internal affairs and peaceful resolution of conflicts.[1]

ASEAN is not, and was not meant to be, a supranational entity acting independently of its members. It has no regional parliament or council of ministers with law-making powers, no power of enforcement, and no judicial system. Much less is it like NATO, with armed forces at its command, or the UN Security Council, which can authorise military action by its members under one flag.[2]

Fundamental Principles[2]

In their relations with one another, the ASEAN Member States have adopted the following fundamental principles, as contained in *The Treaty of Amity and Cooperation in Southeast Asia* (TAC) of 1976:

- Mutual respect for the independence, sovereignty, equality, territorial integrity, and national identity of all nations;
- The right of every State to lead its national existence free from external interference, subversion or coercion;
- Non-interference in the internal affairs of one another;
- Settlement of differences or disputes by peaceful manner;
- Renunciation of the threat or use of force; and
- Effective cooperation among themselves.

The ASEAN Secretariat was set up in February 1976 by the Foreign Ministers of ASEAN. It was then housed at the Department of Foreign Affairs of Indonesia in Jakarta. *The Agreement on the Establishment of the ASEAN Secretariat* states that its basic mandate is "to provide for greater efficiency in the coordination of ASEAN organs and for more effective implementation of ASEAN projects and activities." In 1992, the ASEAN Summit agreed to redesignate the Secretary-General of the ASEAN Secretariat into the Secretary-General of ASEAN with an enlarged mandate to initiate, advise,

---

1　"What is ASEAN?", *Council on Foreign Relations*, April 11th, 2022.

2　Rodolfo C. Severino, "ASEAN and the Growth of Regional Cooperation in Southeast Asia", *Homepage of ASEAN*, August 1st, 1999.

3　Source from the website of the Association of Southeast Asian Nations, "Home/What We Do", accessed on April 25th, 2023.

coordinate, and implement ASEAN activities. Since 1992, the staff of the ASEAN Secretariat has been professionalised through open and competitive recruitment.[1]

The Secretary-General has been accorded ministerial status. He is selected by the ASEAN Ministerial Meeting (AMM) and appointed by the Heads of Government on the basis of merit. His tenure of office is five years. In addition to being in charge of the ASEAN Secretariat, the Secretary-General serves as the spokesman and representative of ASEAN on all matters; addresses the AMM on all aspects of regional cooperation and offers assessments and recommendations on ASEAN's external relations; attends and advises all ASEAN meetings at the ministerial level; and chairs on behalf of the Chairman of the ASEAN Standing Committee (ASC) all meetings of the ASC except the first and last for each year.[2]

Read This[3]

When ASEAN was established in 1967, many were uncertain about its chances of survival. It was born amidst regional tensions—particularly the escalation of the Vietnam War. High in ideals, ASEAN developed an institutional base slowly.

The Treaty of Amity and Cooperation was signed in 1976, stressing core ASEAN principles of mutual respect and non-interference in each others' affairs. ASEAN established a Free Trade Area in 1992 but economic integration made little progress. The first meeting of the ASEAN Regional Forum was held in 1994. It has become a key regional political and security dialogue, with a current membership of twenty-six countries.

Hit by the economic crisis of 1997 and 1998, the region bounced back fairly quickly. Since then, ASEAN has sought greater internal economic, social, political, and cultural cooperation. It is also looking to place itself at the center of greater regional cooperation and integration. First, through the ASEAN plus 3 processes (involving China, Japan and the Republic of Korea). And then by establishing the East Asia Summit, which added New Zealand, Australia, and India to the ASEAN plus 3 grouping.

---

1 Source from the website of the Association of Southeast Asian Nations, "Home/What We Do", accessed on April 25th, 2023.

2 Ibid.

3 Source: Hon Phil Goff, "ASEAN at Forty: Reflections and Visions", *Beehive.govt.nz*, May 26th, 2007.

ASEAN has been, and still is, criticised for being ineffectual. Burdened, so the argument runs, by principles of consensus decision-making and non-interference. But it has attained a notable international standing perhaps exceptional among regional groupings of post-colonial states. It faces many challenges—not least an extraordinary 400 plus meetings a year. But it has survived, and the region has remained remarkably stable.

We should also not underestimate the extent to which the countries have become intertwined in a web of personal and institutional networks. These links can be vital, especially in difficult times, and are slowly creating an ASEAN sense of community.

Section 3
Supranational Organization—The European Union

Supranational organizations are hybrid organizations composed of States. They are structured in a way similar to federal States. They make decisions binding directly on member States and their nationals, and their laws have supremacy over, and override conflicting, national laws of member States. A typical example is the European Union (EU). The EU is established in such a way that EU law does not only bind member States which it regulates but has direct effect on the nationals of these member States. Rights and obligations created by EU law must be upheld by the domestic courts of member States.

The European Union (EU) is a one-of-a-kind international organization comprised of 27 European countries that cover a large portion of the continent. Initially limited to Western Europe, the EU began a significant expansion into Central and Eastern Europe in the early 21st century.[1]

---

1 Source from the website of Britannica, "European Union/ European organization", accessed on September 10th, 2021.

Currently, the EU's members are: Austria, Belgium, Bulgaria, Croatia, Cyprus, the Czech Republic, Denmark, Estonia, Finland, France, Germany, Greece, Hungary, Ireland, Italy, Latvia, Lithuania, Luxembourg, Malta, the Netherlands, Poland, Portugal, Romania, Slovakia, Slovenia, Spain, and Sweden. The United Kingdom, which had been a founding member of the EU, left the organization in 2020.[1]

3.1　What Is the EU?[2]

The EU represents one in a series of efforts to integrate Europe since World War II. At the end of the war, several western European countries sought closer economic, social, and political ties to achieve economic growth and military security and to promote a lasting reconciliation between France and Germany.

To this end, in 1951, the leaders of six countries—Belgium, France, Italy, Luxembourg, the Netherlands, and West Germany—signed *The Treaty of Paris*, thereby, when it took effect in 1952, founding the European Coal and Steel Community (ECSC). (The United Kingdom had been invited to join the ECSC and in 1955, sent a representative to observe discussions about its ongoing development, but the Labour government of Clement Attlee declined membership, owing perhaps to a variety of factors, including the illness of key ministers, a desire to maintain economic independence, and a failure to grasp the community's impending significance.[3])

The ECSC created a free-trade area for several key economic and military resources: coal, coke, steel, scrap, and iron ore. To manage the ECSC, the treaty established several supranational institutions: a High Authority to administrate, a Council of Ministers to legislate, a Common Assembly to formulate policy, and a Court of Justice to interpret the treaty and to resolve related disputes. A series of further international treaties and treaty revisions based largely on this model led eventually to the creation of the EU. The decisive milestone was reached subsequent to the signing of *The Maastricht Treaty* officially titled *The Treaty on European Union*, on February 7th, 1992.

1　On March 29th, 2017, the United Kingdom provided formal notification under Article 50 of *The Treaty on European Union* of its intention to leave the European Union and Euratom.

2　Source from the website of Britannica, "European Union/European Organization", accessed on March 28th, 2022.

3　Matthew J. Gabel, "European Union-European organization", see also in the website of Britannica, "European Union/ARTICLE/Origins", accessed on September 10th, 2021.

What began as a purely economic union has evolved into an organization spanning policy areas, from climate, environment and health to external relations and security, justice, and migration, and continues to develop towards its full potential. A name change from the European Economic Community (EEC) to the European Union (EU) in 1993 reflected this.[1] Treaties after treaties, the EU has now 27 member countries, mainly working together to maintain peace and prosperity in Europe and worldwide.

The EU has achieved a lot. For example, it has built a single market based on "four freedoms", with people, goods, services and capital moving freely between all Member States. The single market means that over 500 million EU citizens are free to move and settle where they wish in the Union. It has also created *The Charter of Fundamental Rights of the European Union*, which protects certain political, social, and economic rights for EU citizens and residents.[2] The EU was awarded the Nobel Prize for Peace in 2012, in recognition of the organization's efforts to promote peace and democracy in Europe.

Read This[3]

The EU's powers and authority come from its member states: it can do only the things that its members have agreed it should be able to do. In that sense, it is no different from other international organisations, such as the United Nations or NATO. However, the EU is different to other international organisations in two key ways.

First, the EU is involved in almost all areas of public policy (though to varying degrees). For example:

- It does a lot of regional development work in poorer parts of the EU.
- It encourages cooperation between countries on issues such as foreign policy, international aid, security and defence, and criminal investigations.
- It runs the Euro currency for the countries that use it.

---

1 Directorate-General for Communication (European Commission), *The European Union: What It Is and What It Does*, Luxembourg: Publications Office of the European Union, 2018.

2 Ibid.

3 Source from: "Background: A Quick Introduction to the EU", *Citizens' Assembly*, September 8th, 2017.

Second, the EU has institutions that in some ways make it look more like a country than an international organisation. In other international organisations, key decisions are made by the governments of the Member States meeting together. This happens in the EU. But in the EU decisions are also made by the European Parliament. The European Parliament is unique. It is the only international body in the world whose members are chosen directly by ordinary voters.

3.2　How Does the EU Work?[1]

The unique feature of the EU is that, although the Member States all remain sovereign and independent states, they have decided to pool some of their "sovereignty" in areas where it makes sense to work together. In practice, this means that the Member States delegate some of their decision-making powers to the shared institutions they have created, so that decisions on specific matters of common interest can be made democratically at the EU level.

There are 3 main institutions involved in EU legislation:

- The European Parliament, which represents the EU's citizens and is directly elected by them.
- The Council of the European Union, which represents the governments of the individual member countries. The Presidency of the Council is shared by the Member States on a rotating basis. When the prime ministers and presidents are meeting, this is called the European Council.
- The European Commission, which manages the EU's work. It is the EU's civil service.

Together, these three institutions produce through the "Ordinary Legislative Procedure" (ex "co-decision") the policies and laws that apply throughout the EU.[2] The Council's main job is to create and propose new policies and legislation for the European

---

1　James McBride, "How Does the European Union Work?", *Council on Foreign Relations*, March 11th, 2022.

2　Source from the website of the European Union, "Home/About the EU/Institutions and bodies", accessed on October 7th, 2021.

Union. Led by its President and comprising national heads of state or government and the President of the Commission, it meets for a few days at a time at least twice every 6 months. The Parliament then debates and passes the laws proposed by the Council, electing members once every five years.

Finally, the Commission enforces and operates the laws for the European Union. Additionally, the European Central Bank serves the EU's financial needs and manages things like inflation rates and foreign exchange reserves. The EU remains focused on making its governing institutions more transparent and democratic. Decisions are taken as openly as possible and as closely as possible to the citizen. More powers have been given to the directly elected European Parliament, while national parliaments play a greater role, working alongside the European institutions.

Two other institutions play vital roles:

● The Court of Justice of the EU upholds the rule of European law.

● The Court of Auditors checks the financing of the EU's activities.

These EU institutions form a complex web of powers and mutual oversight.

How Do the EU Institutions Work Together?

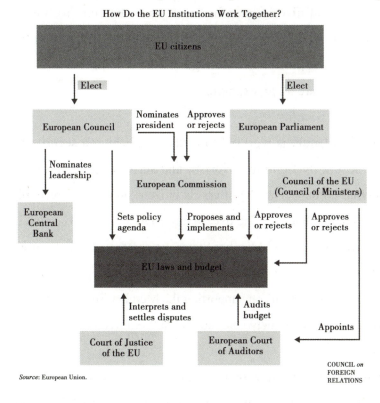

Source: European Union.

At base they draw their democratic legitimacy from elections in two ways. First, the European Council, which sets the bloc's overall political direction, is composed of democratically elected national leaders. Second, the European Parliament is composed of representatives—known as members of the European Parliament, or MEPs—who are directly elected by the citizens of each EU member state.

The European Council and Parliament together determine the composition of the European Commission—the council nominates its members and Parliament must approve them. The commission has the sole authority to propose EU laws and spending, but all EU legislation requires the approval of both Parliament and the Council of Ministers.

3.3　What Does EU Do?

According to the European Union's official website, the union's purpose is to promote peace, establish a unified economic and monetary system, promote inclusion and combat discrimination, break down barriers to trade and borders, encourage technological and scientific developments, champion environmental protection, and, among others, promote goals like a competitive global market and social progress. Here are a few examples.

(1) Borders and Security

The European Union is working towards establishing a security union, making Europe more secure by fighting terrorism and serious crime and by strengthening Europe's external borders. The EU offers its citizens an area of freedom, security and justice without internal borders. The overall objective of a security union is to make this area a safer place. The EU and Member States cooperate to tackle terrorism and violent radicalization, serious and organized crime and cyber-crime.

The EU focuses its actions on supporting the Member States through:

- Information exchange between national law enforcement, customs agencies and border guards;
- Operational cooperation, with the support of EU agencies;
- Training, exchange of best practice, funding, research, and innovation.

The EU has updated and reinforced its laws, harmonizing the definition of terrorist offenses and criminalizing terrorist travel, training, and financing. With the support of the Radicalization Awareness Network Centre of Excellence, the EU is stepping up efforts to prevent radicalization and to address the challenge of returning foreign terrorist fighters. Through the EU Internet Forum, the Commission is facilitating cooperation between key Internet companies, law enforcement agencies and civil society to reduce access to illegal content online and provide effective alternative narratives to counter terrorist propaganda.

(2) Education and Training

The EU helps improve the quality of education by encouraging cooperation between the Member States and by complementing national actions. Erasmus+ provides opportunities for people of all ages and enables young people to study, train, gain work experience or volunteer abroad.

Investing in education and training is the key to people's future, particularly if they are young. The EU has set up a number of other initiatives to make it easier for people to study, train or work abroad. European countries, trade unions and employers cooperate to improve vocational and educational training through the Copenhagen process. One result is the European Credit System for Vocational Education and Training and quality assurance network, which helps people work and study abroad. The Bologna process and the European Higher Education Area make it easier for people to move between education systems within Europe by promoting mutual recognition of periods of study, comparable qualifications, and uniform quality standards.

(3) High Food Standards

Health protection is the aim of all EU laws and standards in the agriculture, animal husbandry and food production sectors. An extensive body of EU-wide law covers the entire food production and processing chain within the EU, as well as imported and exported goods.[1] Four main areas of protection are the focus of EU food safety policy and action:

1　Source from the website of the European Union, "Home/Priorities and Actions/Actions by topic/Food safety in the EU", accessed on April 24th, 2023.

- Food hygiene: food businesses, from farms to restaurants, must comply with EU food law, including those importing food to the EU.

- Animal health: sanitary controls and measures for pets, farmed animals and wildlife, monitoring and managing diseases, and tracing the movement of all farm animals.

- Plant health: detection and eradication of pests at an early stage to prevent spreading and ensure healthy seeds.

- Contaminants and residues: monitoring keeps contaminants away from food and animal feed. Maximum acceptable limits apply to domestic and imported food and feed products.[1]

Thanks to the member countries' cooperation, the food and environment in the EU meet the world's highest quality standards.

(4) Global Clout

The EU promotes cooperation and collaboration among European countries and provides a shared identity for its Member States. Hence, European states find it much easier to cooperate in an organisation like the European Union. Besides, with the 27 member countries working together, there is much more voice than 27 nations acting separately.[2]

The EU is the world's largest trade block and the biggest exporter of manufactured goods and services. Additionally, the organisation plays a significant role when it comes to diplomacy. It promotes security and prosperity, stability, fundamental freedoms, and democracy internationally. Other countries and regions that want coordination in their economic, social, and political systems can use European states policies as a model.[3]

---

1 Source from the website of the European Union, "Home/Priorities and Actions/Actions by topic/Food safety in the EU", accessed on April 24th, 2023.

2 "Goals, Values, and Benefits of the European Union", *Endevio*, accessed on April 24th, 2023.

3 Ibid.

Remember This[1]

Currently, the European Union is described as being in a state of crisis and chaos. This may be the case, but it's important to consider the long-term picture. Apart from Brexit, the European Union has witnessed a continuous increase in its size and competences. The last few decades have seen, for the first time, real progress in increasing the European Union's competency beyond economic aspects. Among the many benefits of European Union, the EU has achieved greater input legitimacy through a stronger and more representative European Parliament in relation to other institutions (although there is still a long way to go).

·Tasks

Activity 1 | Multiple-Choice Test

How well do you know about the above-mentioned organizations? Take this quiz to find out more information about them. Please be noted that, each question only has one answer.

1. Examples of IGOs are_____.

　　A. The United Nations and the EU

　　B. The International Committee of the Red Cross and the G-20

　　C. The International Olympic Committee and Greenpeace

　　D. The G-8 and the Boao Forum for Asia (BFA)

2. Why has the United Nations often been ineffective in maintaining international peace and security?

　　A. Its members regularly withhold funds for the UN.

　　B. The states of the international system place no importance on the resolutions adopted by the UN.

　　C. It fails to adopt resolutions unless there is agreement among the five permanent members of the Security Council.

1　Ricardo Ángel Barrientos, "A Reflection on the Future of the European Union: Towards an EU of Purpose and Promise", *Lawahead*, accessed on April 25th, 2023.

D. All of the options.

3. Missions in which Blue Helmets observe, act as a buffer, and, as a last resort, are allowed to use military force are called_____.

    A. Observer Missions   B. Peacekeeping Missions

    C. Peace Enforcement Missions   D. None of the above.

4. What is the full form of ASEAN?

    A. Association of Southeast Asian Nations.

    B. Administration of Southeast Asian Nations.

    C. Administration of Southern Eastern Asian Nations.

    D. Organisation of Southeast Asian Nations.

5. Which of the following country is not the member of ASEAN?

    A. Mauritius.   B. Laos.   C. Cambodia.   D. Philippines.

6. What is the objective of ASEAN?

    A.To increase competition among the members countries for better products.

    B. To integrate the economies of the region to make region more attractive for investors.

    C. To promote economic cooperation in South East Asia and ensure economic stability in the region.

    D. B and C both.

7. What large international organization had its humble beginnings with the European Coal and Steel Community (ECSC)?

    A. European Atomic Energy Community (Euratom).

    B. European Organization for Nuclear Research (CERN).

    C. Western European Union (WEU).

    D. European Union (EU).

8. Which of the following is not a European Union institution?

    A. European External Action Service.

    B. Court of Justice of the European Union.

    C. European Court of Auditors.

    D. European Court of Human Rights.

9. Which of the following dynamics of globalization have been mirrored by the developments in the EU?

A. EU integration has fed on and contributed to the global trend towards neo-liberal economic policy.

B. The trend towards greater social and cultural exchange has intensified.

C. Despite the growth of an integrated market there is no real integrated civil society.

D. All of the options given are correct.

10. What is regionalism?

A. Creation of a new polity bringing together a number of different constituent parts.

B. Regular and sustained interaction between states on policy issues.

C. Development of institutionalized cooperation among states and other actors on the basis of regional contiguity as a feature of global politics.

D. Creation of institutions having independent decision-making authority.

(Activity 2) Short-answer Questions

Have a discussion with your classmates and choose 3 of the following questions to answer. Think critically. You have 10 minutes to work on it and a computer to help. Support the claims you make.

1. What global organization was founded in the Treaty of Versailles and sought to guarantee global peace through "collective security"?

2. What is the international peacekeeping? What significance does it hold for those wishing to study international organizations and global governance?

3. What is the role of inter-governmental conferences?

4. How long does the Secretary-General of ASEAN serve in one term?

5. Where is the ASEAN Secretariat located?

6. Why are there 12 stars on the European flag?

7. How is the EU relevant to your daily life?

8. Evaluate the contribution of regional security organizations to the maintenance of international security in any region of your choice. The region could be Africa, South East Asia, the North Atlantic Region, or any other region of which you might have some special knowledge.

Activity 3 Gap Filling

Exercise 1 *Fill in the gaps with the right words: states; founded; headquarter; rights; organization; law.*

The United Nations is an international _____ which was _____ in 1945 after World War II, in order to stop conflicts between countries, and to provide a platform for dialogues. Its main goals are facilitating cooperation in international _____ , international security, economic development, social progress, human _____ , and achievement of world peace. The United Nations consists of 193 member_____ . The United Nations' _____ resides in international territory in New York City.

Exercise 2 *Match each organization in the list with its corresponding mission.*
UNESCO, WHO, WTO, UNHCR, WB, UNICEF, UN, IMF, FAO, ILO

1. Provides humanitarian and developmental assistance to children in poor and developing countries: _____

2. Safeguards and protects human including political prisoners' rights: _____

3. Provides medical care during natural and war disasters: _____

4. Founded in 1945 after World War II, to end wars between nations, and provide a platform for dialogue, peace, social and political justice: _____

5. Aims at eradicating hunger and starvation in poor countries, and ensuring food security and good nutrition: _____

6. Is concerned with public health: _____

7. Seeks to promote labors rights: _____

8. Promotes international collaboration through education, science, and culture to ensure universal respect for justice: _____

Activity 4 Writing Practice

In this chapter, we have looked at many different types of international organizations and UN agencies. Now, pick one. Research your favourite subject (be it health, education, development, peace, etc.) and find an international organization or UN agency working in this area. You can find a list of UN agencies or look up organizations working on each SDG online.

Directory of United Nations Systen Organizations

CEB Member Organizations		United Nations	UN Funds & Programmes	Specialized Agencies	
	Regional Commissions		Research & TrainingInstitutes		Jointly Financed Bodies
		Related Organizations		Other Entities	
			Inter–Agency Coordination Mechanisms		

Visit the organization's website and read about their mandate, history, founding document, and day-to-day work on the ground.

Then Write a short paragraph (3—4 sentences) to share with your instructor and fellow students why you chose the organization and what you have learned about their work. This way you can learn together about the scope and variety of international organizations.

(Activity 5) **Extended Reading**

Fostering High-quality Partnership and Embarking

on a New Journey of BRICS Cooperation

(An Excerpt)

Remarks by H.E. Xi Jinping, President of the People's Republic of China

at the 14th BRICS Summit (June 23rd, 2022)

Dear Colleagues,

Our world today is living through accelerating changes unseen in a century and continued spread of the COVID-19 pandemic. They confront humanity with unprecedented challenges and usher in a new phase of instability and transformation for global development.

The Chinese people often say, "True gold can stand the test of fire." Over the past 16 years, the giant ship of BRICS has sailed forward tenaciously against raging torrents and storms. Riding the wind and cleaving the waves, it has embarked on a righteous course of mutual support and win-win cooperation. Standing at the crossroads of history, we should both look back at the journey we have traveled and keep in mind why we established BRICS in the first place, and look forward to a shared future of a more comprehensive, close, practical and inclusive high-quality partnership so as to jointly embark on a new journey of BRICS cooperation.

First, we need to uphold solidarity and safeguard world peace and tranquility. Our world today is overshadowed by the dark clouds of Cold War mentality and power politics, and beset by constantly emerging traditional and non-traditional security threats. Some countries attempt to expand military alliances to seek absolute security, stoke bloc-based confrontation by coercing other countries into picking sides, and pursue unilateral dominance at the expense of others' rights and interests. If such dangerous trends are allowed to continue, the world will witness even more turbulence and insecurity.

　... ...

Not long ago, I put forward the Global Security Initiative (GSI), which advocates a vision of common, comprehensive, cooperative and sustainable security, follows the philosophy that humanity is an indivisible security community, and aims to create a new path to security that features dialogue over confrontation, partnership over alliance and win-win over zero-sum. China would like to work with BRICS partners to operationalize the GSI and bring more stability and positive energy to the world.

Second, we need to uphold cooperation to boost development and jointly tackle risks and challenges. The combination of the COVID-19 pandemic and the Ukraine crisis has resulted in disruptions to global industrial and supply chains, sustained hikes of commodity prices, and weaker international monetary and financial systems. All these have cast shadows over development worldwide, and emerging markets and developing countries bear the brunt. But just as a crisis may bring chaos, it can also spur change. A lot will ride on how we handle the crisis.

This year, we launched the BRICS Initiative on Enhancing Cooperation on Supply Chains and the Initiative on Trade and Investment for Sustainable Development, adopted *The Agreement on Cooperation and Mutual Administrative Assistance in Customs Matters and the Strategy on Food Security Cooperation,* and held a High-level Meeting on Climate Change for the first time. We should make good use of these new platforms to boost connectivity of industrial and supply chains and jointly meet challenges in poverty reduction, agriculture, energy, logistics and other fields. We should support greater development of the New Development Bank and a steady process to admit new members, and improve the Contingent Reserve Arrangement to cement the BRICS financial safety net and firewall. We should also expand BRICS cooperation on cross-border payment and credit rating to facilitate trade, investment and financing among our countries.

... ...

Third, we need to uphold the pioneering spirit and innovation and unleash the potential and vitality of cooperation. Those who seize the opportunities of the new economy, such as big data and artificial intelligence, are in sync with the pulse of the times. Those who seek to create monopoly, blockades and barriers in science and technology in order to disrupt other countries' innovation and development and hold on to their dominant position are doomed to fail.

We need to improve global science and technology governance and allow more people to access and benefit from the fruits of scientific and technological advances. This year, we have accelerated the building of the BRICS Partnership on New Industrial Revolution Innovation Center in Xiamen, hosted the Forum on the Development of Industrial Internet and Digital Manufacturing and the Forum on Big Data for Sustainable Development, reached the Digital Economy Partnership Framework, issued *The Initiative for Cooperation on Digitalization of Manufacturing*, and established a network of technology transfer centers and an aerospace cooperation mechanism. All these have opened new channels for closer industrial policy coordination between BRICS countries. Recognizing the importance of talents in the digital age, we have set up the Alliance for Vocational Education, and organized the Skills Competition and the Women Innovation Contest to build a talent pool for stronger BRICS cooperation in innovation and entrepreneurship.

Fourth, we need to uphold openness and inclusiveness and pool collective wisdom and strength. BRICS countries gather not in a closed club or an exclusive circle, but a big family of mutual support and a partnership for win-win cooperation. At the Xiamen Summit in 2017, I proposed the "BRICS Plus" cooperation approach. Over the past five years, "BRICS Plus" cooperation has deepened and expanded, setting a prime example of South-South cooperation and seeking strength through unity among emerging markets and developing countries.

Under the new circumstances, it is all the more important for BRICS countries to pursue development with open doors and boost cooperation with open arms. This year we, for the first time, invited guest countries to attend the BRICS Foreign Ministers' Meeting. The newly established BRICS Vaccine R&D Center has an unequivocal commitment to openness. Step by step, we have organized a variety of "BRICS Plus" events in such areas as scientific and technological innovation, people-to-people exchanges and sustainable development. All these provide new platforms for cooperation among emerging markets and developing countries.

Colleagues, as representatives of emerging markets and developing countries, we must make the right decision and take responsible actions at this critical juncture in history. What we do will have a significant impact on the world. Let us stay united, pool strength and forge ahead to build a community with a shared future for mankind and jointly create a bright future for humanity.

Thank you.

Chapter 3

An Introduction to the International Civil Service

The principles of the Charter are, by far, greater than the Organization in which they are embodied, and the aims which they are to safeguard are holier than the policies of any single nation or people.

—Dag Hammarskjöld, the second Secretary-General of the United Nations[1]

---

1 Dag Hammarskjöld, Statement to the United Nations Security Council during the Suez Crisis, October 31st, 1956, Official Records of the United Nations Security Council, 751st meeting,

Overview

Learning Objectives

a. To explore the origins of the concept, problems, the logic of reform, and specific improvements of the international civil service;

b. To grasp the significance of the international civil service as an interesting and viable approach to Inter-Governmental Organizations and international law;

c. To think critically and conclude with the specifics of the accountability and morality expected of an international civil servant.

Main Contents

The international civil service holds an important position in the evolution of international organizations. As Langrod (1963) wrote, "[i]t is nowhere possible to administer without administrators. At every level this remains axiomatic."[1] The origin of international civil service was a practical response to administrative demands: in line with increasing international regulation and cooperation, there arose the need for logistical support, so as to plan, promote, and implement international policies and agendas.[2]

It is basing on this that, this chapter launches the topic with an introduction to the administrative Secretariat of international organizations. It then moves on to a more specific discussion of the United Nations Secretariat, the organ that administers and coordinates the activities of the United Nations. From this it follows that, Kofi Annan, the seventh Secretary-General of the United Nations, brings to the position a wealth of experience and expertise gained through more than three decades of service with the world Organization.[3]

---

1 Georges Langrod, *The International Civil Service*, New York: Oceana Publications, 1963, p.24.

2 Edward Newman, "*The International Civil Service*: Still a Viable Concept?", *Global Society*, v.21, n.3, 2007, p.431.

3 "Kofi Annan, United Nations Secretary-General", Press Release SG/2031 BIO/3053*, January 10th, 1997, source from the official website of the United Nations "Press Release/Secretary-General/Miscellaneous", accessed on January 10th, 2022.

Warm-up[1]

This year marks a century since a formal international civil service was introduced into the world. The first time this breed of professionals came into existence was at the signing of *The Versailles Peace Conference* during 1919 and the subsequent establishment of the League of Nations in January 1920.

For global governance, an international civil service matters. Simply because it would be impossible to promote and maintain a rules-based world order without it. An autonomous civil service is crucial for operations within the global governance system—an idea conceptualized 100 years ago at the League of Nations. Already then, international civil servants were expected to be loyal to the aspirations of the international community and to remain neutral and independent of any authority outside their organization.

Eric Drummond, a British diplomat involved in the drafting of the League of Nations Covenant and the first Secretary General of the League of Nations (1919—1933), played a crucial and pioneering role in conceptualizing an independent international civil service. But it was Dag Hammarskjöld, the UN's second Secretary General (1953—1961), who elaborated the concept. He set lasting standards that survive to this day.

An independent civil service was a huge part of Hammarskjöld's arsenal. As his numerous statements and speeches document, his terms in office were guided by strong and coherent ethics concerning the independence of the international civil service. At the core of his ethics were integrity, loyalty to the principles of *The UN Charter*, independence from any national or regional interests and the courage to uphold these values

◀ • Questions

(1) What are the core values adopted by the UN for an independent civil servant?

(2) Can you discuss with your partners and present evidence why the international civil service matters?

---

1 The passage was excerpted from: "It's a Century since an International Civil Service Came into Being. Why It Matters?", *The Conversation*, April 22nd, 2019.

(3) Pause a little bit and do some research into Eric Drummond's and Dag Hammarskjöld's life and thinking. Also remember to take into considerations of their growth background and the environment back then.

Section 1
The Basics about the International Civil Service

For any multilateral organization today, an "international civil service" is crucial. Without "diverse", "independent" and "loyal" professionals to manage its day-to-day operations, it is impossible to plan, promote and implement international polices and agendas. And today, when global efforts are essential to address issues such as climate change and the spread of new digital technologies, the world needs high-quality international civil servants more than ever to assist the world public service to succeed in its global mandate.[1]

1.1   Historical Development of the International Civil Service

International civil service is the brainchild of World War I. The first time the notion of an "international civil service" came into existence was at the signing of *The Treaty of Versailles* during 1919 and the subsequent establishment of the League of Nations in January 1920.[2]

Considering the state of the world at that time, and the objectives of the League,[3] the assembly unanimously voted for the establishment of an international bureaucracy and the appointment of staff. There was no mention of international civil service or international civil servants during this assembly of the League. However, it set up a commission to study and make recommendations to the League on matters relating to

---

1   Kemal Dervis, "The Case for International Civil Servants", *Brookings*, November 1st, 2019.

2   Marco Moraes, *Internationalism as an Organisational Practice: The League of Nations Secretary-General*,1918-1946, DPhil Thesis in the Department of Politics and International Relations, University of Oxford, 2020, p.95.

3   The League of Nations was established to promote international co-operation and to achieve international peace and security by the acceptance of obligations not to resort to war but to settle disputes by peaceful negotiations.

the recruitment and remuneration of the staff.

The concept of the international civil service was clearly illuminated in the commission's report to the Council of the League. The commission report to the Council of the League set in motion a supranational spirit and paved the way for the establishment of a true international civil service. It recommended appointment of staff of the League, under the supervision of the Secretary-General. In making the appointment, the report drew the attention of the Secretary-General to the need to select the best men and women for the particular duties that have to be performed, and the importance of selecting the staff from various nations. The report referred to the staff thus selected as "international staff of the League".

The significance of the word "international" has been used to this date to illustrate the fact that although national governments determine the missions of multilateral institutions, once appointed to the UN system organization, the appointees cease to be the servants of the country of which they are citizens, but become, for the time being, the servants only of the international organization; their duties are no longer national, but international. This concept was translated into *The League Staff Regulations*: "They may not seek or receive instructions from any government or other authority external to the secretariat of the League of Nations".[1]

With the creation of the United Nations, the experiments and experiences of the League were transformed into fully fledged, formalized concepts and principles and lifted to the highest legal level enshrined in *The UN Charter*,[2] thus endowing it with an even more solemn statutory character.[3] Paradoxically, nationality is of primary importance in an international civil service. Allied to the concept of such a service is the concept of a proper spread of nationalities, or as it is now commonly called, "geographical

---

1　Aamir Ali, "The International Civil Service: The Idea and the Reality", in 90th Anniversary of the Founding of the International Civil Service, *AAFI-AFICS Commemorative Report*, December 2009, p.3.

2　"In the performance of their duties the Secretary-General and the staff shall not seek or receive instructions from any government or from any other authority external to the Organization. They shall refrain from any action which might reflect on their position as international officials responsible only to the Organization." Source from *Article 100 of the Charter of the United Nations*, see also the website of the Codification Division Publications: Repertory of Practice of United Nations Organs, last update: March 31st, 2021.

3　Frédéric Mégret, "What Is 'International Impartiality'?", in Vesselin Popovski(ed.), *International Rule of Law and Professional Ethics*, United Nations University Institute for Sustainability and Peace(UNU-ISP), Japan, New York: Routledge, 2016, p.105.

distribution". This, too, is enshrined in the charters and the constitutions of the agencies. Quite rightly, the two provisions are linked closely together. "So far as is possible with due regard to the efficiency of the work of the Office, the Director-General selects persons of different nationalities", says *The ILO Constitution*.[1]

The new and enhanced legal status of the international civil servant was substantiated by the creation of a new *UN Standard of Conduct for International Civil Service*. In 1949, the International Civil Service Advisory Board was set up to develop a standard of conduct for international civil servants. Here too, the continuities from the League, are clear. The Board was chaired by the long-term League official Thanassis Aghnides and in its work the Board drew heavily on the so-called *London Report*, which had been drawn up by Sir Eric Drummond and other leading ex-League officials in London during the war. In the report they collected what they considered the most important institutional know-how of the League Secretariat to subsequent international organizations.

The work of the Board resulted in *The Report on Standards of Conduct in the International Civil Service* (1st edition, 1954), which came to serve as a handbook for international civil servants in the UN, the ILO, the WHO, GATT and many other international organizations. *The Standards of Conduct* remained relatively unchanged until 2001, getting its last major update in 2013. It is still an important document for international civil servants today.

Like the League, the UN experienced growing pains during its early years of operation that tested the international civil service. In addition to hindering the UN's ability to intervene in global conflicts, polarization between the United States and the Soviet Union during the Cold War permeated internal decision-making at the UN. In the most high-profile example, in 1952 the first UN Secretary-General, Trygve Lie (1946—1952), capitulated to US pressure and dismissed 18 US nationals employed by the UN who had been accused of harbouring communist sympathies. The subsequent decision by the UN Administrative Tribunal to award compensation to those who appealed their wrongful dismissal re-asserted the independence of the international

---

1　Aamir Ali, "The International Civil Service: The Idea and the Reality", in 90th Anniversary of the Founding of the International Civil Service, *AAFI-AFICS Commemorative Report*, December 2009, p.5.

civil service after Lie's lapse.[1]

In the 1960s, the process of decolonization contributed significantly to the enlargement of the UN and its global representation. The emergence of new states also permanently altered the global geopolitical landscape, prompting questions about the relevance and legitimacy of multilateral structures and processes that replicated post-war power dynamics.[2] In 1965, the number of non-permanent members of the Security Council was increased, from 11 to 15.[3]

As its membership grew, so did the UN's funds and programmes and the number of specialized agencies and related organizations in the UN system. With the creation of bodies such as the World Health Organization (1948), the Office of the UN High Commissioner for Refugees (1950), the International Atomic Energy Agency (1957), the World Food Programme (1963), the UN Development Programme (1965) and the UN Environment Programme (1972), the international civil service grew organically to accommodate this expansion. This, in turn, led to a gradual increase in the need for a broader range of technical and local competencies among UN staff.

The size and structure of the international civil service present it with additional challenges and opportunities unforeseen by its founders. For instance, non-staff personnel—which includes consultants, commercial contractors, volunteers, interns, government-provided personnel and military observers—make up roughly 40 percent of the total UN workforce.[4] Because they are often funded by extra-budgetary resources, non-staff personnel are increasingly being hired on short-term contracts, which can contribute to feelings of insecurity and vulnerability and may discourage innovation and investments in staff development.

Together with the large number of international civil servants, who are distributed across a myriad of funds, programmes, agencies and other bodies that did not exist in

---

1　United Nations General Assembly, "Report of the Secretary-General on Personnel Policy", A/2364, January 30th, 1953, pp. 6-10; and "UN unit reverses Lie rule on ouster; Administrative Tribunal Rules employee's service may not be ended without reason", *New York Times*, August 12th, 1952.

2　Alanna O'Malley, "Turning Points: Defining Moments for the International Civil Service at the United Nations", Dag Hammarskjöld Foundation, 100 Years of International Civil Service Paper No. 7, May 6th, 2020.

3　United Nations General Assembly, 20th session, 1392nd plenary meeting, December 10th, 1965.

4　Cihan Terzi, *Review of Individual Consultancies in the United Nations System*, Geneva: United Nations Joint Inspection Unit, 2012.

1945, the sheer number of non-staff personnel may challenge the idea of a discernible UN identity rooted in common values and principles. This raises the question of how the international civil service can adapt to these new circumstances, for example by providing all personnel with the right tools to serve the organization and ensuring that they receive adequate protections.[1]

1.2 Core Principles[2] of the International Civil Service

Up to the 1920's, with the notable and trend-setting exceptions of the small secretarial services of the International Telegraphic Union (1868) and the Universal Postal Union (1874), permanent secretariats of international organizations had practically been non-existent.[3] In the 19th century, the secretarial functions of international organizations were normally entrusted to the so-called *edétat directeur*, i.e., one of the member countries.[4] The true predecessor of a modern independent international secretariat and civil service was the staff of the International Institute of Agriculture established in Rome in 1905.[5] Yet it is Sir Eric Drummond, the first Secretary-General of the League of Nations, who is generally regarded as mainly responsible for building "an international secretariat, lifted above all national contexts", which is the genesis of the international civil service (ICS) that emerged in 1919 and 1920.[6]

Eric Drummond, a British diplomat involved in the drafting of *The Covenant of the League of Nations* and the first Secretary General of the League of Nations (1919—1933), played a crucial and pioneering role in conceptualizing an independent international

---

1 Alain Sibenaler, "The United Nations: A Unique Ecosystem for Leadership and Innovation", in T*he Art of Leadership in the United Nations: Framing What's Blue*, Uppsala: Dag Hammarskjöld Foundation, 2020, pp. 66-69.

2 Karen Gram-Skjoldager, "From the League of Nations to the United Nations: Milestones for the International Civil Service", part of a series issued by Dag Hammarskjöld Foundation commemorating 100 Years of International Civil Service, No.3; John Burley, "The Independence of the International Civil Service, 1919-2019: Minority Rights at the League of Nations and Human Rights at the United Nations", Universal Rights Group, May 16th, 2019.

3 Inis L. Claude, Jr., *Swords into Plowshares: The Problems and Progress of International Organization*(4th edition), Random House, 1988, pp.37-38.

4 M.B. Akehurst, "Unilaterateral Amendment of Conditions of Employment in International Organizations", *British Yearbook of International Law*, 1964, p.286.

5 José Gascon y Marin, "Les transformations du droit administratif international", in *Collected Courses of the Hague Academy of International Law*, first published online in 1930, p.53.

6 Dag Hammarskjöld, *The International Civil Servant in Law and in Fact: A Lecture Delivered to the Congregation at Oxford on 30 May 1961*, Dag Hammarskjöld Foundation, 2021, pp.5-31.

civil service. Drummond was a great believer in international administration, and deserves recognition for having conceived a new permanent element of world life— impartial multilateral cooperation. The essential elements of Drummond's vision, ideas of ***internationality, independence,*** and ***loyalty***, were recognized as crucial cornerstones with the creation of the League of Nations, and still shape the organization and operation of the UN secretariat today.

(1) Warranting Internationality

When the UN was created after the Second World War, the principle of national diversity became enshrined in *The UN Charter*, where Article 101(3) today states that [*d*]*ue regard shall be paid to the importance of recruiting the staff on as wide a geographical basis as possible.* However, as was the case after the First World War, the UN started out being heavily dominated by one benevolent hegemon: in 1919, Britain had dominated the Secretariat, in 1946, the US held 50% of all posts in the Secretariat— a number that only gradually dropped to 25% in 1961.[1]

Why was the issue of national diversity critically important from the earliest beginnings of modern international civil service and remained so in the UN system? Two answers present themselves. At one level, the competition over representation in the Secretariat can be seen as a symbolic struggle over international prestige and relative power among member states. An international administration that wished to create ownership and legitimacy for itself needed to take this symbolic economy into account and make the staffing of the Secretariat reflect the geopolitical power structures it operated within.

At another, more practical, level, a broad multinational representation secured a wide range of competencies in the Secretariat and created a multitude of valuable contact points between the Secretariat and different national elite networks and public opinions, which were key to the efficient running of the Secretariat.[2] However, attempting to achieve broad representation and close interactions with its surroundings was inherently

---

1　Sydney D. Bailey, *The Secretariat of the United Nations*, New York: Carnegie Endowment for International Peace, 1962, p.82.

2　Karen Gram-Skjoldager and Haakon A. Ikonomou, "The Construction of the League of Nations Secretariat. Formative Practices of Autonomy and Legitimacy in International Organizations", *International History Review*, v. 41, n.2, 2019, pp.257-279.

at odds with the principles of institutional independence and undivided international loyalty. Balancing out these principles has been a continuous challenge, as could be discussed below.

(2) Ensuring Independence

The multi-nationality of the Secretariat could only function if at the same time the Secretariat had a high degree of institutional independence that could keep it one step removed from member states' pressures and conflicts.

The League Secretariat's independence was only scantly described in *The Covenant of the League of Nations*. The only regulation of the League's authority and relationship to the other League bodies was Article 6, which stated that the Secretary-General had the authority to appoint Secretariat staff—with the subsequent approval of the League Council, the equivalent of today's UN Security Council.[1] Given the high level of member-state interest in pushing candidates for positions within the Secretariat, it was key to the independence of the administration that the Secretary-General was able to uphold this provision and assert his authority to set up his own team.

However, while the Council rarely used its right to veto appointments, the Assembly pushed to break Drummond's monopoly on staff appointments from the get-go. At the 1920 Assembly, South African representative, Sir Reginald Blankenberg, proposed to set up a joint committee consisting of Drummond and two Council members who were to approve all new appointments. Based on this experience, *The UN Charter* (Article 1010) set up a new and clearer work division, asserting the General Assembly's right to draw up the regulations of staff appointments but specifying the sole autonomy of the Secretary-General in appointing his staff within this framework.[2]

(3) Upholding Loyalty

The formal institutional independence of an international civil service is worth little if the civil servants inhabiting the administration are not loyal to the organization. As *The Covenant* was entirely silent on this issue, Drummond established and fleshed out this principle in the Secretariat's 1922 staff regulations, which opened with this poignant phrase:

1　Karen Gram-Skjoldager, "From the League of Nations to the United Nations: Milestones for the International Civil Service", Paper Series No. 3, *100 Years of International Civil Service*, 2019.

2　More details can be found in *The Charter of the United Nations*, Article 1010 (I).

The officials of the Secretariat of the League of Nations are international officials, responsible for the execution of their duties to the Secretary-General alone. They may not seek or receive instructions from any other authority.[1]

The regulations went on to spell out what this undivided loyalty to the organization entailed: League officials, according to the staff regulations, could not hold any kind of political office or side job without the Secretary General's consent; they were not allowed to receive any honors or decorations while serving in the Secretariat; they could not publish or lecture on matters relating to the League without the Secretary General's permission and they were to maintain strict secrecy on all confidential matters relating to the League.

In 1932 the fourth milestone in the creation of the new international civil service was reached when an explicit oath of loyalty was introduced. From then on, all new League officials were required to sign a declaration in which they swore:

...to exercise in all loyalty, discretion and conscience the functions that have been entrusted to me as an official of the Secretariat of the League of Nations, to discharge my functions and to regulate my conduct with the interests of the League alone in view and not to seek or receive instructions from any Government or other authority external to the Secretariat of the League of Nations.

After the outbreak of the Second World War, it was clear to most political observers that the damages the League had suffered were critical and irreversible and that the organization would not serve as the institutional centre of the post-Second World War international order. Nonetheless, the victorious powers at the San Francisco Conference fundamentally agreed that the institutional invention of an international civil service responsible only to the organization had proven workable and efficient. This is why we see the League's notion of loyalty making it almost verbatim into *The UN Charter.*

Here, Article 100(1) states that [*i*]*n the performance of their duties the Secretary-General and the staff shall not seek or receive instructions from any government or from any other authority external to the Organization.*[2] With this article, the issue of

---

1   *LONA-R1460: Staff Regulations (1 edition)*, Geneva, June 1922, Article I.

2   More details can be found in *The Charter of the United Nations*, Article 100 b (I).

international loyalty had moved from being an internal staff matter and become part of the foundational treaty of the UN—a clear expression of the importance ascribed to it.

1.3　Practical Legitimacy of the International Civil Service[1]

The international civil service (ICS) developed both as an ideal type and an empirical reality in the League of Nations, the United Nations (UN), and related organizations. The normative expectations linked to this concept have their roots in liberal internationalism and a vision of an effective and professional bureaucracy based on Max Weber's ideal type.[2] As an empirical category, it refers to the staff employed by Inter-Governmental Organizations. It was first developed to describe the staff of the League of Nations, and the UN system later retained the label for its secretariat staff. As such, tension between ideal and reality has been present in the ICS from the start.

Several high-profile scandals connected to the conduct of the UN Secretariat in recent decades have served to highlight difficulties in implementing the ICS ideal in the realities of the modern world. The so-called "oil-for-food" scandal drew attention to management problems within the Secretariat. This scandal implicated some UN officials—along with private companies and national officials—in financial impropriety in connection with the programme which allowed Iraq to export oil in the 1990s in return for food and other supplies to mitigate the humanitarian effects of UN sanctions. While UN Secretary-General Kofi Annan was personally cleared of improper behaviour, the independent inquiry into the scandal pointed to serious management failures in the UN Secretariat.[3]

A further challenge comes from problems with neutrality and impartiality, mainstays of the classical model of the ICS. During the Cold War, UN peace operations were premised upon the principles of neutrality, impartiality, and the consent of the

---

1　Edward Newman and Ellen Jenny Ravndal, "International Civil Service", in Diane Stone and Kim Moloney (eds), *The Oxford Handbook of Global Policy and Transnational Administration,* Oxford: Oxford University Press, 2019, pp.165-181.

2　Guenther Roth and Claus Wittich (eds.), *Max Webber's Economy and Society*, Berkeley: University of California Press, 2013.

3　Paul A. Volcker, Richard J. Goldstone and Mark Pieth, "Manipulation of the Oil-for-Food Programme by the Iraqi Regime", Independent Inquiry Committee into the United Nations Oil-for-Food Programme, October 27th, 2005.

sovereign government and other parties. In situations where peacekeepers formed an inter-positional line between national armies this made sense and was necessary. However, a continuation of these principles in situations of civil conflict has come close to undermining UN legitimacy.

During the Bosnian civil war, the UN bore witness to a series of atrocities committed against non-combatants by all sides, culminating in a massacre of Bosnian Muslims at the UN "safe haven" of Srebrenica in 1995, where approximately 7,000 men and boys were killed. A similar case occurred in Rwanda, where signs that genocide was being prepared were apparently ignored in New York.[1]

Many of the problems discussed above concern the performance of IO staff in relation to the ICS ideal. International civil servants, like any civil servants, potentially face serious conflicts of interest in their work. Dilemmas related to gifts and honorary distinctions, financial advantages, opportunities for recruitment or advancement of relatives or friends, relations with businesses or NGOs, and protection of confidential information, occur for both domestic and international civil servants.[2]

International civil servants additionally face unique conflicts of interest connected to their status as "international". As "international", the ICS is supposed to be neutral and impartial in relation to conflicting parties, but such neutrality causes problems for UN peacekeepers when faced with complex civil wars and atrocities.[3] The dilemmas faced by the ICS deployed in field operations, just as much as those faced by Secretaries-General and senior management, will influence public perceptions of IO legitimacy.

A recent study of two UN humanitarian agencies sought to assess the prevalence of conflicts of interest between the national and international identities of international civil servants among different groups of staff. It found that locally-recruited general

---

1   Roméo Dallaire, *Shake Hands with the Devil: The Failure of Humanity in Rwanda*, New York: Carroll & Graf, 2004, pp.6-7.

2   Auguste Nganga Malonga, "Conflict of Interest of International Civil Servants". In Anne Peters, Lukas Handschin (eds), *Conflict of Interest in Global, Public and Corporate Governance*, Cambridge: Cambridge University Press, 2012, pp.63-84.

3   Patrick Weller and Yi-Chong Xu, "Agents of Influence: Country Directors at the World Bank". *Public Administration*, v.88, n.1, 2010, pp.211-231.

service staff reported the highest level of loyalty conflict.[1] This finding cautions us against focusing solely on senior management and professional staff when studying the legitimacy of the ICS.

Tensions between the ICS as ideal and reality are inevitable. The ICS takes its normative content both from Weberian rationalization and liberal internationalism. As Barnett and Finnemore (2004) also observed, this tension can make it difficult for the ICS to maintain both procedural and substantial legitimacy.[2] Koppell (2010) further showed that it is near impossible for IOs to reconcile the conflicting demands of accountability—transparency, liability, controllability, responsibility, and responsiveness.[3] In some ways recent developments have only served to make the job of the ICS even more difficult.

Section 2

The International Civil Servants within the UN System

To clarify the distinctive role of international organizations and the individuals who work in the world organization, Claude (1996) long ago used the concepts of the "First UN" and the "Second UN", and argued that the "First UN" is constituted by its Member States,[4] whereas the "Second UN" is constituted by the heads of Secretariats and staff members who are recruited internationally and locally, and work in duty stations and on peacekeeping missions.[5] Resulting from the fact that the international organizations

---

1 Valentina Mele, Simon Anderfuhren-Biget and Frédéric Varone, "Conflicts of Interest in International Organizations: Evidence from Two United Nations Humanitarian Agencies", *Public Administration*, v.94, n.2, 2016, pp.490-508.

2 Michael N. Barnett and Martha Finnemore, *Rules for the World: International Organizations in Global Politics.* Ithaca, New York: Cornell University Press, 2004.

3 Jonathan G.S. Koppell, *World Rule: Accountability, Legitimacy, and the Design of Global Governance.* Chicago, London: University of Chicago Press, 2010.

4 Inis L. Claude Jr., "Peace and Security: Prospective Roles for the Two United Nations", *Global Governance*, v.2, n.3, 1996, pp.289-298; Also see, Nejat Dogan, *Pragmatic Liberal Approach to World Order: The Scholarship of Inis L. Claude, Jr.*, Lanham, Maryland: University Press of America, 2012, p.152.

5 The "Third UN" of Non-Governmental Organizations, experts, commissions, and academics is a more recent addition to analytical perspectives that first appeared in these stages. See more in Thomas G. Weiss, "The John W. Homes Lecture: Reinvigorating the International Civil Service", *Global Governance*, v.16, n.1, 2010, pp.39-57.

employ staff of one kind or another to carry out their objectives, these non-state actors owe their power to their titles and function, whether we call them "Secretary-General", "UN Expert", or "Special Rapporteur", or "International Judge".[1]

2.1　Staff Categories

The United Nations workforce is made up of different categories of staff. Within each category there are different levels, which reflect increasing levels of responsibilities and requirements.[2] According to the location of recruitment, it can be divided into global recruitment and local recruitment; according to the nature of the post, it can be divided into geographical quotas and not subject to geographical quotas; according to the type of appointment contract, it can be divided into three types: long-term contracts, regular contracts and temporary contracts.

By the work nature, the posts of United Nations general staff are divided into the following five categories:

(1) Professional and Higher Categories (P and D)

Staff members in the Professional and higher categories ("Professionals"[P] and/ or "Directors"[D]) are normally internationally recruited, meaning that they are hired to work at an office (duty station) throughout their career outside of their home country. There are a variety of jobs within these categories, ranging from programme specialists and operation experts to communication specialists, information system professionals, and many others.

Directors [D-1 and D-2 levels] represent the highest level on the career staffing structure of the Organization, and are normally expected to provide leadership in formulating and implementing the substantive work programme of an office, determine priorities, and allocate resources for the completion of outputs and their timely delivery.

Senior professionals hired for positions at the P-6 and P-7 level typically work as senior advisers or experts, bringing several years of analytical and research experience

---

1　Jose E. Alvarez, "Distinguished Speaker Series: Governing the World: International Organizations as Lawmakers", *31 Suffolk Transnational Law Review*, 2008, pp.597-98.

2　Source from the website of the United Nations Careers, "Home/What are my career options/Staff categories", accessed on October 8th, 2021.

to the United Nations.

Table 1　UN Hierarchy: Professionals[P] and Directors[D] Positions

Category	Required Experience	Level
P-2	min. 2 years of work experience [no experience is required if applying to the young professional programme]	Entry level
P-3	min. 5 years of work experience	Entry level
P-4	min. 7 years of work experience	Mid-level
P-5	min. 10 years of work experience	Mid-level
P-6/D-1	min. 15 years of work experience	Senior level
P-7/D-2	more than 15 years of work experience	Senior level

Work in the Professional category generally demands strong analytical and communication skills, substantial experience, and, often, solid leadership ability. Typically, these positions require judgment in analyzing and evaluating problems as well as in decision-making involving discretionary choices between alternative courses of action. They also require the understanding of an organized body of theoretical knowledge at a level equivalent to that represented by a university degree. While this knowledge is customarily and characteristically acquired through formal education, it may, in some fields of learning or specialized disciplines, be acquired through other training, self-study, or practical experience.

The work experience requirements for each level can be found in Table 1. As the amount of experience increases, so does the professional level. For headquarters and regional office posts, all nationalities are welcome to apply. Openings for professional jobs can be found at all duty stations across the global United Nations Secretariat.

(2) General Service and Related Categories (G, TC, S, PIA, LT)

The functions in the General Service and related categories include administrative, secretarial and clerical support as well as specialized technical functions such as printing, security and buildings maintenance. There are jobs in all the eight job networks: management and operations support; economic and social development; political, peace and security; information systems and communication technology; legal; public information and external relations; conference management; and safety and security.

The work carried out by General Service staff supports the functioning of the Organization and is typically procedural, operational or technical in nature. The work in these categories ranges from routine duties to varied and complex assignments. The knowledge of the subject matter and higher-level skills are generally developed through long experience and familiarity with applicable procedures, regulations and precedents or projects of the Organization in a narrow technical field or in an administrative support activity. The higher the level of the job, the more complex the functions become along with higher levels of responsibility.

Completion of secondary (high school) education is a requirement. These are the work experience requirements for each level:

G1—No work experience required

G2—Minimum of 2 years of work experience

G3—Minimum of 3 years of work experience

G4—Minimum of 4 years of work experience

G5—Minimum of 5 years of work experience

G6—Minimum of 6 years of work experience

G7—Minimum of 7 years of work experience

Staff in the General Service and related categories are generally recruited locally from the area in which the particular office is located. They can be of any nationality, but should be legally permitted to work in the country where the office/duty station is located. As a result, such staff members are usually not expected to move between different duty stations.

From these, as anticipated, it is possible to continue to the professional category by internal examinations. With the exception of certain cases, the hierarchical subdivision just described is also applied to the autonomous agencies and organizations affiliated to the United Nations. For this reason, reference can be made to it even when speaking of the employment of personnel in the UNDP and UNICEF.

(3) National Professional Officers (NO)

NO roles are similar to Professional (P) roles, but they are normally locally recruited, meaning these staff are recruited to work at a duty station in their home country. The qualifications for National Professional Officers are the same as for the Professional category and require as a minimum a first-level university degree. Jobs for National Professional Officers can only be found in non-headquarters duty stations.

These are the work experience requirements for each level:

NOA — No work experience required

NOB — Minimum of 2 years of work experience

NOC — Minimum of 5 years of work experience

NOD — Minimum of 7 years of work experience

National Professional Officers are nationals of the country in which they are serving and their functions must have a national context, i.e. functions that require national experience or knowledge of the national language, culture, institutions, and systems. Examples of these positions include human rights officers, political affairs officers, legal officers, medical officers, child protection officers, humanitarian affairs officers, interpreters and civil engineers.

(4) Field Service (FS)

Staff in the Field Service category are normally recruited internationally to serve in field missions. You are expected to be highly mobile and to serve in different locations during your career.

Field Service staff members provide administrative, technical, logistics and other support services to United Nations field missions. You are required to have as a minimum a High School diploma or equivalent; some positions may require a technical or vocational certificate.

(5) Senior Appointments (SG, DSG, USG and ASG)

As is the practice in many other international institutions, one arrives at the highest positions in the Secretariat either by appointment of the Organization's legislative organs or Chief Administrative Officer. These positions include:

a. Secretary-General (SG): The chief administrative officer of the United Nations and head of the UN Secretariat, appointed by the General Assembly, on the recommendation of the Security Council, for a period of five years;

b. Deputy Secretary-General (DSG): Appointed by the Secretary-General following consultations with Member States;

c. Under-Secretary-General (USG): A Head of Department, appointed by the Secretary-General;

d. Assistant Secretary-General (ASG): A Head of Office, appointed by the Secretary-General

The Secretary-General has wide authority to appoint senior staff at the ASG and USG levels as well as special envoys at all levels. However, the appointment of a number of senior officials is subject to specific requirements set forth in General Assembly resolutions or related legislative documents

2.2   Staff Benefits

It is also important to realize that for many graduates, a role in an international organization is part of their longer-term career plan rather than an immediate post-graduate destination. It is critical to have a good understanding of how recruitment is managed, the skills, expertise and broader profiles sought, and where you will be able to develop useful experience.

2.2.1   Career Support

Career support in short:

- Several week-long Orientation and Development Programmes for entry-level professionals;
- A wide menu of workshops at the Career Resource Centre/New York;
- One-on-one career consultations with senior career counsellors;
- 10 years of Mentoring at the UN;
- On-line courses and books on career development;
- Regular information sessions for spouses/ partners of UN staff, including on "dual career";
- Bi-annual pre-retirement information sessions.

From the moment you join the United Nations' dynamic team of staff members, you can be certain of one thing—their support system will ensure that you are not left alone to figure out your career. The development of every staff member is very important to the United Nations—helping you to grow helps them to become better at what they do. They are therefore committed to providing all the available tools to respond to your needs.

They are serious about career support at the United Nations and their approach is firmly rooted in a solid and interactive partnership between the staff members, the manager and the Organization. Although you are primarily responsible for your professional and personal development, and are the key driver in your career planning process, managers are always there to provide you with the necessary direction, information as well as a work environment to positively and qualitatively support your career development.

The Organization provides real and valuable opportunities through a competency model based on a diverse range of programmes that include a wide selection of career planning and development workshops. These exciting opportunities and tangible career support services are naturally extended across all the Organization's established job network:

- Political, Peace and Security
- Management and Operations Support
- Economic and Social Development
- Information Systems and Communication Technology
- Legal
- Public Information and External Relations
- Conference Management
- Safety and Security

Through Career Resource Centers or Training Centers, the following services are available:

- Career and life planning information
- Learning opportunities

- Mobility support

- Confidential career coaching

- Guidance with career consultants as well as Human Resources experts

- Workshops to develop skills in networking, performance management and competency-based interviewing; as well as information sessions on diverse human resources management and development issues.

2.2.2   Pay and Benefits

The United Nations offers you an attractive remuneration package with competitive pay and benefits. The level of pay for staff in the Professional and higher categories that are recruited internationally is set by reference to the highest paying national civil service. Staff members in categories that are locally recruited are compensated in accordance with the best prevailing conditions of service locally.

The following information is provided to give a general overview of the United Nations conditions of service. The actual employment contracts of staff are based on *The UN Staff Regulations and Rules*, which remains the definitive source of any legal and administrative interpretation.

(1) Professional and Higher Categories

In the Professional and higher categories, you are normally recruited internationally. You will receive a salary which is paid on the basis of a worldwide scale and benefits which take account of your dependants and the cost of living at your duty station.

A. Base Salary

The base salary, which is determined by the grade of the post specified in the job opening and by the existence of any dependants, is the same throughout the United Nations system. Annual net base salary ranges approximately in US$:

Categories	Levels to be specific	Salaries
P1-P3	entry level Professionals	37,000—80,000
P4-P5	mid-career Professionals	67,000—106,000
P6/D1-P7/D2	senior level Professionals	95,000—123,000
Tax exemption: salaries grants and allowances paid by the United Nations are normally exempt from income tax.		

B. Post Adjustment

The base salary is supplemented by a post adjustment which varies according to the cost of living in the duty station and the exchange rate of the United States dollar. The post adjustment, set by the United Nations as a percentage of the base salary, ensures that all staff members at the same salary level have a similar purchasing power in every duty station by compensating for the differences in cost of living while taking currency fluctuations into account.

For example, if your annual base salary is US$ 64,000 and the post adjustment multiplier for your duty station is 65.7%, your salary will be calculated based on the following:

Post adjustment per year: US$ 64,000 x 0.657 = US$ 42,048

Total annual salary: US$ 64,000+42,048=US$ 106,048

To see the current post adjustment rates, visit the International Civil Service Commission website.

C. Other Benefits

As a United Nations staff member, you may also be entitled to other allowances and benefits including:

- *Rental subsidy* if you are newly arrived at the duty station and your rent represents a high proportion of the total remuneration.
- *Dependency allowances* if you have an eligible dependent spouse and/or child(ren).
- Under certain conditions an *education grant* if you have eligible children in school.
- *Travel and shipping expenses* when you are moving from one duty station to another.
- *Assignment grant* to assist you in meeting initial extraordinary costs when arriving at or relocating to a new duty station.
- At some duty stations, *a hardship allowance* linked to living and working conditions is paid and where there are restrictions on bringing family members, a non-family hardship allowance is also paid.

- *Hazard pay and rest and recuperation break* when you serve in locations where the conditions are particularly hazardous, stressful and difficult.

(2) General Services and Related Categories

Staff members in these categories are normally recruited and paid on a local basis. You will be paid a salary according to a local salary scale. Salary scales are reviewed periodically on the basis of comprehensive surveys of the best prevailing conditions of employment in the locality.

You may be entitled to other allowances and benefits including: *Family allowances* if you have eligible children in school; and in some locations if you have an eligible dependent spouse.

(3) National Professional Officers

Staff members in this category are recruited and paid on a local basis. You will be paid a salary according to a local salary scale. Salary scales are reviewed periodically on the basis of comprehensive surveys of the best prevailing conditions of employment in the locality.

You may be entitled to other allowances and benefits including: *Family allowances* if you have eligible children in school; and in some locations if you have an eligible dependent spouse.

(4) Field Services

In the Field Service category, you are normally recruited internationally. You will receive a salary which is paid on the basis of a worldwide scale and benefits which take account of your dependants and the cost of living at your duty station.

As a staff of the United Nations in the Field Service category you are paid: a) a base (minimum) salary and b) post adjustment.

A. Annual Net Base Salary Ranges Approximately in US$

Categories	Levels to be specific	Salaries
FS 1—FS 3	entry level Field Service staff	31,000—54,000
FS 4—FS 5	mid-career Field Service staff	44,000—68,000
FS 6—FS 7	senior level Field Service staff	56,000—90,000
Tax exemption: salaries grants and allowances paid by the United Nations are normally exempt from income tax.		

B. Post Adjustment

The base salary is supplemented by a post adjustment which varies according to the cost of living in the duty station and the exchange rate of the United States dollar. The post adjustment, set by the United Nations as a percentage of the base salary, ensures that all staff members at the same salary level have a similar purchasing power in every duty station by compensating for the differences in cost of living while taking currency fluctuations into account.

For example, if your annual base salary is US$ 42,000 and and the post adjustment multiplier for your duty station is 55.5% your salary will be the following:

Post adjustment per year: US$ 42,000 x 0.555 = US$23,310

Total annual salary: US$42,000+23,310=US$65,310

To see the current post adjustment rates, visit the International Civil Service Commission website.

C. Other Allowances and Benefits

You may also be entitled to other allowances and benefits including:

- *Rental subsidy* if you are newly arrived at the duty station and your rent represents a high proportion of the total remuneration.
- *Dependency allowances* if you have an eligible dependent spouse and/or child(ren).
- Under certain conditions *an education* grant if you have eligible children in school.
- *Travel and shipping expenses* when you are moving from one duty station to another.
- *Assignment grant* to assist you in meeting initial extraordinary costs when arriving at or relocating to a new duty station.
- At some duty stations, *a hardship allowance* linked to living and working conditions is paid, and where there are restrictions on bringing family members, a non-family hardship allowance is also paid.
- *Hazard pay and rest and recuperation break* when you serve in locations where the conditions are particularly hazardous, stressful and difficult.

2.3   Career Paths

Career development and promotions modalities vary in each UN organization. For example, some UN organizations (such as WFP and UNHCR) have a rotation system for staff members, which offers certain job security. Others have such rotation systems only for senior management, or do not have any career development planning systems at all. While some organizations such as UNICEF allow their interns and consultants to apply for staff positions in the same organization, others, including the UN Secretariat, require interns and consultants to take a break in service and are not eligible to apply for a staff position within 6 months after completion of their contract.[1]

Career progression to senior levels depends, in part, on evidence of mobility, including service in difficult locations. To advance within a UN organization, you will normally need to submit an application for your next career move or promotion. Therefore, your own career planning initiative is key. Generally, the process of staff promotion will be as follows:

a. **General Category (G, General Service).** These staff are engaged in general clerical work, typically recruited from the location of an international organization and mainly engaged in secretarial and administrative work. There are seven levels from the G1 to the G7, mainly including secretary, service and security personnel. G1 to G3 are the lowest levels, mostly recruited from the public on condition that they pass certain simple examinations with required language skills. Additionally, G5 to G7 are mostly internal assignation and promotion.

b. **Professional Category (P, Professional Officers).** These staff are recruited from various countries in the world and engaged in various business work of international organizations. For example, more than 60% of the WHO's business personnel have a professional background in medicine and biology related to medicine and health, and other specialties include information, finance, personnel, law, diplomacy and languages. There are five levels of these employees, from the lowest P1 to the highest P5. The P5 level personnel enjoy diplomatic treatment.

---

1   Sources from the website of cinfo (The Swiss Center of Competence for International Cooperation), "Individuals/Get informed/Staff positions at the UN", accessed on July 9th, 2022.

Some international organizations, such as the World Health Organization, put up P6, which is equivalent to D1.

c. **Directory Category (D, Directors).** These staff are generally the heads of the internal departments of international organizations, and they are D1 and D2 respectively. Most of them are appointed by the executive heads of international organizations, and some of them also participate in the competition in form.

d. **Senior Category (S, Senior Official).** These staff, controlling the senior management of the United Nations, are divided into two levels, D1 and D2. They are either the chief executives at the United Nations or the heads of the UN specialized agencies.

G-level staff must pass the annual examinations held within the United Nations if they wish to be converted to P-level. It takes about 12 years or more to move from P2, a comparatively lower position, to P5, a higher position, if very smoothly, but this is seldom the case. Each promotion of a staff member will be based on the job vacancy application, and then they will participate in the interview after which qualified staff can be promoted to the new position.

The top post in the United Nations staff is the United Nations Secretary-General, recommended by the Security Council and elected by the General Assembly. Under the Secretary-General are the Under-Secretary-General, Assistant Secretary-General and Special Envoy of the Secretary-General appointed by the Secretary-General. Competition for any post in the United Nations, with the exception of those directly appointed by the Secretary-General, means that competition is the most common routine for United Nations staff. Therefore, international staff must be universally competitive and irreplaceable.

There are few clearly marked career paths in the United Nations. The diversity of occupations and multidisciplinary mandates means that a staff may not only change functions, departments but even organizations or fields of work. While such shifts require learning, time and effort, they also provide valuable experience, broader perspectives and challenging work. Geographic mobility is yet another way for you to positively affect your career in the United Nations.

A few examples of staff members' career paths can be found below[1]:

---

1   Source from the website of the United Nations, "United Nations Career/What can I do at the UN?/Career paths", accessed on October 14th, 2021.

Anastasia WILSON
Chief, Human Resources
Duty Station: Beirut, LEBANON

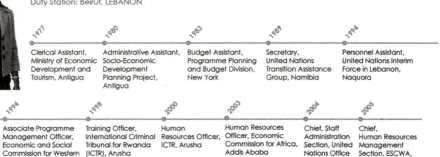

1977	1980	1983	1989	1994
Clerical Assistant, Ministry of Economic Development and Tourism, Antigua	Administrative Assistant, Socio-Economic Development Planning Project, Antigua	Budget Assistant, Programme Planning and Budget Division, New York	Secretary, United Nations Transition Assistance Group, Namibia	Personnel Assistant, United Nations Interim Force in Lebanon, Naquora

1994	1994	1998	2000	2003	2004	2005
G to P examination in Administration	Associate Programme Management Officer, Economic and Social Commission for Western Asia (ESCWA), Amman	Training Officer, International Criminal Tribunal for Rwanda (ICTR), Arusha	Human Resources Officer, ICTR, Arusha	Human Resources Officer, Economic Commission for Africa, Addis Ababa	Chief, Staff Administration Section, United Nations Office at Nairobi	Chief, Human Resources Management Section, ESCWA, Beirut

Barbara RUIS
Legal Officer
Duty Station: Geneva, SWITZERLAND

1992	1993	1995	1997
Coordinator Human Rights Policy, Foundation Justitia et Pax, Oegstgeest	Junior Programme Officer, UNEP, Nairobi	Associate Expert, UN Division for Sustainable Development, New York	Consultant, UN Intergovernmental Forum on Forests, Netherlands

1998	1999	2002	2004	2008
Lecturer, Business School, Haarlem, Netherlands	Researcher and Lecturer, Department of Law, Vrije Universiteit, Amsterdam	Legal Officer, Division of Policy, Development and Law, UNEP, Nairobi	Legal Officer, Division of Environmental Law and Conventions, UNEP, Nairobi	Legal Officer, Regional Office for Europe, UNEP, Geneva

Weihua TANG
Chinese Interpreter
Duty Station: Nairobi, KENYA

1970	1978	1982	1983	1987
Platoon leader at an Army farm, Heilongjiang Province, China	Teacher of Business English and International Trade, Beijing	Masters in Simultaneous Interpretation and International Affairs	Conference Interpreter, UN Secretariat, New York	Editor, International Law Journal, New York Law School, New York

1988	1990	1990	1992	2004
International Law Clerk, Pennie & Edmonds (Intellectual Property Law Firm), New York	Juris Doctor	Attorney-at-Law, Pennie & Edmonds, New York	Attorney-at-Law, Venture, Rebeiro & Tang, partner, jurisdictions of practice, New York, New Jersey and Washington, DC	Conference Interpreter, United Nations Office at Nairobi, Kenya

Section 3

The Secretary-General as an International Civil Servant

3.1 Brief Introduction[1]

(1) What Is the UN Secretary-General?

Though U.S. President Franklin D. Roosevelt, several years before the United Nations' creation, saw the Secretary-General's role as that of a "world moderator," the UN website describes the Secretary-General's role as "equal parts diplomat and advocate, civil servant and CEO." *The UN Charter* designates the Secretary-General as the Organization's "chief administrative officer", and head of the UN Secretariat with its 50,000 international civil service officers. The General Assembly, Security Council and other organs of the UN may also assign the Secretary-General certain tasks to perform. This means the Secretary-General has to oversee hundreds of programs, funds and agencies, and balance the budget—a large portion of which is often overdue—plus represent the UN to the media and in conferences around the world.

The Secretary-General also has the authority, under Article 99 of *The Charter*, to bring to the attention of the Security Council matters that threaten international peace and security. Article 99 is interpreted as providing the Secretary-General with an independent political role on issues before the Security Council.

Past Secretaries-General have helped shape the office of the Secretary-General as it is today. Dag Hammarskjöld, considered the most effective and dynamic Secretary-General, widened the role of the Secretary-General to act, according to UN historian Brian Urquhart, as "negotiator, crisis manager and director of active peace operations." Trygve Lie[2] was the first Secretary-General to bring an international crisis (Soviet troops in Iran) to the attention of the Security Council—this now standard practice was highly controversial at the time.

Aside from his formal functions, the Secretary-General is expected to uphold

---

1 Paul B. Stares, Nathalie Tocci, Dhruva Jaishankar and Qingguo Jia, "The Role of the UN Secretary-General", *Council on Foreign Relations*, last updated on October 5th, 2021.

2 Norwegian lawyer and politician Trygve Lie (1896-1968) was the United Nations first Secretary-General. He held the post for seven years, from 1946 to 1953, and famously described it as "the most difficult job in the world".

the values of the United Nations and act as its moral authority, even at the risk of challenging Member States. For example, when tensions escalated between Serbs and ethnic Albanians in Kosovo in 1999, Annan famously said that "no government has the right to hide behind national sovereignty in order to violate human rights." Still, in the book *Secretary or General?*, Simon Chesterman and Thomas M. Franck write that the officeholder is sometimes treated as "an errand boy and punching bag," expected to be both an independent political force and a public servant.

(2) What Are the Main Responsibilities of the Secretary-General?

a. **Administrative**. The Ssecretary-General oversees the UN Secretariat, which functions as the United Nations' Executive Officer and handles operations, including research, translation, and media relations. The Secretariat has a staff of more than thirty-six thousand. Each Secretary-General has handled his administrative responsibilities differently. Hammarskjöld established a system of offices in charge of legal, political, personnel, and budgetary aspects of the secretariat, while Boutros Boutros-Ghali (1992—1996) added Under-Secretaries-General to oversee operations. During Annan's administration, the Deputy Secretary-General position was created to handle day-to-day operations. Under Guterres, the protocol for delegating authority in the Secretariat was revised and two new management departments were created.

b. **Human Resources**. The Secretary-General appoints Under-Secretaries for approximately fifty UN posts, including the heads of funds such as the UN Children's Fund (UNICEF) and UN Development Program (UNDP). An important aspect of the appointment process involves lobbying efforts by Member States to fill these posts with their nationals, highlighting the Secretary-General's role in ensuring broad regional representation in UN leadership.

c. **Peacekeeping**. The Secretary-General's office oversees peacekeeping missions and appoints the Under-Secretary in charge of that department, which manages a dozen operations worldwide as of 2021. While the General Assembly or Security Council can initiate a peacekeeping mission (though the General Assembly has only done so once), operational control rests with the Secretariat. António Guterres has introduced several reforms to the UN peace and security framework, including his *Action for Peacekeeping* (*A4P*) initiative, an effort to strengthen peacekeeping operations by implementing reforms across eight major areas, including increasing gender parity among peacekeepers, improving coordination with local governments, and strengthening accountability for misconduct.

d. **Mediation**. As part of the "good offices" responsibility of the position, the Secretary-General practices independence and impartiality to prevent and limit conflict. Examples of UN leaders taking on mediation roles in the past include Hammarskjöld's promotion of an armistice between Israel and Arab states and Javier Perez de Cuellar's (1982—1991) negotiation of a cease-fire to end the Iran-Iraq War. The Secretary-General also appoints envoys charged with brokering peace deals. Such envoys report to the Security Council, and their appointments can be influenced by the preferences of the council's members. In 2017, for example, the United States objected to Guterres's appointment of former Palestinian Prime Minister Salam Fayyad as envoy to Libya. The intervention raised the question of whether such appointments are subject to approval by the Security Council, even if *The UN Charter* authorizes the Secretary-General to make the decision.

(3) How Is the Secretary-General Appointed?

The Secretary-General is appointed by the General Assembly, upon the recommendation of the Security Council. As the recommendation must come from the Security Council, the Secretary-General's selection is therefore subject to the veto of any of the five permanent members of the council. Any one of them can eliminate a nominee with a veto. For example, China vetoed a third term for the fourth Secretary-General, Austria's Waldheim, while the United States vetoed a second term for the fifth, Egypt's Boutros-Ghali. Although the ten elected members of the Security Council do not have veto power, their votes are still crucial, as candidates need at least nine votes to be recommended as Secretary-General.

The selection process is opaque and is often compared to a papal conclave.[1] Since 1981, the Security Council has voted in secret in a series of straw polls; it then submits the winning candidate to the General Assembly for ratification. Critics of

---

1 Somini Sengupta, "Secrecy Reigns as U.N. Seeks a New Secretary General", *The New York Times*, July 21st, 2016.

the appointment process say it lacks transparency and falls prey to cronyism due to the permanent Security Council members' veto power and their secret negotiations over candidates. A number of advocacy groups have chosen to focus on this issue in order to bring greater transparency and inclusiveness to the selection process.[1] Coupled with the changes in technology and communications, the selection of Guterres in 2016 was more open than any previous election, with a televised town hall meeting and informal dialogues between the candidates and the General Assembly. However, the Security Council voted in private and followed the same process as previous selections, leading the president of the General Assembly to complain that it "adds little value and does not live up to the expectations of the membership and the new standard of openness and transparency".[2]

Despite the broad and vague requirements of the job, some unofficial qualifications have been set by precedent in previous selections. The General Assembly *Resolution 51/241 in 1997* stated that, in the appointment of "the best candidate", due regard should be given to regional (continental) rotation of the appointee's national origin and to gender equality,[3] although no woman has yet served as Secretary-General. Most Secretaries-General are compromise candidates from countries considered to be small- or medium-sized neutral powers and have little prior fame. By custom, the appointee may not be a citizen of any of the Security Council's five permanent members (China, France, Russia, the United Kingdom, and the United States).

One quality shared by past Secretaries-General is that they have all been career diplomats for their own countries. Kofi Annan is the first Secretary-General who has been chosen from the United Nations staff. Another essential skill is the ability to speak English and French, two of the six official languages of the UN.

1　"Research Report on Appointing the UN Secretary-General", *Security Council Report*, October 16th, 2015.

2　Mogens Lykketoft, "Letter to All Permanent Representatives and Permanent Observers to the United Nations", The President of the General Assembly, July 21st, 2016.

3　Typically, the post of the Secretary-General is rotated after two five-year terms so that the position is held by someone from another region of the world. Member States belong to one of the five regional groups: African States, Asian States, Eastern European States, Latin American and Caribbean States, and Western European and Other States. Kofi Annan, who succeeded Boutros Boutros-Ghali of Egypt in 1997, was re-elected in 2001 although Africa had already held the seat for two terms. Because of Annan's popularity among Member States and UN staff, the Asia States, who were up for the seat, did not challenge Annan's re-election. See more from "Life Map/On the Job/Job at a Glance", in *Kofi Annan: Center of the Storm*, 2003.

Although *The Charter* does not specify the length of time the Secretary-General serves, but all Secretaries-General since 1971 have been appointed to five-year terms. After five years he can be re-elected for an additional term. Every Secretary-General since 1961 has been re-selected for a second term, with the exception of Boutros Boutros-Ghali, who was vetoed by the United States in the 1996 selection. Traditionally, there is a term limit of two full terms, established when China, in the 1981 selection, cast a record 16 vetoes against a third term for Kurt Waldheim. No Secretary-General since 1981 has attempted to secure a third term.

In June 2021, Guterres was unanimously reelected as Secretary-General for a second five-year term after being nominated by his home country and approved by the 193 Member States. His predecessors were:

- Ban Ki-moon (the Republic of Korea), who held office from January 2007 to December 2016;

- Kofi A. Annan (Ghana), who held office from January 1997 to December 2006;

- Boutros Boutros-Ghali (Egypt), who held office from January 1992 to December 1996;

- Javier Pérez de Cuéllar (Peru), who served from January 1982 to December 1991;

- Kurt Waldheim (Austria), who held office from January 1972 to December 1981;

- U Thant (Burma, now Myanmar), who served from November 1961, when he was appointed acting Secretary-General (he was formally appointed Secretary-General in November 1962) to December 1971;

- Dag Hammarskjöld (Sweden), who served from April 1953 until his death in a plane crash in Africa in September 1961; and

- Trygve Lie (Norway), who held office from February 1946 to his resignation in November 1952.

3.2　The Evolving Roles[1]

From the beginning of the Secretariat's existence, scholars and practitioners argued for a political role of the Secretary-General, often conceptualizing this role as one of

---

1　Excerpted and adapted from Jodok Troy, "The United Nations Secretary-General as an International Civil Servant", *The International History Review*, v.43, n.4, 2021, pp.908-909.

the international moral authorities.[1] In fact, other than commonly assumed, the legal and administrative set-up of international organizations tends to strengthen Secretaries-General's political performance.[2] The staffing practice of the League of Nations, for example, helped to balance legitimacy between state interests and the independence of the Secretariat—illustrating that international civil servants and executive heads can push back on a variety of constraints.[3] This is not much different in the case of the UN's Secretary-General.

The aspiration and advocacy of Secretaries-General for a broader engagement (beyond serving the interests of the organization) "has evolved in and through practice."[4] The international system certainly influenced these practices. Throughout the Cold War, for example, the role of the Secretary-General has predominantly been attributed to one of the "two UNs"—the Secretariat, but even more so, the inter-governmental arena of states.[5]

Yet, amidst an evolutionary UN and a changing world, there were always calls for

1   Leon Gordenker, "U Thant and the Office of U.N. Secretary-General", *International Journal*, v.22, 1966/1967, p.6.

2   Georges Langrod, *The International Civil Service: Its Origins, Its Nature, Its Evolution*, Leyden: A.W. Sythoff, 1963, p.309.

3   Karen Gram-Skjoldager, Haakon A. Ikonomou, "The Construction of the League of Nations Secretariat: Formative Practices of Autonomy and Legitimacy in International Organisations", *The International History Review*, 2017, pp.1-23; K. Dykmann, "How International was the Secretariat of the League of Nations?", *The International History Review*, v.37, 2015, pp.721-744; see also N. Hall, N. Woods, "Theorizing the Role of Executive Heads in International Organizations", *European Journal of International Relations*, v.36, 2017, pp.1-22.

4   Ole Jacob Sending, *The Politics of Expertise: Competing for Authority in Global Governance*, Ann Arbor: University of Michigan Press, 2015, p.52.

5   K. Haack, K. J. Kille, "The UN Secretary-General and Self-Directed Leadership: Development of the Democracy Agenda" in Joel E. Oestreich (ed), *International Organizations as Self-directed Actors: A Framework for Analysis*, Abingdon, Oxon, New York: Routledge, 2012, pp.29-59; I. Johnston, "The Role of the UN Secretary General: The Power of Persuasion Based on Law", *Global Governance*, v.9, 2003, pp.441-458; J. Karlsrud, "Special Representatives of the Secretary-General as Norm Arbitrators?: Understanding Bottom-up Authority in UN Peacekeeping", *Global Governance*, v.19, 2013, pp.525-544; M. Fröhlich, "Representing the United Nations—Individual Actors, International Agency, and Leadership", *Global Governance*, v.20, 2014, pp.169-193; Inis L. Claude, "Peace and Security: Prospective Roles for the Two United Nations", *Global Governance*, v.2, 1996, pp.289-298.

a stronger political role of the Secretary-General.[1] These calls have gained traction, not least because of an even more evolving dynamic interpretation of *The Charter* and the widening scope and tasks of the Secretary-General's role over time (e.g., overseeing expanding peacekeeping missions; attempts of moral entrepreneurship, etc.).[2] The Secretary-General might as well have the responsibility to heighten international awareness in the service for peace in the words of Secretary-General Boutros-Ghali[3] or to "draw the line between struggle and conflict."[4] The following analysis points out that this aspiration of serving peace was destined to be present from the beginnings because of the institutional preconditions of the office holder as an international civil servant, however sparingly described in *The UN Charter*.

The establishment of a civil service has a solid trajectory in domestic and international politics. Since the nineteenth century, the concept of an international civil service kept spreading among governments and international organizations.[5] Although international organizations in the nineteenth century had secretariats, bringing the concept of an international civil service up front and center on the stage of international interaction was developed in the context of the League of Nations. This was not least

1   See e.g., Deborah D. Avant, Martha Finnemore, Susan K. Sell (eds), *Who Governs the Globe?* , Cambridge: Cambridge University Press, 2010; "End of Assignment Report" by Inga-Britt Ahlenius, former Under-Secretary-General for Oversight Services; "Our Global Neighborhood: 'A Timely Work Deserving Our Full Attention'", *The Report of the Commission on Global Governance* (1st edition), Oxford University Press, February 16th, 1995; R. C. Thakur, "Choosing the Ninth United Nations Secretary-General: Looking Back, Looking Ahead," *Global Governance*, v.23, 2017; Simon Chesterman, "The Secretary-General We Deserve?", *Global Governance*, v.21, n.4, 2015, pp.505-513; Brian Urquhart, Erskine Childers, "A World in Need of Leadership: Tomorrow's United Nations", published under the joint auspices of the Ford Foundation and Dag Hammarskjöld Foundation, 1990.

2   G. F. Sinclair, "The International Civil Servant in Theory and Practice: Law, Morality, and Expertise", *European Journal of International Law*, v.26, 2015, pp.747-766; see also M.W. Manulak, "Leading by Design: Informal Influence and International Secretariats", *The Review of International Organizations*, v.12, 2017, pp.497-522.

3   B. Boutros-Ghali, "Global Leadership after the Cold War", *Foreign Affairs*, v.75, 1996, p.88.

4   Acceptance by Javier Pérez de Cuéllar, on the occasion of the award of the Nobel Peace Prize in Oslo, December 10th, 1988.

5   John Mathiason, *Invisible Governance: International Secretariats in Global Politics*, Bloomfield: Kumarian Press, 2007, Chapter 2; see also T.G. Weiss, "International Bureaucracy: The Myth and Reality of the International Civil Service", *International Affairs*, v.58, 1982, p.287-306, here 288-92.

because of the ambitions of the Organization's first Secretary General, Eric Drummond.[1] International history, however, continues to neglect the "endangered species"[2] of the civil servant.[3]

Arthur Balfour outlined the principles of the international civil service, emphasizing that "members of the secretariat once appointed are no longer the servants of the country of which they are citizens, but become for the time being the servants only of the League of Nations. Their duties are not national but international."[4] In other words, an "international civil servant is a person to whom the representatives of several States, or an organ acting on their behalf, have entrusted, in virtue of an inter-State agreement and under their supervision, the continuous and exclusive exercise of functions in the common interests of the States in question subject to special legal rules."[5] The international dedication locates the international civil servant "in a hierarchy of values in which 'the necessities peculiar to an international organization should completely exclude the idea of representation.'" Whatever the task and purpose of the organization,

1   Sir Eric Drummond (1876–1951) was the first Secretary-General of the League of Nations. As a member of the British delegation to the Paris Peace Conference of 1919 he was involved in the drafting of the Covenant of the League of Nations. With strong backing from British and American leaders, he was appointed League Secretary-General in May 1919. Drummond's accomplishments included creating the international body's multinational Permanent Secretariat and establishing patterns of relationships between the Secretariat and the League's other bodies, the Council and the Assembly, and with the permanent missions of the Member States. Drummond sought to use his office to help resolve disputes brought before the League, such as Japan's invasion of Manchuria in 1931. See, in particular, David Macfadyen, Michael D. V. Davies, Marilyn Norah Carr and John Burley, *Eric Drummond and His Legacies: The League of Nations and the Beginnings of Global Governance*, Cham: Springer International Publishing, 2019, pp.71-112; see also in Lorna Lloyd, "Drummond, (James) Eric, Seventh Earl of Perth (1876–1951)", *Oxford Dictionary of National Biography*, Oxford: Oxford University Press, 2004.

2   Jacques Lemoine, *The International Civil Servant: An Endangered Species*, Dordrecht: Kluwer Academic Publishers, 1995; Inis L. Claude, *Swords into Plowshares: The Problems and Progress of International Organization*, New York: Random House, 1971, pp.191; see also Hylke Dijkstra, 'Collusion in International Organizations: How States Benefit from the Authority of Secretariats', *Global Governance: A Review of Multilateralism and International Organizations*, v.23, 2017, pp.601-618.

3   See also T. G. Weiss, "International Bureaucracy: The Myth and Reality of the International Civil Service", *International Affairs*, v.58, 1982, pp.287-306; T.G. Weiss, "The John W. Holmes Lecture: Reinvigorating the International Civil Service", *Global Governance*, v.16, 2010, pp.39-57. For a current engagement, see, E. Newman, E. J. Ravndal, "The International Civil Service" in Diane Stone and Kim Moloney (eds), *The Oxford Handbook of Global Policy and Transnational Administration*, Oxford: Oxford University Press, 2019.

4   Cited in Colum Lynch, "The Decline of the International Civil Servant", *Foreign Policy*, March 2nd, 2010; see also "Chapter 2 Evolution of the International Pubic Service (1919-2006), in John Mathiason, *Invisible Governance: International Secretariats in Global Politics*, Lynne Rienner Publishers, 2007.

5   Ibid.

its international administration "serves institutionalized international co-operation—that is to say unity in plurality."[1]

This is particularly obvious in the case of the UN. The UN Secretary-General, then, seeks to bridge the gap between being chief administrative officer serving the organization, consisting of nation states, but who also serves the international interest, detached from and impartial to national interests.

Toward this end, the UN's *Standards of Conduct for the International Civil Service* holds that they are tasked to "serve the ideals of peace, respect for fundamental rights, economic and social progress, and international cooperation."[2] *The UN Charter* stresses the impartiality of the Secretary-General and the staff of the organization and calls on its members to abstain from seeking influence on the Secretariat. This led Secretary-General Dag Hammarskjöld, for example, to formulate his position as one to serve as a civil servant of the organization but who is, at the same time, "active as an instrument, a catalyst, perhaps an inspirer—he serves."[3] While those are high aspirations, their standards are often left unfulfilled as many international civil servants are political appointees rather than chosen or elected based on their experience.[4]

Secretaries General are also often politically compromised and lack the authority that they are supposed to possess based on their impartiality. "The" international civil servant, in other words, often remains an ideal-type.[5] Peace, cooperation, etc. are rather abstract and how they are achieved depends a lot on who the Secretaries-General—as well as the leading states—are at various times and conditions.

3.3　Former Secretary-General Kofi Annan

Kofi Annan (1938—2018), in full Kofi Atta Annan, Ghanaian international civil

---

1　Georges Langrod, *The International Civil Service: Its Origins, Its Nature, Its Evolution*, Leyden: A.W.Sythoff, 1963, pp.49-50.

2　International Civil Service Commission, *Standards of Conduct for the International Civil Servant*, New York, 2013, p.3.

3　Wilder Foote(ed.), *The Servant of Peace: A Selection of His Speeches and Statements*(1st edition), Harper and Row, 1961, p.348.

4　Colum Lynch, "The Decline of the International Civil Servant", *Foreign Policy*, March 2nd, 2010; see also Jacques Lemoine, *The International Civil Servant: An Endangered Species*, The Hague, London, Boston: Kluwer Law International, 1995.

5　Georges Langrod, *The International Civil Service: Its Origins, Its Nature, Its Evolution*, Leyden: A.W.Sythoff, 1963, p.184.

servant, was the Secretary-General of the United Nations from 1997 to 2006. He was the co-recipient, with the United Nations, of the Nobel Prize for Peace in 2001.[1]

(1) Career with the United Nations

Annan's career with the United Nations began in 1962, when he got a job working as a budget and administrative officer for the World Health Organization (WHO), a UN agency in Geneva. With the exception of a brief stint as the director of tourism in Ghana (1974—1976), Annan spent his entire career working as an international civil servant, serving in several administrative posts.

For a nine-year period from 1987 to 1996, Annan was appointed to serve as an Assistant Secretary-General in three consecutive positions: Human Resources, Management and Security Coordinator; Program Planning, Budget and Finance, and Controller; and Peacekeeping Operations. While he served in that last capacity, he distinguished himself during the civil war in Bosnia and Herzegovina, particularly in his skillful handling of the transition of peacekeeping operations from UN forces to NATO forces. Mr. Annan also served as Special Representative of the Secretary-General to the former Yugoslavia (1995—1996), and facilitated the repatriation from Iraq of more than 900 international staff and other non-Iraqi nationals (1990).

The United Nations Security Council recommended Annan to replace the previous Secretary-General, Dr. Boutros Boutros-Ghali of Egypt, in late 1996. The General Assembly voted in his favor, and he began his first term as the seventh Secretary-General of the United Nations on January 1, 1997. This was the first time in the history of the United Nations that a Secretary-General had come up through the ranks of the UN staff, and Annan, a Ghanian national, was also the first and only black African to be appointed as the world's top diplomat, a tenure that saw him mediate in some of the biggest crises of the 21st century.[2]

(2) Career Highlights

One of Mr. Annan's main priorities as Secretary-General was a comprehensive programme of reform aimed at revitalizing the United Nations and making the

---

1 Source from the website of Britannica, "Kofi Atta Annan", edited by the editors of Encyclopedia Britannica, accessed on July 4th, 2021.

2 Linda Melvern, "Kofi Annan: Former UN Secretary-General and Nobel Peace Prize Laureate", *The Independent*, August 20th, 2018.

international system more effective. He was a constant advocate for human rights, the rule of law, the Millennium Development Goals and Africa, and sought to bring the Organization closer to the global public by forging ties with civil society, the private sector and other partners.

Read This[1]

The Millennium Development Goals (MDGs) are 8 international development goals that UN Member States have agreed to try to achieve by the year 2015:

Goal 1. To eradicate extreme poverty and hunger

Goal 2. To achieve universal primary education

Goal 3. To promote gender equality and empower women

Goal 4. To reduce child mortality rates

Goal 5. To improve maternal health

Goal 6. To combat HIV/AIDS, malaria, and other diseases

Goal 7. To ensure environmental sustainability

Goal 8. To develop a global partnership for development

The MDGs were developed out of several commitments set forth in *The United Nations Millennium Declaration*, signed in September 2000. The MDGs emphasized three areas: human capital, infrastructure and human rights, with the intent of increasing living standards.

- Human capital objectives include nutrition, healthcare (including child mortality, HIV/AIDS, tuberculosis and malaria, and reproductive health) and education.

- Infrastructure objectives include access to safe drinking water, energy and modern information/communication technology; increased farm outputs using sustainable practices; transportation; and environment.

- Human rights objectives include empowering women, reducing violence, increasing political voice, ensuring equal access to public services and increasing security of property rights.

---

1 Source from the website of the United Nations "Millennium Development Goals and Beyond 2015".

Each MDG has specific targets set for 2015 and measurable indicators to monitor progress from 1990 levels. They have galvanized unprecedented efforts to meet the needs of the world's poorest. The Sustainable Development Goals (SDGs) succeeded to the MDGs in 2016. The UN is also working with governments, civil society and other partners to build on the momentum generated by the MDGs and carry on with an ambitious post-2015 development agenda.

At Mr. Annan's initiative, UN peacekeeping was strengthened in ways that enabled the United Nations to cope with a rapid rise in the number of operations and personnel. It was also at Mr. Annan's urging that, in 2005, Member States established two new inter- governmental bodies: the Peacebuilding Commission and the Human Rights Council. Mr. Annan likewise played a central role in the creation of a global fund to fight AIDS, tuberculosis and malaria,[1] the adoption of the UN's first-ever counter-terrorism strategy, and the acceptance by Member States of the "responsibility to protect" people from genocide, war crimes, ethnic cleansing and crimes against humanity. His "Global Compact" initiative, launched in 1999, has become the world's largest effort to promote corporate social responsibility.

Mr. Annan undertook wide-ranging diplomatic initiatives. In 1998, he helped to ease the transition to civilian rule in Nigeria. Also, that year, he visited Iraq in an effort to resolve an impasse between that country and the Security Council over compliance with resolutions involving weapons inspections and other matters—an effort that helped to avoid an outbreak of hostilities, which was imminent at that time. In 1999, he was deeply involved in the process by which Timor-Leste gained independence from Indonesia. He was responsible for certifying Israel's withdrawal from Lebanon in 2000, and in 2006, his efforts contributed to securing a cessation of hostilities between Israel and Hizbollah. Also, in 2006, he mediated a settlement of the dispute between Cameroon and Nigeria over the Bakassi peninsula through implementation of the judgement of the International Court of Justice. Annan is also known for his opposition to the 2003

1　Among Annan's most well-known accomplishments were his issuance of a five-point *Call to Action* in April 2001 to address the HIV/AIDS pandemic and his proposal to create a *Global AIDS and Health Fund*. He and the United Nations were jointly awarded the Nobel Peace Prize in December of 2001 "for their work for a better organized and more peaceful world."

invasion of Iraq and to Iran's nuclear program.

Later in 2003, Annan appointed a panel to explore the UN's response to global threats, and he included many of its recommendations in a major reform package presented to the UN General Assembly in 2005. His efforts to strengthen the Organization's management, coherence and accountability involved major investments in training and technology, the introduction of a new whistleblower policy and financial disclosure requirements, and steps aimed at improving coordination at the country level.[1]

In 2005 Annan was at the center of controversy following an investigation into the oil-for-food program, which had allowed Iraq—under UN supervision—to sell a set amount of oil in order to purchase food, medicine, and other necessities. A report described major corruption within the program and revealed that Annan's son was part of a Swiss business that had won an oil-for-food contract. Although Annan was cleared of wrongdoing, he was criticized for his failure to properly oversee the program. In 2006, Annan's term ended, and he was succeeded by Ban Ki-Moon.

(3) After the United Nations

In 2007 Annan was named chairperson of the Alliance for a Green Revolution in Africa (AGRA), an organization aiding small-scale farmers; AGRA was funded by the Bill & Melinda Gates Foundation and the Rockefeller Foundation. He later played a crucial role in resolving the Kenyan election crisis that began in late December 2007, eventually brokering a power-sharing agreement between the government and the opposition on February 28, 2008. In the same year, he received the Peace of Westphalia Prize, awarded biannually for contributions to unity and peace in Europe, and became chancellor of the University of Ghana. In 2007, he founded the Kofi Annan Foundation, a not-for-profit organization that promotes peace, sustainable development, human rights, and the rule of law.

In February 2012 Annan was appointed Joint Special Envoy for Syria by the United Nations and the League of Arab States. His core diplomatic effort consisted in delivering to the Syrian government a six-point proposal for ending the country's civil war, a plan endorsed by the Security Council. The proposal enjoined Pres. Bashar al-Assad's

---

1   Source from the United Nations Secretary-General website, "Home/On the Job/Former Secretaries-General/Kofi Annan", accessed on July 10th, 2021.

government to take significant steps, including ending all fighting operations. The Syrian government formally accepted the plan in March but continued its attacks on rebel forces and on popular demonstrations. In August, Annan announced his demission as Joint Special Envoy, citing a lack of unity and political will among world powers to resolve the conflict.

Annan passed away after a short illness in a hospital in Bern, Switzerland, on August 18, 2018, at the age of 80. His wife Nane and children Ama, Kojo and Nina were by his side. "Kofi Annan was a global statesman and a deeply committed internationalist who fought throughout his life for a fairer and more peaceful world. During his distinguished career and leadership of the United Nations he was an ardent champion of peace, sustainable development, human rights and the rule of law," the Kofi Annan Foundation and Annan family said in a statement.

Tasks

Activity 1 Quick-Quiz Questions

One Day at UNHCR (Bangkok, Thailand)

Assume that you are a young female staff of UNHCR (Bangkok, Thailand) now, who used to live in Chongqing, China for a long time.

*In the morning, you read interior newsletters, surprisingly finding that more and more refugees tried to head for another country through Bangkok. You are upset about their condition. Limited by weak individual capacity, you decide to participate in group work to collect more donations from society to make a difference.

*At noon, you scan a menu at a Spanish restaurant. As a super Chongqing gourmet, you cannot stand a meal without spicy food. But here in Bangkok, you choose to abandon your chance to enjoy hot-pot and Chuanchuan with your friends and to eat sea-food noodles to reduce her inadaptation and homesickness.

*In the afternoon, you collect information of enterprises and institutions with your departmental colleagues from the United States, Japan, the Philippines and Malaysia. Then you chat with them in your leisure time and exchange opinions on the concrete solutions to tackle refugee issues.

*At night, the leader of your department sends you an e-mail which asks if you have time to go to Geneva Headquarters and hand in some documents at weekends. Though you have intendency to eat hot-pot with your friends, you give up this relaxing weekend and accept this task considering of human resource limitations of your department.

After this occupied but rich day, could you answer the following questions?

1. Does making a difference motivate you?

2. Are you selfless and driven to be a part of a bigger purpose in the service of humanity?

3. Are hope and strength of character attributes which will guide your zeal to make a difference in a complex world?

4. Are you the type of person who will travel and work anywhere at a moment's notice?

5. Do you thrive in an environment that is truly international and multi-cultural, which respects as well as promotes diversity and functions at its best through the efforts of teams of different people?

If your answers are yes, congratulations! These are some of the characteristics that you will find in an INTERNATIONAL CIVIL SERVANT.

Activity 2 Blank Filling

Major Organs ot the United Nations

Objectives:

- Identify the particulars of each of the major UN organs.
- Match the answers to the appropriate question box.
- Have a general understanding of the different functions of the major UN organs.

Requirements

(1) Time: 40—60 minutes

(2) Materials Needed:

- Handout Sheet: The United Nations Organs Puzzle
- Scissors and Glue (optional)

Procedure

A. Lesson Introduction/Activation of Prior Knowledge

KWL (Know-Want-Learned) Discussion on UN major organs: please create a KWL chart on your papers and individually fill in the "Know" and "What they Want to Know" of the KWL chart regarding the UN major organs. Discuss your responses with the class.

It is okay if you do not have much completed on your charts because this activity will help you learn about the major organs and their functions.

B. Activity

- Distribute Handout Sheet: The United Nations Organs Puzzle
- Match "answer squares" with "question squares". You may cut and paste.

C. Closing 3/Wrap-Up

- Once you are done, review answers.
- Fill in "Learned" section of KWL activity.

Handout Sheets—United Nations Puzzle

Please place the number of the answer in the correct box. You can only use each description once.

Sheet 1

	Secretariat	General Assembly	Security Council	International Court of Justice	Economic and Social Council	Trusteeship Council
Who are the members?						
What do they do?/ What topics do they discuss?						
If it is a voting body, how do they vote?						
When and where do they meet?						
What makes it different from other organs?						

Sheet 2

1	2	3	4	5	6
Simple majority, but the permanent members have a veto.	These are the employees of the United Nations; they do the actual work of the United Nations.	They meet yearly at UN Headquarters beginning 3rd week of September.	15 Member States: 5 permanent and 10 rotating	They do not vote, due to the fact that they are functionaries.	54 member-state regional body that is elected by the General Assembly.
7	**8**	**9**	**10**	**11**	**12**
Simple majority or if declared an important question, a 2/3 majority.	This body needs a simple majority vote, but Member States are expected to confer with their region before voting.	This organ meets when it is asked by the Secretary General or a Member State in crisis at UNHQ.	This organ is located in the same city as the International Criminal Court. The term runs from August 1st through July 31st.	Debates international economic and social issues.	Oversaw Trust Territories.
13	**14**	**15**	**16**	**17**	**18**
All 192 Member States of the United Nations. Discusses issues of peace and security.	This body provides legal opinions on cases.	The 5 permanent representatives ran this council when it was active.	15 judges are elected by the General Assembly for their expertise; they do not represent countries.	Members must be available at a moment's notice.	This council no longer meets because it has fulfilled its mission. If necessary, it will be recalled by the General Assembly.
19	**20**	**21**	**22**	**23**	**24**
This body can discuss any topic their members wish to speak on.	These individuals work all over the world implementing the work of the United Nations.	This body regularly works with Non-Governmental Organizations (NGOs) to promote economic and social welfare.	The decisions are legally binding and may be enforced through sanctions.	This body did not vote, it had monitored newly-emerged nations.	Settles legal disputes among nations, not individuals.
25	**26**	**27**	**28**	**29**	**30**
This body ceased to exist with the independence of Palau.	This body meets regionally and then sends its elected representatives to serve the plenary at UNHQ in New York.	This is the only body that regularly meets with a representative of all Member States.	There are offices all around the world where the UN's mission is being carried out.	The composition of the court of this organ cannot have more than one member of a nationality represented at a time.	This is not made up of Member States.

Activity 3 ⎟ Group Discussions

Today's workforce is very international and diverse. People of different ages and backgrounds are working alongside one another more so today than ever before. The purpose of this activity is to consider how we perceive others and how others may perceive us, as well as whether or not these perceptions paint an accurate picture of who we are. Consider and discuss with your partner about the following situations:

a. Sandra is 19 years old and has her first job as an administrative assistant. She wears very low-cut shirts, short skirts, heels, and lots of perfume. What might Sandra's attire lead others to believe about her? What might the reality be?

b. Tony is 24 years old. He has tattoo sleeves on both of his arms, as well as a name tattooed on his neck. Tony would like to be a waiter at a very fancy restaurant. He has his first interview today. What might a job interviewer think of Tony? What might the reality be?

c. Terrence is 18 years old and just graduated high school (where he had a 4.0 average). Terrence has an interview today for a summer internship. Terrence is a wheelchair user. Do you think there is a chance that the interviewer might not ask Terrence the same interview questions he or she would ask of someone who isn't in a wheelchair? Why or why not?

d. Marissa is in 10th grade. She comes from a family of mechanics. Her dad and three brothers are mechanics, and her grandfather owns a garage. Marissa has secretly wanted to work on cars but has been afraid to tell her family. She now wants to approach her grandfather for a summer job. Why do you think Marissa has kept her career dream a secret? How might she ask her grandfather for a summer job?

e. Ruthie is 62 years old and is looking for a job. She loves one of the local clothing stores and applied online for a job as a sales clerk. She has an interview today and is afraid the store manager will be much younger than her. Ruthie considers canceling the interview. Why do you think Ruthie is worried about her interview? What would you tell Ruthie?

f. Sam is 20 years old, a sophomore in college and is looking for an engineering internship. Sam has Asperger syndrome (a form of autism), and while he has an

A average in his engineering courses, he recognizes the fact that he has trouble interacting socially and is worried about his interviews. Why do you think Sam is worried about his interviews? What advice would you give Sam?

Activity 4 | Sociodrama

The Declaration on the Elimination of Violence against Women (VAW) which was adopted by the General Assembly on December 20, 1993 defined "violence against women" as "any act of gender-based violence that results in, or is likely to result in, physical, sexual, or psychological harm or suffering to women, including threats of such acts, coercion or arbitrary deprivation of liberty, whether occurring in public or in private life."

Violence against women encompasses domestic violence, threats of violence, threats of divorce by husband, rape, incest, child marriage, and honor killing for choosing a partner or taking divorce, acid burns, and trafficking. Violence in the family also includes battering, preference for a son and female genital mutilation. In the community, violence against women also includes sexual harassment and violence against domestic workers. All these acts reflect the gender bias in society and which by being perpetuated and condoned has social, psychological and economic impacts on the individual, family, the nation, and the world.

Work in groups and discuss what the impact of VAW is on: (a) women; (b) the family; (c) society.

- Each group should prepare a sociodrama describing the impact of violence against women from a different aspect in relation to self, family, and society;
- After each group has presented its sociodrama, the other groups should describe what they have seen and analyze or interpret it. The group which has just presented should then explain what they were trying to convey in their sociodrama.

NOTE: *You are allowed some more time for discussion, as the aim is to stimulate thought about the effects of violence against women.*

a. Is the impact of violence against women accurately portrayed in the drama?

b. Were there issues that were not sufficiently portrayed?

c. What can society do to reduce or eliminate this violence against women?

d. What would the world be like if violence against women and girls ended?

Here are some prompts to help you take the first step.

—there will be no child marriage, or sale of brides;

—divorce will all be done in a respectable way;

—women refugee centers will no longer be needed...

Activity 5 Extended Reading

Remarks at Memorial for Kofi Annan[1]

António Guterres

September 21st, 2018

Mrs. Nane Annan and members of the Annan family, we are deeply honoured and graced by your presence.

The United Nations and Kofi Annan were inseparable. It is impossible to say where one ended and the other began. And so, dear Annan family, we say to you today not only welcome, but welcome home. To so many of us, Kofi Annan was more than just a dear friend. He was family. And I know you all feel in this room the profound sorrow that accompanies the sudden passing of such a beloved leader, mentor and guide.

Kofi Annan was uncommonly warm, accessible and of the people—but above all he was principled and forceful in battling for the values of *The UN Charter*. In recent weeks, so many of his former colleagues have fondly recalled a workplace encounter or an unexpected phone call asking after their well-being, or that of their family. He had a knack for assembling solid teams and winning their allegiance by giving them room to do their best. He was charming and wise, kind and courageous. But he also knew how to deliver the barb—in his masterly subtle way. "I wonder if that's the best approach", he would muse. Or perhaps he might say, "I would want to be sure..." And sometimes, people were so captivated by his presence that they did not realize that they were being admonished!

I have an enormous debt of gratitude towards Kofi Annan. […] I would very

---

1　The passage was from the United Nations Secretary-General website, accessed on December 28th, 2022.

probably not be here if he had not chosen me to become, thirteen years ago, United Nations High Commissioner for Refugees. That was probably his worst mistake.

At the funeral service in Accra last week, Kofi Annan was described as a "good and faithful servant". [He] was indeed good at everything he did across a life of service. He would be the first to describe any achievements as the product of teamwork. But let me mention just two of the so many examples of where his individual brilliance shone through.

His personal advocacy to mobilize a global response to the HIV/AIDS epidemic led to actions that saved millions of lives.

His efforts to articulate the Millennium Development Goals rallied the world behind poverty eradication and paved the way for the 2030 Agenda, today's ambitious blueprint for a better world.

In a world of impunity and buck-passing, his willingness to own up to setbacks was also refreshing and a remarkable example. And his moral voice led the world toward ground-breaking understandings about defending our common humanity. Throughout his tenure Kofi Annan urged us never to be bystanders in life. He summoned us all to act against bias, brutality and bloodshed. He was a multilateralist through and through, a true UN-blue believer in a rules-based global order. And, I must say, his loss cuts even deeper because we have never needed that faith and inspiration more.

Kofi Annan called the United Nations the "last best hope of humanity". He burned with the flame of human rights, dignity and justice. We shall miss him every day. But we vow, here in the heart of his beloved home, that we will carry forward his torch now and forever more. And in the exercise of my duties, he will always be my central inspiration and my deepest reference.

Thank you very much.

PART II

Part II

Practice-Based Guideline

Chapter 4

Conduct Standards for International Civil Servants

I believe that a shared view of the standards we are striving to achieve will assist us in our continuing efforts to prepare the Organization to meet the challenges of the 21st century.

—Kofi Annan, former Secretary-General of the United Nations[1]

---

1   In "Building the Future", the Secretary-General has indicated that the Organization's greatest strength—and the key to our success—is the quality of our staff and managers. For more information, see *United Nations Competencies for the Future.*

Overview

Learning Objectives

a. To identify and analyse actual job tasks and projects offered or required by employers in the real-world organizations;

b. To get familiar with the key values and competencies which are considered important for international civil servants in their daily work;

c. To better understand cultural competence and its components, and to develop and enhance "the ability to communicate effectively and appropriately in intercultural situations based on one's intercultural knowledge, skills and attitudes".[1]

Main Contents

Noting that the international civil service is the embodiment of the will of so many diverse cultures,[2] this chapter articulates, and draws reasonable conclusions about the nature of services provided by United Nations common system organizations, as well as the universal standard for all staff members employed by the United Nations as the "highest standards of efficiency, competence and integrity".[3] On the basis of *A Guide to a Career with the United Nations*, it further explains in detail the common characteristics and skills needed to become a qualified international civil servant. This chapter stands, humbly, that, in this context, the attributes essential to foster professional competence might include: commitment to the process of continuous learning and reflection; adoption of shared responsibility and cooperative action; openness to new opportunities, ideas and ways of thinking; self-awareness about identity and culture; and, sensitivity and respect for differences, etc.

---

1 Darla K. Deardorff, "Identification and Assessment of Intercultural Competence as a Student Outcome of Internationalization", *Journal of Studies in International Education*, 2006, pp.247-248.

2 David Owen, "Reflections of an International Civil Service", *Public Administration Review*, v.30, n.3, 1970, pp.207-211.

3   United Nations Secretariat, *Status, Basic Rights and Duties of United Nations Staff Members: Secretary-General's Bulletin*, ST/SG/2016/9, July 21st, 2016, p.3.

Warm-up

Activity: Baseline Targets (10 minutes)

Note: This session aims to see how much you know about key subjects of international civil servants by placing dots on a flipchart which represents degrees of understanding. The closer to the centre, the greater the knowledge. It also enables you to note your starting point and monitor your progress during the workshop.

Preparation and materials:

Flip-chart, flip-chart pens and post-its. Draw diagram below on a large flipchart drawing (four sheets of flip-chart sellotaped together).

Approach:

a. Identify the three expected learning outcomes which you wrote most, for example "understand the role and responsibilities of international civil servants";

b. Write one of these expectations above each flipchart;

c. Take a color marker pen and place a dot on the flipchart. Place the dot towards the centre indicates you are already close to achieving this expectation, whereas placing the dot towards the outside indicates you still have a long way to go;

d. Keep these targets throughout the workshop. On the last day of this chapter, return to these targets and mark a dot again using a different coloured marker. This will tell you how successful this chapter has been in fulfilling your expectations.

Section 1

What Are the Core Values for International Civil Servants?

The UN Organizational core values are the shared principles and beliefs underpinning the work of the Organization and its agencies; they are also the guiding actions and behaviors of UN employees and UN staff members in carrying out their individual work.[1] *So what are these core values that all United Nations staff members are not only expected to follow but will be appraised on?*

- **Integrity** which involves among others the obligation to include impartiality, fairness, honesty and truthfulness, in an international civil servant's daily activities and behaviors, and to stand by decisions that are in the Organization's interest even if some of them might be unpopular;

- **Professionalism** aiming to among others for UN staff members to show pride in their daily work and persistence when faced with difficult problems or challenges;

- **Respect for Diversity and Gender** aiming to among others for UN staff members to work effectively with people from all backgrounds, treat all people with dignity and respect as well as men and women equally.

1.1   Core Value 1: Integrity

- *Upholds* the principles of *The United Nations Charter*;
- *Demonstrates* the values of the United Nations, including impartiality, fairness, honesty and truthfulness, in daily activities and behaviors;
- *Acts* without consideration of personal gain;
- *Resists* undue political pressure in decision-making;
- *Does* not abuse power or authority;
- *Stands by* decisions that are in the Organization's interest even if they are unpopular;
- *Takes* prompt action in cases of unprofessional or unethical behaviour.

The concept of ***integrity*** enshrined in *The Charter of the United Nations* embraces all aspects of an international civil servant's behaviour, including such qualities as honesty, truthfulness, impartiality and incorruptibility. The following examples are contrary to the concept of integrity: theft, falsification of official documents, falsification

---

1   "What Are the Core Values, Principles and Competencies of the United Nations?", *United Career Coalition (UCC)*, " UN Career/UN applications/UN cover letter/UN interview May 26".

of the amount of medical expenses or school fees, false statements of travel expenses, false statements in reference to a family situation, establishment of contracts for fictitious temporary assistance or for the benefit of close family members, personal use of extra-budgetary funds, misappropriation of funds, manipulation of the rules and procedures governing purchases and corruption.[1]

On top of that, international civil servants should abide by the principle of *political neutrality*. The so-called "political neutrality" originally refers to the fact that the official working in the government should be detached from party politics and personal political ideas in the process of performing official duties.[2] Evolved to the present, political neutrality means that staff transcend the boundaries of the state, the nation, and the party, and consider the general interests. When staffs are engaged in administrative management and public affairs management, they should suppress their personal feelings to the utmost extent, take the law and objective facts as the criteria, aim at the interests of all the people, and do their duty to do the best for the people of the world. Although this does not necessarily mean that international civil servants must abandon their personal political views or national opinions, they must be requested to always maintain a broad international outlook and an understanding of the entire international community.

Quick Quiz

How can international civil servants possibly achieve integrity? Demonstrates the values of the United Nations in daily activities and behaviors? Acts without consideration of personal gain? Resists undue political pressure in decision-making? Does not abuse power or authority? Stands by decisions that are in the Organization's interest, even if they are unpopular? Takes prompt action in cases of unprofessional or unethical behaviour? *Are there anymore?*

1　United Nations Education, Scientific and Cultural Organization, *Standards of Conduct for the International Civil Service*, 2014, pp.7.

2　Xie Songsong and Cao Jie, "Analysis of the Meaning of the 'Political Neutrality' Principle in the Civil Servant System", *Principles of the Law* , 2009(7)

1.2　Core Value 2: Professionalism

- **Shows** pride in work and in achievements;
- **Demonstrates** professional competence and mastery of subject matter;
- **Is** conscientious and efficient in meeting commitments, observing deadlines and achieving results;
- **Is** motivated by professional rather than personal concerns;
- **Shows** persistence when faced with difficult problems or challenges;
- **Remains** calm in stressful situations.

The competency of professionalism is a core value for the United Nations. It refers to an ability to work in a calm, competent and committed manner. All staff members are required to demonstrate this value, irrespective of the nature of their role.

But what does "being professional" actually mean? For some, being professional might mean dressing smartly at work, or doing a good job. For others, being professional means having advanced degrees or other certifications, framed and hung on the office wall. Professionalism isn't one thing; it's a combination of all of these definitions. But it also covers more.

To work with professionalism is to be dedicated, conscientious and efficient in meeting deadlines and achieving results. A professional employee arrives on time for work and in any situation, presenting the best possible appearance, commitment, and pride in his or her work. Professional workers take responsibility for their own behavior and work effectively with others. High-quality work standards, honesty, and integrity are also part of the package. Professional employees look clean and neat and dress appropriately for the job. Communicating effectively and appropriately for the workplace is also an essential part of professionalism.

Toward its realization, international civil servants must also have an **international outlook**. International outlook comes from the understanding and loyalty of the purposes and objectives regulated in their legal instruments by international organizations. This means, among other things, respecting the rights of others to disagree and comply with different cultural patterns. And it requires willingness to work with people of different nationalities, religions, and cultures without prejudice; sensitiveness at all times; attention to what proposals, activities and statements will be at others' opinion, and to cautiously avoid any statements that can be understood as biased or intolerant. Working methods can vary from culture to culture. International staff should not be rigidly attached to their own national or regional attitudes, working methods or work habits.

1.3　Core Value 3: Respect for Diversity

> - *Works* effectively with people from all backgrounds;
> - *Treats* all people (including all persons of concern) with dignity and respect, and with a sense of fairness;
> - *Treats* men and women equally;
> - *Shows* respect for, and understanding of, diverse points of view and demonstrates this understanding in daily work and decision-making;
> - *Examines* own biases and behaviors to avoid stereotypical responses;
> - *Does* not discriminate against any individual or group;
> - *Develops* skills in age, gender, and diversity analysis as applicable to the area of work;
> - *Seeks* to understand and respect differences in people, in the professional and personal domain.

Diversity is one of the defining features of the United Nations. With talent and resources coming from every walk of life, respect is the foundation of all positive successes that arise from living and working in a diverse environment. The concept of "respect" encompasses acceptance and compassion. It means understanding that each individual is unique and moving beyond simple tolerance to embracing and celebrating the rich dimensions of diversity contained within each individual. These can be along the dimensions of *race, ethnicity, gender, sexual orientation, socio-economic status, age, physical abilities, religious beliefs, political beliefs, or other ideologies.*

(1) Employee Diversity

"... Due regard shall be paid to the importance of recruiting the staff on as wide a geographical basis as possible."

—Article 101(3), *The UN Charter*

The United Nations Secretariat which commenced operations in early 1946 was staffed with a mere 300 people working primarily for the Preparatory Commission and engaged in providing conference services for a fledgling world body that was beginning to chart a course to positively change the world. From that nucleus, it expanded within six months to about 3,000 employees. Three years later, in October 1949, the cornerstone was laid for what would evolve into the Organization's sprawling Headquarters in midtown Manhattan in New York. Today, the United Nations has evolved beyond the conference management services and gradually transformed itself into a global Secretariat with a workforce that now numbers some 44,000 specialized men and women.

The United Nations encourages employees from various backgrounds and respects employees' differences by offering opportunities for employees to work in various global locations as part of the multi-cultural communication training program.

Today the United Nations has become a more reactive field-based operation with 60 percent of its staff working away from Headquarters in locations all over the world.[1]

(2) Empowering Women in the Workplace

"The United Nations shall place no restrictions on the eligibility of men and women to participate in any capacity and under conditions of equality in its principal and subsidiary organs."

—Article 8, *The UN Charter*

One of the main tenets of *The Charter* is the principle of equality of men and women, which is about empowering women to reach their full potential to contribute to and benefit from economic, social, and cultural participation. To demonstrate a commitment to gender equality requires every employee's commitment to developing gender awareness and applying this sensitivity in their day-to-day activities.[2] In this context, consciousness-raising campaign about the equal participation of women in the public sphere, leadership training and transparent hiring practices are all very important.

To operationalize the goal of gender parity, all UN personnel:

---

1   Source from the website of United Nations Careers, "Home/Why work at the UN/Where we are".

2   To know more about UN Women, see the official website of the UN Women.

- Take consideration of gender equality and women's empowerment issues and the application of this awareness by treating all members of UN equally and with respect;
- Have knowledge of gender-based disadvantages, discrimination and inequality; formed from a shared understanding that there are socially determined differences between women and men, which affect women and girls experience of equality;
- Modify behavior and interactions at work to overcome biases and assumptions regarding socially constructed roles of men and women, girls and boys;
- Ensure all actions demonstrate zero tolerance for sexual harassment and abuse of power to ensure that all behavior supports UN Women's commitment to gender equality practices.

In addition to demonstrating the above, leaders at UN are required to have substantive knowledge of gender equality practices and women's empowerment issues and exemplify this understanding in their daily behaviour. Leaders also need to provide team members with coaching and support as to how they can further develop and demonstrate sensitivity to gender issues in their day-to-day work.

Featured History[1]

For many years, the United Nations faced serious challenges in its efforts to promote gender equality globally, including inadequate funding and no single recognized driver to direct UN activities on gender equality issues. In July 2010, the United Nations General Assembly created *UN Women*, the United Nations Entity for Gender Equality and the Empowerment of Women, to address such challenges. In doing so, UN Member States took an historic step in accelerating the Organization's goals on gender equality and the empowerment of women.

UN Women supports UN Member States as they set global standards for achieving gender equality and works with governments and civil society to design laws, policies, programmes and services needed to ensure that the standards are effectively implemented and truly benefit women and girls worldwide. It works globally to make the vision of *The Sustainable Development Goals* a reality for women and girls and stands behind women's equal participation in all aspects of life, focusing on four strategic priorities:

1　Source from the website of UN Women, "Home/About us/Work and priorities", accessed on August 21st, 2022.

a. Women lead, participate in and benefit equally from governance systems;

b. Women have income security, decent work, and economic autonomy;

c. All women and girls live a life free from all forms of violence ;

d. Women and girls contribute to and have greater influence in building sustainable peace and resilience, and benefit equally from the prevention of natural disasters and conflicts and humanitarian action.

UN Women also coordinates and promotes the UN system's work in advancing gender equality, and in all deliberations and agreements linked to *The 2030 Agenda*. The entity works to position gender equality as fundamental to *The Sustainable Development Goals*, and a more inclusive world.

(3) Hiring People with Disabilities

Freedom from discrimination is a basic human right. International civil servants are expected to respect the dignity, worth and equality of all people without any distinction whatsoever. Assumptions based on stereotypes must be assiduously avoided. The United Nations has an office which works to make sure that all persons have the same rights. It is called the Office of the High Commissioner for Human Rights, "OHCHR" for short.

Persons with disabilities often find it hard to get a job or to keep it. In developing countries, 80% to 90% of persons with disabilities of working age are unemployed, whereas in industrialized countries the figure is between 50% and 70%.[1] The OHCHR wants to make sure that persons with disabilities can use their right to work. They wrote *The Convention on the Rights of Persons with Disabilities (CRPD). The Convention* is made up of articles which recognize the right of persons with disabilities to work, on an equal basis with others. This includes the right to the opportunity to gain a living by work freely chosen or accepted in a labour market and work environment that is open, inclusive, and accessible to persons with disabilities.[2]

Disability is also referenced in various parts of the Sustainable Development

---

1　Source from the website of the Department of Economic and Social Affairs Disability, "Home/Resources/Factsheet on Persons with Disabilities/Disability and Employment", accessed on October 2nd, 2021.

2　Source from the website of the Department of Economic and Social Affairs Disability, "Home/Convention on the Rights of Persons with Disabilities (CRPD)/Article 27-Work and employment", accessed on October 2nd, 2021.

Goals and specifically in parts related to education, growth and employment, inequality, accessibility of human settlements, as well as data collection and monitoring of the SDGs, for instance:

Goal 4 forces on inclusive and equitable quality education and promotion of life-long learning opportunities. It emphasizes eliminating gender disparities in education and ensuring equal access to all levels of education and vocational training for the vulnerable, including persons with disabilities. In addition, the proposal calls for building and upgrading education facilities that are child, disability and gender sensitive and also provide safe, non-violent, inclusive and effective learning environments for all.

Read This[1]

I was born in the Italian countryside and at the age of six, I was diagnosed with a very rare tumour pressing on my spine. I survived but I became paraplegic. Growing up, there were no specific laws in favour of children with disabilities, so my parents and I had to be creative in pioneering different ways of overcoming physical and attitudinal barriers, along with stigma and discrimination. This made me resilient, persistent and a quick problem solver—qualities that have been valuable to me in life.

I have always been interested in the world, and in learning more about different groups and cultures. When I was at university, my class was visited by a diplomat from the Italian Ministry of Foreign Affairs. As I was interested in international organizations, I asked how one could work for the United Nations. That's how I found out about the Junior Professional Officer Programme (JPO, also called the Associate Expert Programme). It seemed like the perfect opportunity to follow my passion for empowering others through international development.

I started my career at the United Nations in Vienna as a JPO in what used to be the Centre for Social Development and Humanitarian Affairs (CSDHA), which hosted the Unit of Disabled Persons, the Youth Unit, the Aging Unit, the Family Unit and the Division for the Advancement of Women. Except for the Division for

---

1　Personal narrative of Daniela Bas, Director of the Division for Social Policy and Development, Economic, Social and Development Network. See also the website of the United Nations Careers.

the Advancement of Women, these CSDHA units would later form the Division for Social Policy and Development (DSPD) of the Department for Economic and Social Development (DESA)—the Division I have had the honour of leading since 2011!

Between 1986 and 1993, I worked in the area of social development and human rights. I left the Organization in 1995 and held a number of significant assignments, including as Special Adviser on "Fundamental Rights" to the former Vice President of the European Commission and as Chief Executive Officer for private enterprises in Italy. In May 2011, I was appointed to my current position as Director of DSPD at the United Nations. I have to thank the United Nations. I am here because the Organization started promoting equal opportunities for people with disabilities decades ago.

I am intrigued by cultures, people, and social groups, and using communication to reach out and empower them. In this regard, my position as Director of a Division which advocates for society and development is important. Our mandate allows us to reach out to the world, and to all relevant stakeholders to raise awareness of important social issues. We can give grassroots organizations the tools and confidence to empower their local communities—where it matters most.

Through my work at the United Nations, I have become highly familiar with the World Programme of Action concerning Disabled Persons, which provided a blueprint for governments to develop their national policies to ensure the full and equal participation of persons with disabilities in society and development. It was an inspiring and empowering document that worked towards promoting real changes on the ground in the lives of people with disabilities. In 2006, the General Assembly adopted *The Convention on the Rights of Persons with Disabilities. The Convention* elevated the work of the United Nations for persons with disabilities to new heights by changing the perception of disability and promoting the human rights and well-being of persons with disabilities in society and development.

Since the adoption of *The Convention*, the United Nations Headquarters in New York is undergoing major transformations and across the Secretariat, a new policy is being implemented on the employment and accessibility of persons with disabilities since the United Nations does not discriminate on the basis of disability.

The Organization takes measures to provide reasonable accommodation to ensure that staff with disabilities can fully perform the functions of their job.

If you are curious about life and want to be a part of the United Nations, you must relentlessly pursue your dreams, no matter what disability, barriers or challenges you may face. By being willing and open to change, I can see results as I continue to realize my dream of empowering vulnerable groups. My passion for my work as a United Nations staff member grows every day as it is my motivation to bring hope, development and positive change to social policies and people around the world.

Section 2

What Are the Core Competencies for International Civil Servants?

The concept of "competency" in the UN vocabulary, cannot be dissociated from the history of UN personnel, being quoted in Article 101 of *The UN Charter: "The paramount consideration in the employment of the staff and in the determination of the conditions of service shall be the necessity of securing the highest standards of efficiency, competence, and integrity"*. Along the history of the United Nations, Secretaries-General have put emphasis on the excellence and motivation of the personnel.

From 1999 on, the competencies have been used in the United Nations system at the step of recruitment, through competency-based interviews: "United Nations managers select core values and competencies to fit the requirements of the post from a menu of originally three core values (integrity, professionalism and respect for diversity), eight core competencies (communication, teamwork, planning and organizing, accountability, client orientation, creativity, technological awareness and commitment to continuous learning) and six managerial competencies (vision, leadership, empowering others, managing performance, building trust and judgement/decision making)"[1].

---

1 Papa Louis Fall, Yishan Zhang, *Staff Recruitment in United Nations System Organizations: A Comparative Analysis and Benchmarking Framework: Institutional Framework*, Joint Inspection Unit, 2012, p.17.

2.1 Core Competencies[1]

(1) Communication

- ***Speaks*** and writes clearly and effectively;
- ***Listens*** to others, correctly interprets messages from others and responds appropriately;
- ***Asks*** questions to clarify, and exhibits interest in having two-way communication;
- ***Tailors*** language, tone, style and format to match the audience;
- ***Demonstrates*** openness in sharing information and keeping people informed.

Language ability refers to the ability of information transmitters and receivers to communicate through words, tone, expressions, and appropriate body movements in different environments. At the United Nations good communication goes beyond merely disseminating information effectively in a written or verbal manner. It is also the ability to use good judgment in each situation, to tailor the tone and content so that a message is well understood.

Moreover, it is also required that international staff to possess strong social skills and wide social contacts so as to build wide working relationships and a harmonious atmosphere. Interpersonal skills mean the capacity of international staff to control, mobilize and coordinate activities between different persons through exchange of feelings, attitudes, thoughts, opinions, etc.[2] Thus, all concerned parties can cooperate with each other, establishing great collaborate relationships.

At all levels, effectiveness in this area is about leading from the front and communicating with clarity, conviction, and enthusiasm. It's about supporting principles of fairness of opportunity for all and a dedication to a diverse range of citizens. At senior levels, it is about establishing a strong direction and a persuasive future vision; managing

---

1 Source from *UN Competency Development: A Practical Guide*, United Nations Office of Human Resources Management, April, 2010.

2 Luo Shuangping, "Abilities and Qualities a Civil Servant Should Have", *Chinese Talents*, 2005.

and engaging with people with honesty and integrity, and upholding the reputation of the international civil service.

(2) Teamwork

- **Works** collaboratively with colleagues to achieve organizational goals;
- **Solicits** input by genuinely valuing others' ideas and expertise; is willing to learn from others;
- **Places** team agenda before personal agenda;
- **Supports** and acts in accordance with final group decision, even when such decisions may not entirely reflect own position;
- **Shares** credit for team accomplishments and accepts joint responsibility for team shortcomings.

At the United Nations, teamwork is essential. Daily work of international staff will inevitably be exposed to different customs, which requires them to have an open mind and inclusive attitude to improve self-cultivation in order to work smoothly in a friendly and harmonious atmosphere. According to Teng et al. (2014), "those who work at the United Nations should be open-minded and can't gauge others with their own inherent values. Only then they can be fair and efficient when fulfilling duties."[1]

People skilled in this area create and maintain positive, professional, and trusting working relationships with a wide range of people within and outside the international civil service to help get business done. At all levels, it requires working collaboratively, sharing information, and building supportive, responsive relationships with colleagues and stakeholders, whilst having the confidence to challenge assumptions. At senior levels, it's about delivering business objectives through creating an inclusive environment, encouraging collaboration, and building effective partnerships including relationships with Ministers.

1　Teng Jun, Qu Mei, Zhu Xiaoling and Zhang Tingting, "What Capacities Are Important for International Organizations: Case Study on Professional Position Recruitment Standards in UN's Special Institutes", *Comparative Education Review* (Chinese), v.10, n.297, 2014, pp.78-84.

(3) Planning and Organizing

- *Develops* clear goals that are consistent with agreed strategies;
- *Identifies* priority activities and assignments; adjusts priorities as required;
- *Allocates* appropriate amount of time and resources for completing work;
- *Foresees* risks and allows for contingencies when planning;
- *Monitors* and adjusts plans and actions as necessary;
- *Uses time* efficiently.

Each department and office have a work plan that outlines what has to be accomplished and each unit and individual develops goals that support the Organization's larger vision. Staff members have to identify the priorities but also adjust them when needed. Time and resources have to be used efficiently and one has to allow for contingencies when planning. The following principles can be considered as a reference:

- Plans, organizes and/or monitors one's own work or the work of others to ensure achievement of desired results;
- Identifies and/or assigns resources (human or other resources) for one's self or the team to meet objectives in an optimal fashion;
- Establishes goals and objectives that align with *The Corporate Business Plan* and meets the needs/targets set by their work area;
- Reports on results to promote accountability and takes action as appropriate;
- Assigns priorities to multiple competing and important activities quickly and effectively;
- Demonstrates a keen understanding of the relationships between different organizations;
- Takes timely, strategic actions in designing and leads groups and organizations to facilitate their working together effectively;
- Is always planful and prepared, anticipates the impact of industry trends, and develops strategic plans in the best interest of the company.

(4) Accountability

- *Takes* ownership of all responsibilities and honors commitments;
- *Delivers* outputs for which one has responsibility within prescribed time, cost and quality standards;
- *Operates* in compliance with organizational regulations and rules;
- *Supports* subordinates, provides oversight and takes responsibility for delegated assignments;
- *Takes* personal responsibility for his/her own shortcomings and those of the work unit, where applicable.

As a United Nations employee, you have to take responsibility for your role in a larger project and for specific tasks. In honoring your commitment, you have to be mindful of the Organization's regulations and rules, programme beneficiaries and Member States. You can consider the following principles as a reference: allocating decision-making authority and/or responsibility as appropriate to maximize the Organization's and individuals' effectiveness; inspiring collective ownership of decisions and required actions

(5) Client Orientation

- *Considers* all those to whom services are provided to be "clients" and seeks to see things from clients' point of view;
- *Establishes* and maintains productive partnerships with clients by gaining their trust and respect;
- *Identifies* clients' needs and matches them to appropriate solutions;
- *Monitors* ongoing developments inside and outside the clients' environment to keep informed and anticipate problems;
- *Keeps* clients informed of progress or setbacks in projects;
- *Meets* timeline for delivery of products or services to clients.

A customer is defined as any person inside or outside the Organization with whom you have a service relationship. The United Nations puts all those it serve first and makes sure that the clients feel valued. It is important to have productive relationships with people based on trust and respect. You have to listen to what they need and find appropriate solutions for them. The reward comes when you feel you have made a difference to those you serve. You can consider the following principles as a reference:

Competency Indicators		
1	2	3
Provides help and assistance wherever possible; correctly refers customers elsewhere when unable to help; Maintains a calm composure and responds appropriately and professionally in difficult situations; Understands the range of services provided by area of work; Learns from complaints.	Provides accurate and timely help and assistance to students, staff, and visitors in accordance with MMU policy and procedures; correctly refers customers elsewhere when unable to help; Ensures that the experience of each customer is positive and satisfactory; Has accurate and up-to-date knowledge of services available in own and related areas of work and use it to provide accurate and timely information to customers; Learns from complaints and takes action to resolve them.	Creates a positive image of MMU by being responsive and prompt in responding to requests from a wide range of individuals; Helps others beyond their expectations and reacts appropriately to unexpected events or questions; Has broad knowledge of all services within the institution and uses it to refer people where appropriate.

(6) Creativity

- Actively *seeks* to improve programmes or services;
- *Offers* new and different options to solve problems or meet client needs;
- *Promotes* and persuades others to consider new ideas;
- *Takes* calculated risks on new and unusual ideas; think "outside the box";
- *Takes* an interest in new ideas and new ways of doing things;
- *Is* not bound by current thinking or traditional approaches.

Ways to demonstrate this skill:

a. Find new and creative ways to accomplish existing tasks and routines in your area of responsibility;

b. Identify significant (existing or upcoming) work issues in your area of responsibility that have not yet been dealt with, and that you think require an innovative approach;

c. Volunteer to lead the effort to develop a creative solution;

d. When you must solve a problem, acquire a resource, initiate a new procedure, or decide on a course of action, first develop several alternatives and evaluate which one will best achieve your objectives, considering the realities of your situation. Document your options and the reasons for making the choice you made;

e. If others will make the final decision, present the alternatives you developed. Highlight your own recommendation and why you think it is the best choice.

(7) Technology Awareness

- *Sees* technology as an ongoing aspect of all work and keeps abreast of available technology.
- *Understands* applicability and limitations of technology to the work of the office.
- Actively *seeks* to apply technology to appropriate tasks for maximum benefit.
- *Invests* time and energy in incorporating new technology.

It is hard to keep up with the fast pace of technological change, but the Organization offers training as well as support and consistently presents opportunities to keep abreast of technological development. You can consider the following principles as a reference:

- Shows interest in and ability to work with software and technology tools.
- Actively pursues technological solutions to work tasks; seeks training when needed.
- Participates in technology groups and other knowledge management circles in order to stay on top of useful application of technology for solutions.
- Values technology and mobilizes resources to ensure its use to perform tasks and carry out the team's workplans.

(8) Commitment to Continuous Learning

- ***Keeps*** abreast of new developments in own occupation/profession.
- Actively ***seeks*** to develop oneself professionally and personally.
- ***Contributes*** to the learning of colleagues and subordinates.
- ***Shows*** willingness to learn from others.
- ***Seeks*** feedback to learn and improve.

There are many great workshops and programmes available for professional growth and development. The United Nations is committed to a process of continuous learning and encourages each staff to keep abreast of the latest trends in our respective areas of expertise. You never stop learning. You are required to demonstrate this competency in your work:

- You provide expert or professional advice which needs to be kept current;
- You work in a professional field where new approaches are continually emerging;
- You are relatively new to the UN or your current post and need to understand the organization, department or role in more depth;
- You have current development needs which would enhance your performance;
- You have career aspirations which will require you to develop new skills;
- You are motivated to learn more and develop yourself.

2.2 Managerial Competencies[1]

If you have ever baked cakes, you will know that there are certain types and amounts of ingredients that go into the cake so it will turn out correctly. Too much of one ingredient or not enough of another, and your cake could turn out more like a door stop than a tasty treat. The same holds true when we look at managerial functions in international organizations. What ingredients you have and how you add them to the mixture will determine your leadership success.

1　Source from *UN Competency Development: A Practical Guide*, United Nations Office of Human Resources Management, April, 2010; see also the publication titled *United Nations Competencies for the Future* from the website of United Nations Careers.

For a person to be an effective manager, they will have to take the ingredients and change a little to make them work in an international setting. The ingredients, if you will, are:

- **Vision:** Developing and implementing strategy for the Organization to function;
- **Leadership**: Serving as a role model that other people want to follow, and showing the courage to take unpopular stands;
- **Empowering Others**: Delegating responsibility, clarifying expectations, and giving staff autonomy in important areas of their work;
- **Managing Performances**: Monitoring progress against milestones and deadlines, and actively supporting the development and career aspirations of staff;
- **Building Trust**: Following through on agreed upon actions, and providing an environment in which others can talk and act without fear of repercussion;
- **Judgment/Decision-making**: Taking decisions with an eye to the impact on others and on the Organization, and making tough decisions when necessary.

(1) Vision

It is important for staff to have a vision of how the Organization will fulfil its mandates and carry out its work. Understanding the Organization's direction provides clarity and makes people enthusiastic about the future. It also helps staff members to see the link between what they do every day and the overarching goals of the Organization.

Therefore, for a manager to be effective, he or she has to have a clear vision for managing and growing their organization over time. In an international setting, planning takes on a different feel because the manager has to take into account all the different aspects present in an international environment. They have to understand aspects such as:

- Clearly communicate links between the Organization's strategy and the work unit's goals;
- Inspire loyalty and caring through the involvement of all employees;
- Display and reflect the unique strengths, culture, values, beliefs, and direction of the Organization;
- Help employees believe that they are part of something bigger than themselves and their daily work;
- Be regularly communicated and shared, not just through monthly announcements and reminders at the company meeting, it must permeate all communication at every level of the organization every day;
- Serve as the reason for why courses of action are chosen, people are hired, markets are selected, and products are developed;
- Convey enthusiasm about future possibilities;
- Challenge people to outdo themselves, to stretch and reach.

These are the fundamentals necessary for a vision that excites and motivates people to follow the leader. They need to give the best candidates, the employees what they really want, compelling reasons to choose your organization over any other organization—this becomes even more important as the war for the most talented employees escalates. The vision may have changed along the way, but as long as the leader continuously shares the vision, employees can adapt and adjust. Sharing that vision with others in a way that compels them to act is the secret to a successful leadership vision.

(2) Leadership

There are various definitions of leadership, like "the activity of leading a group of people or an organization or the ability to do this", and "the act of inspiring subordinates to perform and engage in achieving a goal."[1] But the way John C. Maxwell defines leadership is most favorable, "*A leader is one who knows the way, goes the way, and shows the way.*" At the United Nations, leaders serve as role models for the staff. They listen before they act; and while they nurture relationships and gain broad support, they also make tough decisions and drive change that is necessary. They make things happen

---

1 Paul Thares, "What Is the Definition of Leadership?", *South Dakota State University Extension*, April 17th, 2019.

with the support of others. He or she can prove to be a difference maker between success and failure.

UNDP's *Core Competency Framework*, clearly sets out what is essential for a manager to fulfill his or her leadership role, by scaling leadership from level 1-6. Starting out with positive behavior at level 1, it describes the expected behaviors, skills and knowledge that enable excellence on the job (see Table 1 below).[1]

Table 1   Detailed Scale on Leadership

Level	Description	Specific Indicators
Level 1	Responsible for own work	Takes responsibility for quality of own work; Uses resources, methods, partners, and information effectively; Acts as an individual contributor.
Level 2	Takes initiative	Identifies opportunities and challenges and recommends options; Checks assumptions against facts; Assumes responsibility for decisions and outcomes; Shares information proactively, also when not required to do so.
Level 3	Inclusive in decision making	Seeks and recognizes individual contributions; Encourages dialogue and acts in accordance with team inputs; Anticipates differing opinions seeing them as opportunities for improvement; Gives credit to others; Determines appropriate resources, methods, partners, information and solutions.
Level 4	Creates excitement for work through demonstrated excellence	Generates individual commitment, excitement and excellence; Creates opportunities for team to learn and take on new responsibilities; Shares experience and knowledge.
Level 5	Empowers individuals and teams to act independently	Ensures people and teams are resourced for success; Plans and acts transparently; Creates awareness of substantive opportunities and risks; Enables individual growth and responsibility; Holds staff accountable; Recognizes and rewards success; Empowers the team to identify and solve problems; Rewards individuals initiatives that goes beyond expectations; Removes barriers or provides resources to further teams' progress; Champions a culture of coaching and empowerment.

---

1   United Nations Development Programme, *"Core Competency Framework"*, Integrated Talent Management, p.7-9.

continued

Level	Description	Specific Indicators
Level 6	Inspires an organization to take on new challenges, reach higher performance	Inspires others to reach new heights; Conveys a vision that staff and clients can see and charts a clear course to achievement; Positions the Organization as a center of expertise and influence; Inspires sustainable high-performing teams across geographic boundaries and in the face.

(3) Empowering Others

Research has regularly demonstrated that when employees feel empowered at work, they are more likely to make decisions that are in the best interest of the Organization and the customers as well.[1] As more and more leaders come to understand that employee empowerment is paramount to achieving organizational goals, they realize that people are their most strategic asset; all other organizational elements—technology, products, processes—result from the actions of workers. To that end, leaders are increasingly concerned about ensuring that their employees feel truly empowered to contribute to the company's mission and drive value to customers.

So, *what does it mean to empower and how can leaders go about it?* Empowering employees to achieve something requires alignment between individual aspirations and organizational goals. It takes a genuine two-way conversation to achieve alignment:

- On the one hand, leaders need to be deliberate about sharing a broader perspective on the Organization's performance and focus, as well as implications for the Organization. Here are four themes leaders must consider as they strive to understand their subordinates' needs and work with them to define the right path toward empowerment: (a) your employees' values might differ from yours; (b) your employees' skill sets may not be on par with competences required for the job; (c) your employees may not be fully aware of your intentions; (d) your employees' decisions may differ from yours, but it does not mean they're bad.

- On the other hand, employees should be able to express thoughts about their

---

1　Allan Lee and Sara Willis, Amy Wei Tian, "When Empowering Employees Works, and When It Doesn't", *Harvard Business Review*, March 2nd, 2018.

individual work and the role they see themselves playing in driving success. It is important to note that the more employees are given room to lead this part of the exercise, sharing not only ideas but also execution strategies, the more engaged and transparent they are likely to be. Once a decision has led to a positive outcome, it is the time to reward the employee for their success with acknowledgement, incentives, and the like.[1]

(4) Managing Performances

Organization and management ability is the external comprehensive performance of a person's knowledge, quality and other basic conditions. It refers to adopting various methods, selecting appropriate organizational forms, designing highly effective working mechanisms and control systems, and carrying out scientific division of labor and appropriate authorization, as well as establishing and improving various rules and regulations according to the characteristics and needs of the work task, in order to effectively achieve the objective. It is the ability to reasonably organize and effectively coordinate various forces, including organization and command ability, coordination and control ability, planning and decision-making ability, ability to analyze problem and handle personnel, as well as leadership and execution ability.

Too many organizations try to create leaders from people who are simply good at their jobs. To be clear, those who emerge to be very good workers often have important qualities. They are the ones who have a strong understanding of the company's products and services. They understand company goals, processes, and procedures. All of these are important.

On the other hand, being good at one's job doesn't prove that someone possesses the other competencies they need. For example, can they inspire, motivate, mentor and direct? Wang illustrates this with major league baseball. While nearly all coaches have backgrounds as major league players, the most winning players aren't necessarily the most successful coaches.

1　Murielle Tiambo, "Leaders Can Cultivate True Employee Empowerment", *Forbes*, February 19th, 2019.

(5) Building Trust

- ***Provides*** an environment in which others can talk and act without fear or repercussion;
- ***Manages*** in a deliberate and predictable way;
- ***Operates*** with transparency, has no hidden agenda;
- ***Places*** confidence in colleagues, staff members and clients;
- ***Gives*** proper credit to others;
- ***Follows*** through on agreed upon actions;
- ***Treats*** sensitive or confidential information appropriately.

The 34th President of the United States, Dwight. D. Eisenhower once said, "*The supreme quality of leadership is unquestionably integrity. Without it, no real success is possible, no matter whether it is on a section gang, a football field, in an army, or in an office.*" Honesty and integrity are two important ingredients which make a good leader. Whether it's giving proper credit for accomplishments, acknowledging mistakes, or putting safety and quality first, great leaders always exhibit integrity. They do what's right, even if that isn't the best thing for the current project or even the bottom line. Leaders succeed when they stick to their values and core beliefs and without ethics, this will not be possible.

At the United Nations, teamwork is essential. People work collectively towards a common goal.[1] When a leader of a team trusts his/her team members, it empowers them and makes them proud to be part of that team. A good manager is open to other people's views and expertise, follows up as promised and gives the team due credit. It is great working in an environment where everyone feels free to speak openly and know that their opinions are valued.

1　Source from the website of United Nations Careers, "Home/What can I do at the UN/What we look for", accessed on October 14th, 2021.

(6) Judgement/Decision-Making

- ***Identifies*** the key issues in a complex situation, and comes to the heart of the problem quickly;
- ***Gathers*** relevant information before making a decision;
- ***Considers*** positive and negative impact on others and on the Organization;
- ***Proposes*** a course of action or makes a recommendation based on all available information;
- ***Checks*** assumptions against facts;
- ***Determines*** that the actions proposed will satisfy the expressed and underlying needs for the decision;
- ***Makes*** tough decisions when necessary.

Judgment—the ability to combine personal qualities with relevant knowledge and experience to form opinions and make decisions—is "the core of exemplary leadership," according to Noel Tichy and Warren Bennis (the authors of *Judgment: How Winning Leaders Make Great Calls*).[1] Apart from having a futuristic vision, a leader should have the ability to take the right decision at the right time. Decisions taken by leaders have a profound impact on masses. Great leaders understand how to use objective reasoning and insight to take into consideration critical aspects of medium- and long-term decisions that positively impact themselves, their employees, their customers and stakeholders, and their organizations. In the face of ambiguity, uncertainty, and conflicting demands, the quality of a leader's overall judgment determines the fate of the entire Organization.[2]

Great leaders also know when to move quickly and proceed with the available information, versus when to take more time and gather additional information. When leaders opt to pursue additional information or avenues, they must also know when to stop. While a large amount of data may be desirable in a perfect world, the data gathering process can take too much time, and the vast amount of data can also be

---

1   Andrew Likierman, "The Elements of Good Judgment: How to Improve Your Decision-Making", *Harvard Business Review*, January-February 2020.

2   Noel M. Tichy and Warren G. Bennis, *Judgment: How Winning Leaders Make Great Calls*(1st edition), Portfolio, 2007.

paralyzing and take attention away from the big picture or key data points.[1]

Section 3
What Are the Status, Basic Rights and Duties of International Civil Servants?

Although national governments determine the missions of multilateral institutions, international civil servants do not resort to any national legislation (from which they have immunity of jurisdiction) but are bound by internal codes and staff regulations.[2] The international civil servants' positive and active approach to fulfilling job responsibilities enables that the international civil service will continue to be an effective instrument to fulfill the aspirations of the public worldwide.[3] Below is further information on their status, basic rights and duties as international civil servants and United Nations staff members.

3.1 Obligations[4]

While the early Inter-Governmental Organizations founded before World War I were often staffed by seconded officials, Sir Eric Drummond, the British diplomat and the first Secretary-General of the League of Nations, set the ground for creation of an "international" secretariat, composed of professional public servants of various backgrounds, who were ready to commit to the goals of the League and carry out their functions under the sole direction of a non-national leader. The principles of

---

1 Larna Kase, "Great Leaders Are Great Decision-Makers: Three Qualities to Take the Paralysis out of Decision Analysis", *Graziadio Business Review*, v.3, n.4, 2010.

2 Source from the website of OECD, "Glossary of Statistical Terms/International Civil Servants", accessed on June 6th, 2021.

3 Julejda Gërxhi, "Ethical Standards in the International Civil Service", *Mediterranean Journal of Social Sciences*, v.5, n.20, 2014, p.892.

4 Source from: Neagr Mansouri, "International Civil Servants and Their Unexplored Role in International Law", *EJIL:Talk!*(Blog of the European Journal of International Law), October 3rd, 2019; Dag Hammarskjöld, "The International Civil Servant in Law and in Fact", Lecture Delivered to Congregation at Oxford University, May 30th, 1961, pp. 329-338

an international civil service he first espoused is found in the report submitted to the Council of the League by its British member, Arther Balfour:

> I emphasize the word "international", because the members of the Secretariat once appointed are no longer the servants of the country of which they are citizens, but become for the time being the servants only of the League of Nations. Their duties are not national but international.[1]

The concepts and approaches introduced by Drummond were later inherited by the United Nations and other IOs. Built essentially on the experience of the League, Article 100 of *The Charter of the United Nations* follows almost verbatim the League regulations on "independence" and "international responsibility"—barring the seeking or receiving of instructions from any government or other authority external to the Secretariat. Similarly in line with Article 100, the Preparatory Commission laid emphasis on the fact that the Secretary-General "alone is responsible to the other principal organs for the Secretariat's work", and that all officials in the Organization must recognize the exclusive authority of the Secretary-General and submit themselves to rules of discipline laid down by him.

Later on, the second UN Secretary-General Dag Hammarskjöld played a major role in concertizing the concepts and principles of international civil service, introducing "independence" and "international responsibility", as the pillars of the work of the Secretariat. Today, the backbone of international bureaucracies are individuals with expertise and diplomatic tact, who altogether constitute a unique body of human resources known as "international civil servants". International civil servants perform their duties in complex legal and political environments; in refugee camps, humanitarian missions, post-conflict administrations, and sometimes in calmer environment of headquarters.

The status, rights and obligations of employees of IOs are rooted in the constituent instruments of their respective organizations and detailed in staff rules and regulations adopted by each organization. International civil servants are also required to comply

---

1　Dag Hammarskjöld, "The International Civil Servant in Law and in Fact", Lecture Delivered to Congregation at Oxford University, May 30th, 1961, p.331.

with standards of conduct applicable to their service.[1]

Under *The Charter*, UN staff members have a special calling to serve the universal ideals of building a more peaceful and prosperous world and are appointed on the basis of meeting the highest aspirations of the peoples of the world.[2] This means that his or her responsibilities as an international civil servant are not national but exclusively international. This is the promise made in the Oath of Office, the declaration that is signed at the time of his or her appointment.

In accordance with *The Staff Regulations and Rules of the United Nations* adopted by the General Assembly (ST/SGB/2018/1), staff members shall make the following written declaration witnessed by the Secretary-General or his or her authorized representative:

"I solemnly declare and promise to exercise in all loyalty, discretion and conscience the functions entrusted to me as an international civil servant of the United Nations, to discharge these functions and regulate my conduct with the interests of the United Nations only in view, and not to seek or accept instructions in regard to the performance of my duties from any Government or other source external to the Organization."

"I also solemnly declare and promise to respect the obligations incumbent upon me as set out in *The Staff Regulations and Rules*."

Important Documents

● *Standards of Conduct for the International Civil Service (2013)*

For more than a half-century the international civil service has been informed and guided by *The Standards of Conduct*. The 2013 edition of *The Standards* was drafted under the guidance of the International Civil Service Commission (ICSC), and approved by the United Nations General Assembly in its resolution 67/257.

---

1 Neagr Mansouri, "International Civil Servants and Their Unexplored Role in International Law", *EJIL:Talk!*(Blog of the European Journal of International Law), October 3rd, 2019.

2 *Putting Ethics to Work: A Guide for UN Staff*, jointly published by the United Nations Ethics Office and the United Nations Office of Human Resources Management, January 2017, p.2.

- ***United Nations Competencies for the Future BookLet***

This booklet has been prepared to inform staff of the United Nations competencies for the future, to describe how these competencies were arrived at, to provide examples of how the competencies look in action and to indicate how they will be applied in the Secretariat.

- ***The Staff Regulations and Rules of the United Nations (ST/SGB/2018/1)***

The Staff Regulations are provided by the General Assembly and describe the fundamental conditions of service and the basic rights, duties and obligations at the United Nations Secretariat. They represent the broad principles of human resources policy for the staffing and administration of the Secretariat.

- ***Putting Ethics to Work—A Guide for UN Staff***

The UN Ethics Office prepared this practical guide to explain the ethical expectations that the United Nations has set for its staff members and to answer frequently asked questions about what is and is not allowable within the context of the UN workplace.

- ***Status, Basic Rights and Duties of United Nations Staff Members— Secretary-General's Bulletin (ST/SGB/2016/9)***

The purpose of this bulletin is to remind staff members of and assist them in understanding their basic rights and duties as international civil servants and United Nations staff members.

3.2   Privileges and Immunities[1]

Recognizing the need for privileges and immunities for the United Nations, the Legal Problems Committee of the San Francisco Conference proposed stipulations to be

---

1   Source from David B. Michaels, "Part II. Organizational Practice—The United Nations System", in *International Privileges and Immunities: A Case for a Universal Statute*, The Hague: Martius Nijhoff, 1971, pp.59-69; August Reinisch, "Introductory Note of Convention on the Privileges and Immunities of the United Nations', United Nations Audiovisual Library of International Law.

added to the Dumbarton Oaks proposals for inclusion in *The Charter*.[1] The committee's draft was adopted by the Conference as Article 105 of *The Charter* with only minor language changes.

Neither the draft, nor the final version of Article 105, stipulated the nature and extent of the imposition on the member states. It was believed at the time that:

> The terms *privileges* and *immunities* indicate in a general way all that could be considered necessary to the realization of the purposes of the Organization, to free the functioning of its organs and to the independent exercise of the functions and duties of its officials: exemption from tax, immunity from jurisdiction, facilities for communication, inviolability of buildings, properties and archives, etc. It would moreover have been impossible to establish a list valid for all the Member States and taking account of the special situation in which some of them might find themselves by reasons of the activities of the Organization or of its organs in their territory. But if there is one certain principle it is that no member state may hinder in any way the working of the Organization or take any measures the effect of which might be to increase its burdens, financial or other.[2]

At the time of the adoption of *The Charter of the United Nations*, there were not many legal instruments that could have served as examples for what was intended to be achieved. *The Covenant of the League of Nations* of June 28th, 1919 merely provided for "diplomatic" privileges and immunities of its employees and the inviolability of its property. One of the difficulties with *The Covenant* was that the exact nature and extent of the status conveyed by the broad affirmation of "diplomatic" privileges and immunities remained without definition.[3] In addition, there was no provision for

---

1 Delegates of fifty nations met in San Francisco, California, USA, between April 25th and June 26th, 1945 at the United Nations Conference on International Organization. Working on the Dumbarton Oaks proposals, the Yalta Agreement, and amendments proposed by various governments, the Conference agreed upon the Charter of the United Nations and the Statute of the new International Court of Justice. Source from the website of the United Nations, "About us/History of the United Nations/The San Francisco Conference", accessed on October 25th, 2021.

2 United Nations, *Conference Documents*, XIII, pp. 704-705.

3 Except for Paragraph 5 of Article 7 which stated: "The Buildings and other property occupied by the League or its officials or by Representatives attending its meetings shall be inviolable."

"supervision" and "implementation" of *The Covenant*'s intentions. Consequently, at San Francisco, the Legal Problems Committee included the stipulation that the General Assembly would have authority to act in further definition and application of the privileges and immunities that might be required by the United Nations.[1]

> The juridical basis of the diplomatic privileges and immunities of League officials is to be found in Paragraph 4 of Article 7 of *The Covenant of the League of Nations*, which reads as follows:
>
> Representatives of the Members of the League and officials of the League when engaged in the business of the League shall enjoy diplomatic privileges and immunities.[2]

The Committee did not intend, however, that the General Assembly's power would need to be exercised to create a general convention, nor that this power would in any way impair the provisions of Paragraphs 1 and 2 of Article 105. In addition, the provisions of this article were not intended to apply to the specialized agencies that might become affiliated with the Organization.[3] More significant, however, was the avoidance of the use of the term "diplomatic" in describing the nature and extent of the privileges and immunities that were to be afforded and reserved. The Committee commented that it "preferred to substitute a more appropriate standard, based, for the purposes of the Organization, on the necessity of realizing its purposes and, in the case of the representatives of its members and the officials of the Organization, on providing for the independent exercise of their functions."[4]

It was against this background that *The Convention on the Privileges and*

---

1   United Nations, *Conference Documents*, XIII, p.704.

2   Source from Martin Hill, *Immunities and Privileges of International Officials: The Experience of the League of Nations*, Washington: Carnegie Endowment for International Peace, 1947, pp.3-5.

3   The United Nations systems is composed of the United Nations' six principal organs, the International Court of Justice and many funds, programmes and specialized agencies, i.e., autonomous international organizations which in accordance with Articles 57 and 63 of *The United Nations Charter* have become affiliated with the United Nations.

4   Report of the Rapporteur of Committee IV/2, as approved by the Committee, Document 933 IV/2/42 (2), June 12, 1945, United Nations, *Documents of the United Nations Conference on International Organizations, San Francisco*, XIII (1945), Commission IV, Judicial Organization, pp.703-704.

Immunities of the United Nations, frequently referred to as the *"General Convention"*, was negotiated and adopted in the immediate aftermath of the establishment of the United Nations. As provided for in Article 105, Paragraph 3, of *The Charter of the United Nations*, it was adopted by the General Assembly at its first session on February 13th, 1946 (*Resolution* 22 A (I)) on the basis of a draft of the United Nations Preparatory Commission. It entered into force on 17 September 1946 and was registered with the Secretary-General on December 14th, 1946. It was one of the first treaties to be published in the United Nations Treaty Series. As of February 2016, it has been ratified by 162 of the 193 UN Member States.

The General Convention further contains privileges and immunities for three categories of persons crucial for the work of the Organization: 1) representatives of Member States; 2) United Nations officials; and 3) experts on missions for the United Nations.

While Member State representatives enjoy modified "diplomatic" privileges and immunities, United Nations officials, i.e., permanently employed staff members, enjoy "functional" immunity which is defined in Article V, Section 18 (a), as immunity *"from legal process in respect of words spoken or written and all acts performed by them in their official capacity."* Article V, Section 20, stresses that *"[p]rivileges and immunities are granted to officials in the interests of the United Nations and not for the personal benefit of the individuals themselves"* and that the Secretary-General has to waive the immunity of United Nations officials where it would *"impede the course of justice and can be waived without prejudice to the interests of the United Nations."*

In addition to jurisdictional immunity, officials named by the Secretary-General are tax exempt with regard to their salary received from the United Nations and enjoy a number of other fiscal, travel and residence privileges. Together with their spouses and dependent relatives, the officials are entitled to repatriation facilities in time of crisis as diplomatic envoys. Additionally, they are entitled to diplomatic privileges in respect of exchange facilities. Finally, they have the right to import their furniture and effects free of duty at the time of their assuming their post in a given country.

Under the provisions of Section 19, the Secretary-General, Under-Secretaries-General and Assistant Secretaries-General enjoy full diplomatic privileges and immunities, i.e., being granted, supplementally, the privileges and immunities, facilities and exemptions accorded to diplomatic envoys, in accordance with the international law.

As opposed to United Nations officials, experts on missions for the United Nations, like members of the International Law Commission, Special Rapporteurs, or members of United Nations peacekeeping operations, serve under a temporary and specific mandate. They also enjoy certain functionally limited privileges and immunities necessary for the completion of their mission and in particular those enumerated in Section 22 which prescribes immunity from personal arrest or detention, seizure of their personal baggage, and inviolability for all papers and documents. They have the privileges of using codes, couriers and sealed pouches for their official communications; and enjoy currency and exchange facilities provided by foreign officials on temporary missions, and the same immunities and facilities of diplomatic envoys with respect to their personal baggage. Unlike officials, experts on missions are immune from legal processes of every kind notwithstanding that they are no longer employed on missions for the United Nations.

While this document establishes minimum privileges and immunities to be enjoyed by the officials and experts on missions for the United Nations, it does not define the categories and identities of the personnel to be afforded prerogatives in accordance with its terms. Additionally, references are repeatedly made to: "officials of comparable ranks forming part of diplomatic missions,"[1] "privileges and immunities, exemptions and facilities accorded to diplomatic envoys, in accordance with international law,"[2] and "as are accorded to diplomatic envoys"[3].

To compensate for these imprecise weaknesses in *The Convention*, the document empowers the Secretary-General to specify the categories of officials who will be covered by *The Convention*, and to waive the immunities and privileges whenever waiver will not prejudice the interests of the United Nations. Any differences arising out of interpretation or application of *The Convention* is to be referred, presumably by the Secretary-General, to the International Court of Justice for an advisory opinion under the provisions of Article VIII, Section 30 of *The Convention* which provides that the opinion

---

1　Section 18 (e).

2　Section 19.

3　Section 18 (f), 2.2 (f), 2.7.

given by the Court shall be accepted as decisive by the parties.[1]

3.3 Main Areas of Wrongdoing[2]

Ethical values embodied by the Organization of the United Nations, should also be a guide for international civil servants to focus on all their activities, to maintain respect for social justice, dignity and human values, respect for the equal rights of large and small nations. However, all recruited persons are and will remain human beings, not angels and, thus, the risk of wrongdoing by staff members of the Secretariats of international organizations cannot be completely excluded.

What are the main areas of criminal activities that can be observed among a minority of international civil servants? In essence, these are fraud and embezzlement, theft, and bribery.

As far as fraud to the detriment of an organization is concerned, some cases are spectacular and trigger much interest such as the one of a senior staff member of the United Nations Interim Administration Mission in Kosovo (UNMIK) who misappropriated a seven-digit amount of US$.[3] More frequent are cases of so-called entitlement frauds; when staff members apply for reimbursement of claims in amounts which are higher than justified in legal terms or even totally unfounded (for example: abuse of education grants by blowing up the tuition fees for staff members' children).

These cases can occur in collusion with third parties and in combination with other criminal acts such as falsification or manipulation of documents or alteration of cheques. Similar cases of fraud have been observed in the context of clearances of missions or relocation of staff members from one duty station to another. What is also worth mentioning in this context is the almost "classical" fraudulent abuse of telephone

---

1　The conventions are in force "with regard to each State which has deposited an instrument of accession with the Secretary-General of the United Nations as from the date of its deposit", i.e., not merely by a state's membership in the UN. Several states, for example the United States of America, have accepted the conventions only with some reservations.

2　Wolfgang Münch, "Wrongdoing of International Civil Servants—Referral of Cases to National Authorities for Criminal Prosecution", in A. von Bogdandy, R. Wolfrum (eds.), *Max Planck Yearbook of United Nations Law*, v.10, n.1, 2006, pp.1-34.

3　For further details see the 9th annual report of the Office of Internal Oversight Services contained in Doc. A/58/364, preface and para. 66.

facilities.[1] According to the statements of the Board of Auditors the summary of cases of fraud or presumptive fraud during the biennium 2002—2003 involves 14 cases amounting to US$ 707.304.[2]

The second cluster of criminal acts are cases of theft. Investigators report that duty stations in the field, in particular in certain peacekeeping operations are prone to that type of delinquency. There is a rather simple explanation for that phenomenon: it is the shortage of important goods which are relevant for the staff members' own elementary needs (for example: building material for fixing an apartment) or which can be easily sold on the black market and, thus, be converted into profits (gasoline, sometimes also food stuff). Nevertheless, cases of theft can also occur at Headquarters. The report of the Board of Auditors for the biennium ended December 31st, 2003, contains some information on stolen laser-jet printer toner cartridges at the United Nations Office at Nairobi.[3]

The third cluster of wrongdoing are cases of bribery, very often in the context of infringements of procurement regulations and rules. The reasons for the increase in that type of delinquency can be found, in essence, in the following: first of all, the oversight function is taken much more seriously by Heads of organizations than in old times. Second, because of largely increased engagement of the United Nations in peacekeeping, the purchase of equipment is breaking all records in United Nations history. According to the report of the Board of Auditors on budgetary and administrative aspects of the financing of United Nations peacekeeping operations the overall amount of peace-keeping budgets for the period from July 1st, 2004 to June 30th, 2005[4] stands at US$ 3.807.160.900.[5]

The relevant document is dated April 22nd, 2005 and neither contains any costs

---

1   In the report on implementation of decisions of the 2005 World Summit outcome the Secretary-General mentions an increase of fraud cases in recent years in the Office of the United Nations High Commissioner for Refugees, Doc A/60/568, para.25(a).

2   Doc. A/59/5 (Vol. I), para.335.

3   Ibid.

4   According to Regulation 2.13 of the Financial Regulations of the United Nations (published in Doc. ST/SGB/2003/7) the Secretary-General shall submit twice a year to the General Assembly for informational purposes a table summarizing the budgetary requirements of each peace-keeping operation for the financial period from July 1st to June 30th, including a breakdown of expenditure by major line item and the aggregate total resource requirement.

5   Doc. A/59/736, Annex II.

regarding the new peacekeeping operation in Sudan (United Nations Mission in Sudan, UNMIS) nor smaller items such as the peacekeeping support account. If those additional cost elements were to be considered, the overall amount would rise beyond the 5 billion thresholds. In a recent report the Secretary-General informed Member States that procurement at Headquarters and in peacekeeping missions has significantly increased from US\$ 1.010 million to US\$ 1.774 million over the last two years as a direct result of the unprecedented surge in peace-keeping.[1]

It is worth noting that the Secretary-General, following the advice of the Office of Internal Oversight Services, launched the idea at the time of the negotiations on *The Convention against Corruption*, that international civil servants should also be included in the texts imposing sanctions on bribery and embezzlement and that international organizations as well as State Parties be allowed to have stolen assets returned.[2]

The Convention initiated by the United Nations General Assembly was opened for signature in Merida/Mexico on December 9th 2003 and entered into force on December 14th, 2005.[3] December 14th has henceforth been designated as "International Anti-Corruption Day". *The Convention* is, indeed, applicable, if an international civil servant becomes the target of an act of bribery.[4] However, in the reverse case, when the international civil servant assumes the role of a briber, *The Convention* only requests the State Party to consider how to handle such a case in its domestic legislation.[5] Thus, the good intention of the Secretary-General has not been fully met.

1　Doc. A/60/846, para. 2.

2　Doc. A/58/364, para. 139.

3　On the 90th day after deposit of the 30th ratification instrument according to Article 68.

4　Article 16 para. 1 states: "Each State Party shall adopt such legislative and other measures as may be necessary to establish as a criminal offence, when committed intentionally, the promise, offering or giving to a foreign public official or an official of a public international organization, directly or indirectly, of an undue advantage, for the official himself or herself or another person or entity, in order that the official act or refrain from acting in the exercise of his or her official duties, in order to obtain or retain business or other undue advantage in relation to the conduct of international business."

5　Article 16 para. 2 states: "Each State Party shall consider adopting such legislative and other measures as may be necessary to establish as a criminal offence, when committed intentionally, the solicitation or acceptance by a foreign public official or an official of a public international organization, directly or indirectly, of an undue advantage, for the official himself or herself or another person or entity, in order that the official act or refrain from acting in the exercise of his or her official duties." The full text of the Convention can be accessed electronically on the website of the United Nations Office on Drugs and Crime (UNODC).

Other cases of criminal activities such as sexual exploitation, abuse or harassment trigger a particularly high degree of attention in the media (all the more, if a senior official or even a top official is involved), but are not that frequent among staff members. Unfortunately, it has to be admitted that they do exist and cause a considerable degree of work to the Investigations Division of the Office of Internal Oversight Services. The Secretary-General has taken special measures of protection from such acts of criminality.[1]

Finally, it is also worth mentioning in this context that the Secretary-General has established an Ethics Office implementing a decision of the General Assembly which was taken at the World Summit 2005.[2] Whereas the terms of reference of the Ethics Office go far beyond the pure prevention of criminal acts committed by staff members, the *ralson-d'etre* of the Office ought to be seen as part of the overall endeavour of securing integrity within the Secretariat of the United Nations and creating an atmosphere in which any thought directed at wrongdoing cannot fall on fruitful soil.[3]

Fact Sheet[1]

The UN Ethics Office was established in 2006 to secure the highest standards of integrity of staff members in accordance with Article 101, Paragraph 3, of *The Charter of the United Nations*, taking into consideration Paragraph 161 of the 2005 World Summit Outcome and pursuant to General Assembly Resolution 60/248.

The UN Ethics Office:

- is independent from management and all other UN offices;
- is impartial in how it treats individuals;
- maintains confidentiality of the information entrusted to it;
- is professional in its dealings with its stakeholders.

The Ethics Office promotes an ethical organizational culture based on UN's core values of integrity, professionalism and respect for diversity, and the values outlined in the Code of Ethics for UN Personnel which include independence,

---

1 See Doc. ST/SGB/2003/13.

2 A/RES/60/lof 16 September 2005, para. 161 (d).

3 For further details about the Office, see Doc. A/60/568 and Doc. ST/SGB/2005/22.

4 Source from the Home page of the UN Ethics Office.

loyalty, impartiality, integrity, accountability, and respect for human rights. The Ethics Office assists the Secretary-General in ensuring that all staff members perform their functions consistent with the highest standards of integrity as required by *The Charter of the United Nations*. The Office carries out its work through five strategic functions: (a) advice, (b) protection against retaliation, (c) financial disclosure, (d) ethics training, and (e) coherence of ethical standards.

Once a case of wrongdoing has been discovered in a Secretariat, the initial questions which arise usually are: what has to be done to safeguard the financial interests of the organization? What steps are required in the interest of damage containment? What disciplinary measures can be applied against the staff member concerned?

Staff Rule 110(3) of the United Nations provides the following list of disciplinary measures (which corresponds by and large also to the legal situation and practice in other international organizations):[1]

a. Written censure by the Secretary-General;

b. Loss of one or more steps in grade;

c. Deferment, for a special period of eligibility for within-grade increment;

d. Suspension without pay;

e. Fine;

f. Demotion;

g. Separation from service, with or without notice or compensation in lieu thereof;

h. Summary dismissal.

The list does not include written or oral reprimands by supervisors which are similar to letters of caution but are regarded not as disciplinary, but as managerial measures.[2]

Next to the issue of application of disciplinary measures, the question arises what has to be done to recover assets of the Organization and to compensate financial losses resulting from staff members' wrongdoing. Closely related to the latter is the question of

---

1　Published in Doc. ST/SGB/2002/1.

2　A compilation of disciplinary measures taken by the Secretary-General and cases of criminal behaviour covering the period January 1st, 2004—June 30th, 2005 is published in Doc. A/60/315.

referral of cases to the national judiciary of the country where the criminal act has been committed.[1]

Staff members with a long record of years of service and retirees of the United Nations Secretariat occasionally report the anecdote that, in old times, the worst case scenario—which could have happened if someone was identified as a criminal actor—was summary dismissal. The anecdote, although falling under the category of tavern gossiping and being somewhere in between poetry and reality, sheds some light on the ethical and managerial conditions in a Secretariat how they should not be, if an organization wants to convince its stakeholders that assessed and voluntary contributions are well invested in the interest of the individual Member State and the entire membership.

Tasks

Activity 1   Questionnaire Survey

This survey aims to provide an analysis of your awareness and adaptability regarding global issues. Why not take a moment to think about it? Please select one response in each row. At the end, use one statement that best describe your current situation.

Construct 1: Self-efficacy regarding global issues

How easy do you think it would be for you to perform the following tasks on your own?

	I couldn't do this	I would struggle to do this on my own	I would do this with a bit of effort	I could do this easily
Explain how carbon-dioxide emissions affect global climate change.				

---

1 Staff members with a long record of years of service and retirees of the United Nations Secretariat occasionally report the anecdote that, in old times, the worst case scenario—which could have happened if someone was identififi ed as a criminal actor—was summary dismissal.

continued

	I couldn't do this	I would struggle to do this on my own	I would do this with a bit of effort	I could do this easily
Establish a connection between prices of textiles and working conditions in the countries of production.				
Explain how economic crises in single countries affect the global economy.				
Discuss the different reasons why people become refugees.				

Construct 2: Awareness of intercultural communication

Imagine you are talking in your native language to people whose native language is different from yours. To what extent do you agree with the following statements?

	Strongly disagree	Disagree	Agree	Strongly agree
I carefully observe their reactions.				
I frequently check that we are understanding each other correctly.				
I listen carefully to what they say.				
I choose my words carefully and give concrete examples to explain my ideas.				
If there is a problem with communication, I find ways around it (e.g. by using gestures, re-explaining, writing etc.).				

Construct 3: Global mindedness and respect for others

To what extent do you agree with the following statements?

	Strongly disagree	Disagree	Agree	Strongly agree
I think of myself as a citizen of the world.				
When I see the poor conditions that some people in the world live under, I feel a responsibility to do something about it.				
When I'm upset at someone, I try to take the perspective of that person for a while.				
It is right to boycott companies that are known to provide poor workplace conditions for their employees.				
I give space to people from other cultures to express themselves.				

Construct 4: Global competency activities at school

Do you learn the following at school?

	YES	NO
I learn about the inter-connectedness of countries' economies.		
I learn how to solve conflicts with other people in our classrooms.		
We read newspapers, look for news on the internet or watch the news together during classes.		
I am often invited by my teachers to give my personal opinion about international news.		
I participate in events celebrating cultural diversity throughout the school year.		
I participate in classroom discussions about world events as part of the regular instruction.		
I analyse global issues together with my classmates in small groups during class.		
I learn that people from different cultures can have different perspectives on some issues.		
I learn how to communicate with people from different backgrounds.		

Activity 2 Cultural Iceberg

UN peacekeepers come from all walks of life, with diverse cultural backgrounds and from an ever-growing number of Member States.[1] Imagine you are the members of UN military peacekeepers working together. Brainstorm and discuss with your partners the following questions. After that, fill in the cultural iceburg with the attributes of diversity.

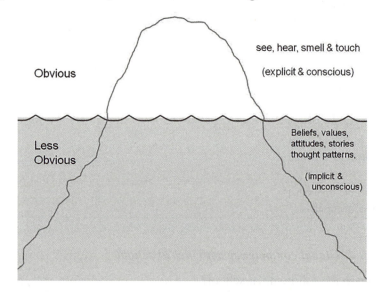

a. Peacekeepers are civilian, military, and police personnel serving under the United Nations. They share a common purpose to protect the most vulnerable and provide support to countries in transition from conflict to peace. Consider the possible differences between individuals, either or not, with diverse nationalities.

b. What differences are obvious? Put them in the above part of the iceberg.

c. What differences are less obvious? Put them in the hidden part of the iceberg.

d. What problems could be brought about if the differences cannot be managed?

e. Conscious diversity management enables organizations to overcome these obstacles. Then how to manage the differences?

f. In all fields of peacekeeping, women peacekeepers have proven that they can perform the same roles, to the same standards and under the same difficult conditions, as their male counterparts. However, women's participation remains low and uneven across the formal implementation and monitoring mechanisms

---

1 Source from the website of the United Nations, "United Nations Peacekeeping/What is peacekeeping/OUR PEACEKEEPERS".

during peace agreements. What is the cause of the problem?

Activity 3   Group Discussions

Please give your specific ways to think about the following questions and bring up information that supports your judgement when the group discussion starts.

    a. *The Charter of the United Nations* is a forceful document with resplendent hopes and aspirations. Under *The Charter*, UN staff are appointed on the basis of exhibiting and securing the highest standards of ethical conduct. At a practical level, *what are the ethical values and principles the international civil servants being held accountable to?*

    b. Warren Buffet once said, "It takes 20 years to build a reputation and five minutes to ruin it. If you think about that, you will do things differently." *What is the logic behind the quote and how does it apply to international civil servants' professional conduct?*

    c. *What is the place of international civil servants in international law? How much do they contribute to making the legal norms and institutions that govern states? To what extent does law sustain and constrain their authority?* These important and difficult questions are raised, directly and indirectly, by several recent works that examine the life and legacy of Dag Hammarskjöld, the second and arguably most influential Secretary-General of the United Nations. After conducting a research study, try to put your thoughts on a piece of paper and share them with the group.

Activity 4   Oral Presentation

In *The International Civil Servant in Law and in Fact*, Dag Hammarskjöld points out that, on a day-to-day basis, individual civil servants make choices based on a continuous moral self-examination, rather than on a fixed idea of what the UN stands for. This "value-scan" is necessary precisely because the international civil service is a collection of people from different backgrounds, who serve in an ever-changing environment. Hammarskjöld also underlined that the source of morality can vary from written to unwritten because,

        the everyday work of international civil servants requires them not only to deal in the currency of legal arguments and instruments but also to draw upon moral purposes and technical means that are present in their institutional settings as well as their own personal values and professional training.[1]

The UN Charter Article 101 (3) establishes that the UN staff has to meet "the highest standards of efficiency, competence and integrity", wherein integrity encompasses the ethical norm of behaviour for the entire UN bureaucracy. This notion has been elaborated in documents like *The Standards of Conduct for the International Civil Service* enacted by the International Civil Service Commission, as well as internal UN regulations. *The UN Staff Regulation 1.2* contains the following "Core values" for UN staff:

    a. Staff members shall uphold and respect the principles set out in the Charter, including faith in fundamental human rights, in the dignity and worth of the human person and in the equal rights of men and women. Consequently, staff members shall exhibit respect for all cultures; they shall not discriminate against any individual or group of individuals or otherwise abuse the power and authority vested in them;

    b. Staff members shall uphold the highest standards of efficiency, competence and integrity. The concept of integrity includes, but is not limited to, **probity, impartiality, fairness, honesty and truthfulness** in all matters affecting their work and status;[2]

In this rule, as a representative of the internal administrative law of the UN, the **internationalism** and **integrity** of the UN civil servants are set at the same level as standards of behaviour. But while internationalism is a cosmopolitan ideal, a model for the organizational culture, integrity is a quality that refers to the moral fiber of the individual as expressed in his or her work. Most significantly, because these values affect concrete actions—speaking the truth, according to fair treatment—the integrity of individual civil servants thus affects the unity and wholeness of the institution that he or she is loyal to more strongly than abstract cosmopolitan ideals.

---

1 Guy Fiti Sinclair, "The International Civil Servant in Theory and Practice: Law, Morality, and Expertise", *European Journal of International Law*, v.26, n.3, 2015, pp.747-766.

2   emphasis added

Of course, the principles and character are not completely divorced and in conflict. Quite the contrary, in order to pursue world peace and universal human rights, international civil servants require an open mind and courage. To quote Dag Hammarskjöld,

At their best the representatives of this legacy show the quiet self-assurance of people firmly rooted in their own world, but they are, at the same time and for that very reason, able to accept and develop a true world citizenship. At the best they are not afraid to like the man in their enemy and they know that such liking gives an insight which is a source of strength. They have learned patience in dealings with mightier powers. They know that their only hope is that justice will prevail and for that reason they like to speak for justice. However, they also know the dangers and temptations of somebody speaking for justice without humility. They have learned that they can stand strong only if faithful to their own ideals, and they have shown the courage to follow the guidance of those ideals to ends which sometimes, temporarily, have been very bitter. And finally, the spirit is one of peace…[1]

◆ **Assignment**

After this reading, please choose 3 statements to summarize the main contents, 2 statements to introduce your favorite merits about international civil servants, and 3 sentences to assume one real ethical test where you have to decide what is the right thing to do. You're highly encouraged to use the materials described above and to add many more to your oral presentations.

Activity 5 | **Extended Reading** [2]

When I attempt to distill my experience to its most precious essence, I come up with a single word: independence. That word encapsulates what gave me the strength

---

1   Dag Hammarskjöld, "On the Uppsala Tradition—From Address after Receiving Honorary Degree at Upsala College", East Orange, N.J., June 4th, 1956, in Andrew W. Cordier, Wilder Foote(eds), *Public Papers of the Secretaries-General of the United Nations, Vol. III: Dag Hammarskjöld, 1956-1957*, New York and London: Columbia University Press, 1973, p.164.

2   Excerpt from: Javier Pérez de Cuéllar, "Independence and Impartiality as the Heart and Soul of the Secretary-General", *The Magazine of the United Nations*, v.52, n.2, 2015, pp.11-12.

and the ability to make a positive difference regarding a number of seemingly intractable issues that had bedeviled the international community, defying solution for years and years. Independence has consistently been my one-word answer to the question, how did you do it?

The word *independence* does not appear in Article 100. Under its second paragraph *"Each Member of the United Nations undertakes to respect the exclusively international character of the responsibilities of the Secretary-General and the staff and not to seek to influence them in the discharge of their responsibilities."* The word "independence" might have been a bridge too far in the 1940s, at a time when sovereignty was still significantly more robust in substance and in the minds of statesmen than it is today. But it was unnecessary: there can be no doubt from the context that that is what *The Charter* enshrines. That is certainly as I saw it. At the time, and all the more so in retrospect, it was invaluable to me. I shall briefly explain why this was so.

Like Hammarskjöld, I did not seek to be Secretary-General. My Government wished me to be a candidate and informed Security Council members that I was available, but I refused to campaign. I did not ask for anyone's support. I did not go to New York. I made no commitments to Member States or anyone else to become Secretary-General; there was no *quid pro quo*, no *do ut des*. I thus came to office having promised no one anything. Nor did I have any desire to remain as Secretary-General beyond the five-year term to which I was appointed.

On 13 May 1986, a few months before the expiry of what turned out to be my first term as Secretary-General, I delivered the Cyril Foster Lecture in the Sheldonian Theatre at Oxford University. Twenty-five years ago Dag Hammarskjöld delivered a similar lecture on the subject of "The International Civil Servant in Law and in Fact". My subject was "The Role of the Secretary-General."

I reviewed the good office's role of the Secretary-General and summarized it in one word—*impartiality*. "Impartiality," I said, "is the heart and soul of the office of the Secretary-General." I took it one step further, suggesting that in order to ensure the impartiality of the Secretary-General, the healthy convention that no person should ever be a candidate for the position should be re-established. It should come unsought to a qualified person. However impeccable a person's integrity may be, he cannot in fact retain the necessary independence if he proclaims his candidacy and conducts a kind of election campaign.

Independence does not mean that the Secretary-General can or should act as a totally free spirit: the Secretary-General is bound by *The Charter of the United Nations*, and for the United Nations to be an effective agent for peace he must work in partnership with the Security Council. But that partnership is strengthened if he takes a perspective broader than that of individual Member States or even the selection of them embodied in the Council. There are instances in which he may feel compelled to distance himself slightly so as to keep channels open to those who feel misunderstood or alienated by it. The maintenance of this discrete position will make him a more effective and credible partner. If he is clear about this with Security Council members, they will see the usefulness of his doing so and respect him for it.

Chapter 5

Landing a Job in International Organizations

The best way to find yourself is to lose yourself in the service of others.

—Mahatma Gandhi, the primary leader of India's Independence Movement[1]

---

1 Mahatma Gandhi, byname of Mohandas Karamchand Gandhi, was Indian lawyer, politician, social activist, and writer who became the leader of the nationalist movement against the British rule of India. Gandhi is internationally esteemed for his doctrine of nonviolent protest (satyagraha) to achieve political and social progress. And his life and teachings inspired activists including Martin Luther King Jr. and Nelson Mandela.

Overview

Learning Objectives

a. To rediscover and comprehend the fundamental concepts and elementary questions of the international civil service;

b. To scan and interpret descriptive position requirements in international organizations, and mark out career development paths for those interested in quality international jobs;

c. To present recent scholarship on job-hunting strategies, which encapsulate a range of skills, attributes, and other measures such as networks, professional identity and active citizenship.

Main Contents

Large numbers of students and college graduates—particularly with a background in international relations—express an interest in "development" work or a career working for international organizations.[1] For some, this is fueled by humanitarian, social conscience or religious reasons. For others, it is part of a long-term career plan to work for a relief or development agency. Whatever the motive, it is important to fully research the opportunities available, develop a well-informed and realistic view of the sector and plan well in advance. This is where this chapter comes in.

In a guide such as this chapter, it is impossible to describe every path into this field. However, what it can provide is a step-by-step guidance on what you should do to get a foot in the door of international development, especially if you are uncertain. And this is something that probably empowers you to start out your job-hunting in the field of global development, while at the same time to develop an inter-information searching capability—which you can benefit from for years to come.

---

1   Source from "Getting into... an International Organization", Careers and Employment Service in University of Exeter.

Warm-up

Internships at the United Nations are a great opportunity for students and recent graduates to acquire direct exposure to UN's work. Opportunities are available in a variety of areas and every attempt is made to match the interests of the intern with the needs of the Organization. Interns are selected on a competitive basis. As an applicant, internship seekers should prepare for common interview questions like "*What are your strengths*", or "*What are your weaknesses*", but they can also expect less conventional queries.

Here are some questions that intern candidates were most frequently asked during UN internship interviews.

a. Why would you like to work for the UN?

b. Why do you want to intern in this specific department?

c. What qualities are you willing and interested in getting from the internship?

d. Why do you think you are a good fit for this internship?

e. Can you describe some of your school involvements or your previous work experiences that relate to this internship?

f. Are you sure that this experience/internship will be useful for you taking into account your previous work experience and educational background?

g. How do you handle a responsibility that you don't like?

h. Tell us a challenging situation where your team had an excellent performance and what was your role in it?

i. What is the last time you had to explain something technical to someone, and how did you do this?

j. What do you know about this specific industry and what are some trends that have occurred in the past few years?

Luckily for applicants, employers aren't looking for the most brilliant answers. They are trying to get a sense of would-be interns' thought processes and how they perform under pressure. Put yourself into the applicant's shoes and take some time to reflect on the possible answers to each question. Write some ideas and discuss them with your partners.

Section 1

How to Start a Career with International Organizations?

Can you communicate in multiple languages? Do you have a knack for seeing things from a broader, more global perspective? Did you major in international studies or international business? Are you looking to broaden your corporate experience with a stint working internationally?

If you answered yes to any and all of these questions, then you are a good fit with the international organizations and you might also be interested in reading the tips for landing a job in overseas international organizations, as follows.

1.1 Types of Jobs

Given the diversity of jobs and roles that exist within international organizations, career opportunities are wide-ranging and cover a tremendous number of issue areas, themes and professions. Jobs can be technical, field-based, policy-based, strategic, or administrative—just as they are within the national civil service and within many other commercial organizations.[1] Below are some common career fields and examples of jobs that are associated with international organizations:

(1) International Development/Aid Workers

International aid/development workers are employed by charities, Non-Governmental Organizations, international aid agencies and volunteer groups. There are thousands of international aid/development workers currently employed across the globe by organizations such as the Red Cross, the Salvation Army and the United Nations.

The primary objective for international aid/development workers is to provide aid and assistance to people in locations around the globe, covering all kinds of issues from healthcare, sanitation, housing, education and construction to agriculture, industrial development, human rights, sustainability and relief from natural disasters.

This is a particularly broad area of work and professionals in this area can

---

1 Source from the website of Oxford University Careers Service, "Home/Explore Careers/Sectors and Occupations/ International Organizations", accessed on July 10th, 2021.

perform a range of different functions, including hands-on relief work, fundraising, project planning and project management. Furthermore, you could be responsible for administrative support, budget control, liaising with local agencies and authorities, training volunteers and preparing recommendations, evaluation reports and other related paperwork.

Some international development workers work on the strategy and policy side of things, conducting research, negotiating with other NGOs and lobbying the government to garner support and sponsorship.[1]

(2) International Organizations Administrator

Understandably, an administrator's responsibilities will vary greatly from organization to organization. However, most administrators perform a range of routine office duties, such as filing, invoicing, data input, diary management, minute taking, photocopying, answering telephone enquiries and responding to letters and emails in a timely manner.

An administrator's job will usually involve a great deal of computer-based work. Consequently, most administrators should be confident of using software packages such as Microsoft Word, Excel, Outlook, Access and PowerPoint, as well as internal databases and CRM systems. As you gain more experience, you'll gradually be given more important responsibilities, such as budget management, training junior admin staff and organizing events.

Any degree subjects are considered, but Politics, International Relations, Law and Language degrees are particularly useful.

(3) Public Diplomatic Officers

The role that public diplomacy officers can carry greatly depends on their particular area of focus, but they generally seek to engage, inform, and influence governments, businesses, academics, thinks tanks, local non-governmental groups, and the full range of civil society through a variety of policies and programs to promote mutual understanding and support for international organizations. They manage cultural and information programs and coordinate exchange programs to strengthen relationships that

---

1   Source from the website of All About Careers, "Careers/Job Profiles/International Aid/Development Worker/Job Description, Salary&Benefits", accessed on July 11th, 2021.

improve foreign insight into how history, values and traditions shape the organizations.[1]

(4) Economics and Finance

If you've focused on economics or finance, the world of international organizations is a particularly good fit—development banks, international research panels and trade organizations all offer highly respected positions for young professionals with qualifications in such disciplines.[2]

In a global organization you might find a role performing research, preparing reports, promoting particular policies, or navigating national and international law as applied to finance. The financial economists are also responsible for collecting and processing the economical and statistical data using various sampling and econometric techniques.

Read This[3]

I joined the United Nations in Guatemala, where I worked for four years before acquiring enough experience to join my first international mission in Timor-Leste. Subsequently, I acquired extensive experience in cashier and treasury functions, as well as in the payroll and payment areas in numerous field missions. I enjoy leveraging my skills to simplify various key tasks by creating automatized solutions. As I have been mobile around the Organization, I have been able to implement information technology-based solutions wherever they were needed in order to standardize specific functions across missions.

Timor-Leste holds a special place in my heart because I served there through various mandates and watched the fledgling country grow to the point when I was required to participate in closing the mission. This experience gave me full exposure to all the key areas in finance, which I subsequently complemented with *The International Public Sector Accounting Standards* (IPSAS) as well as training on the enterprise resource planning system "Umoja" to ensure that my skills remain

---

1 Source from the website of the U.S. Department of State, "Home/Work/Worldwide/Foreign Service/Foreign Service Officer/Career Tracks/Public Diplomacy Career Track", accessed on October 9th, 2021.

2 "Jobs in International Organizations: Top 30 Around the Globe", *INOMICS,* July 8th, 2014.

3 Personal narrative of Byron Estuardo Arriaga Figueroa, see also the website of the United Nations Careers, "Home/What can I do at the UN/Career Paths".

current. I am now an Umoja Local Process Expert (LPE) in Finance. As an LPE, I provide solutions to the most common problems encountered by the Umoja users in my area of expertise, develop solutions for less common problems, escalate more complex problems to the Umoja team and provide guidance on procedures and training to less experienced users.

(5) Legal Affairs and Related Work

Besides solicitors, barristers and judges, there is a massive array of other lawyer and non-lawyer career paths you can take within this sector, from legal journalists, legal secretaries, typists, human resources personnel, paralegals and legal executives to solicitor advocates, coroners, lecturers and court clerks. There is so much variety and there is certainly something for everyone.[1]

Specific job duties of legal affairs staff vary by position level, but they typically include providing management with effective legal advice on business issues and company strategies, selecting and overseeing the work of outside counsel, drafting and editing complex commercial agreements, ensuring the company operates in compliance with applicable laws and regulations, and helping prepare briefs, complaints, motions and other court documents.

Other tasks may include advising the human resources department on employment law and labor and benefit issues, drafting and negotiating contracts and agreements, such as joint venture agreements, government contracts and sales contracts, and providing litigation support.

(6) Information Technology

In the 21st century, everything converges on technology. It has become a part of our lives, and everything we consume is the result of growing technology. The information technology field is among the fastest-growing sectors worldwide and offers millions of jobs with lucrative opportunities.[2] Duties of an information technology

---

1   Source from the website of All About Careers, "Careers/Career Industry/Law careers·A career in law explained", accessed on June 4th, 2021.

2   Source from the website of All About Careers, "Careers/Career Path/Is Information Technology a Good Career Path", accessed on June 4th, 2021.

specialist can include network management, software development and database administration. IT specialists may also provide technical support to a business or an organization's employees and train non-technical workers on the business's information systems. Advanced information technology specialists may design systems and assess the effectiveness of technology resources already in use or new systems that are being implemented. Additionally, they will determine the practicality of changes and modification of systems.

(7) Translator and Interpreter

Interpreters can work in a range of different situations. For instance, they are vital to public sector departments and also play an important role in the media, in international business meetings and in healthcare and legal settings.

The job of an interpreter should not be confused with that of a translator. Sure, both of these careers are designated for language specialists, but interpreters deal with the spoken word and translators work with written texts. However, it's also worth bearing in mind that some people may offer both interpretation and translation services to their clients.

Interpreters can offer a range of verbal translation services, including simultaneous interpretation (i.e., "real-time" translation while the speaker is still speaking) and consecutive interpretation (i.e., the stop-start approach to interpretative communication, where short bursts of conversation are translated while the speaker pauses). Some translators might even use sign language as a way of communicating with their clients.

As you can imagine, it's very important that an interpreter is completely fluent in the languages that they are translating. Consequently, these guys might be required to learn complex terminology, such as business jargon, legislative terms and other industry-specific lingo. Even the slightest misunderstanding could change a whole piece of information and this could have negative implications on the success of the dialogue. Therefore, interpreters need to be sharp, talented and forever up-to-date on the evolution of dialects and specialist terms.[1]

(8) Volunteer Work

Voluntary work is often a crucial starting point whether you are looking for a job

---

1　Source from the website of All About Careers, "Careers/Job Profiles/Interpreter·Job Description, Salary&Benefits", accessed on June 4th, 2021.

or an internship. There are a number of international organizations, working in areas ranging from agriculture and economy to education and security and many others, that recruit volunteers for many parts of the world, which could benefit from your experience, skills and potential. It is still expected that potential volunteers are able to demonstrate a range of relevant skills and qualities before being considered a worthy candidate. Despite having relatively little responsibility, voluntary work often provides a foot in the door and an important stepping stone to building a long term career in the sector.

Read Sheet[1]

Administered by the United Nations Development Programme (UNDP), the United Nations Volunteer (UNV) programme is the focal point for volunteerism in the UN system. It pursues distinctive contributions to effective development by advocating the role and benefits of volunteerism, integrating civic engagement into development programmes and helping to mobilize volunteers worldwide.

UNV volunteers support sustainable human development globally in key areas such as poverty reduction, democratic governance, energy, the environment, crisis prevention and recovery and health. UNV places qualified candidates (who must be aged 25 or above) in posts such as administration, agriculture, communication, community development, commerce, education, engineering, environment, health, human settlements, information communication technology, logistics, media and social sciences, etc.

Since 1971, UNV has mobilized some 40,000 mid-career professionals to serve the causes of peace and development. In 2006, 7600 UNV volunteers, representing 163 nationalities, served in 144 countries worldwide. Reaffirming the programme's commitment to promoting South-South cooperation, the vast majority (76 percent) of UNV volunteers are nationals of developing countries.

1.2   Key Requirements

A passion for working towards the achievement of co-operation, peace, justice and

---

1   Source from the website of UN Volunteers, "Home/About UNV/Who we are".

human rights is key to thriving in this sector. In addition, and just as importantly, you need to offer practical skills, specific knowledge and worldly experience, evidencing that you are flexible in sometimes less than ideal situations, able to work effectively in a multi-national and multi-cultural setting, can cope with unpredictability, re-adjust after setbacks, make tough decisions and display leadership in less-than-ideal circumstances, and sometimes survive hardships.

There are generally four key requirements to aspire to a vacancy in an international organization: experience, specialist qualification, languages, skills/attitudes.

(1) Experience

It is the most restrictive area of selection. You must have the required years of experience at your disposal and know that the experience gained after graduation is considered as a professional experience by international organizations. In some cases, a brief work experience can be equated with a post-graduate degree.

Most entry-level positions require a number of years' experience and open for graduates at the start of their careers are relatively rare. If you are a first-time job seeker in the international affairs sector or a career switcher, then international relations internships or volunteering work with an organization could be a good place to start. Internships offer several advantages: you can get insights into and an understanding of a particular career field, form a network for your future job search, raise your visibility and get access to unadvertised job opportunities. Organizations like the UN, the European Union, international NGOs, and multinational corporations all have annual internship programs for graduate students or recent graduates.[1]

Read This[2]

Some people train for it. Others stumble into it. Being a good humanitarian means understanding humanitarian principles and practice. You should know international humanitarian law (that doesn't mean a law degree, just a thorough understanding) and then understand the tools humanitarians use. Start with *The*

---

1 Laura Bridgestock, "How to Start a Career in International Relations", April 6th, 2021, sponsored by IE University.

2 Materials are provided by Bryan Schaaf (MPH from the George Washington University) in answering the question of "How to Get a Job in Humanitarian Field or International Organizations", in *Quora*, April 1st, 2017

Sphere Handbook.[1] You may come into it with a skill—health, shelter, protection, water/sanitation/hygiene, site planning, education, logistics, nutrition/food security, or something else. Or maybe you come into as a generalist which is OK too—in that case you may be writing proposals for a while, backstopping, and pitching in where needed.

In either case, you need experience in the field:

a. to see if this work is really for you,

b. to learn, and

c. to establish your credibility.

Most people start with Non-Governmental Organizations. It is comparatively rare to start with UN and other multilateral organizations right out of the gate. So, see where the NGOs have the hardest time finding good people and apply. Maybe it's a six-month contract in Chad—but that will turn into another contract, and then another one, and before you know it, you have good experience.

(2) Specialist Qualification

Many individuals working for international organizations will possess a postgraduate qualification, either in a relevant discipline such as international development or in a specialist area such as teaching. Consider sharpening your specialist qualifications in a field appropriate to the direction in which you would like your career to develop. Whether it's an MBA with a specialty in international business or a graduate degree in international affairs, be sure to do your homework on the best programs to fit your needs and goals. You might think, for example, of (development) economics in preparation for the International Monetary Fund or the World Bank; conflict resolution for UNDP; forced migration studies for UNHCR, or physics research for the European

---

1　*The Sphere Handbook* is Sphere's flagship publication. It comprises the Humanitarian Charter, the Protection Principles, the Core Humanitarian Standard, and minimum humanitarian standards in four vital areas of response: (1) Water supply, sanitation and hygiene promotion (WASH); (2) Food security and nutrition; (3) Shelter and settlement; (4) Health. The Handbook is one of the most widely known and internationally recognized tools for the delivery of the quality humanitarian response. National and international NGOs, United Nations agencies, and governmental authorities across the globe make use of its guidance when planning, delivering and evaluating humanitarian operations. See more from the website of the Sphere.

Organization for Nuclear Research (CERN).

(3) Languages

There are six languages used officially at the United Nations. These are Arabic, Chinese, French, English, Russian and Spanish. There are two languages preferably requested: English and French. Knowledge of a particular language may be required. It is good to pay attention to the required level:

    a. "Excellent" (excellent, fluent) implies perfect mastery;

    b. "Working knowledge": means the ability to work independently, prepare any type of document (from a letter to a report), actively participate in professional meetings and discussions in the language indicated;

    c. "Limited knowledge" will put the official in a position to call, read work texts, write short reports, attend meetings or discussions, but choose another official language of the Organization to intervene.

> ## Do You Know?[1]
>
> The Department of Global Communications has established language days for each of the UN's six official languages. The purpose of the UN's language days is to celebrate multilingualism and cultural diversity as well as to promote equal use of all six official languages throughout the Organization. Under the initiative, UN duty stations around the world celebrate six separate days, each dedicated to one of the Organization's six official languages. The days are as follows:
>
> - Arabic (18 December)
> - Russian (6 June)
> - Chinese (20 April)
> - English (23 April)
> - Spanish (23 April)
> - French (20 March)

---

1 Source from the website of the United Nations, "Home/About the UN/Official Languages".

(4) Skills and Attributes

Candidates need a strong portfolio of skills and qualities in order to compete for jobs in this area of work. The specific skills required will depend on the role and the type of organization but among the most requested qualities we find: flexibility, initiative, balance of judgment, ability to work under pressure, design and organize activities, establish and maintain fruitful working relationships, ability to draw up effective documents, manage meetings, public speaking, willingness to travel frequently in developing countries.

In addition to technical skills, recruiters in the international development arena look at candidates' international experience, cross-cultural awareness and language skills. A proven ability to work well in cross-cultural teams, evidence of an international mind-set, field experience in developing countries, and fluency in a foreign language will definitely help you in your search for international relations careers.[1]

1.3　Job-Hunting Tactics[2]

The high level of interest in employment opportunities in this sector leads to competitive entry standards, particularly as there are normally quotas for nationals of different member countries. Knowing how to navigate the opportunities that do exist and planning how best to access them, through building and marketing your skills effectively, is essential.

1.3.1　Develop a Job-Search Strategy

The first thing you need to do is to develop an overall job-search strategy that is geared towards your values, goals, and education. It's imperative that you develop a plan for finding employment because if you don't, your job-search experience will likely lead to frustrations and missed opportunities.

What's involved in developing a job-search strategy? Research the area and group of organizations within which you want to work, consider what kind of role you want to undertake and work backwards to plan milestones and your immediate next steps. You

---

1　Laura Bridgestock, "How to Start a Career in International Relations", April 6th, 2021, sponsored by IE University.

2　Source from Randall S. Hansen, "10 Essential Tips for Landing a Job Overseas", Live Career.

may well also re-define and re-focus along the way.

Researching a job, industry, or organization can be conducted online and in person. But *what are the best job-search tools at your disposal for tracking down job leads*? Here are some tools to help you in your job search:

- Networking (with members of professional organizations, alumni, former supervisors and co-workers, family, friends, etc.)
- Cold-Calling (direct mail campaign to selected organizations; communicate via phone with organization representatives)
- Corporate Websites (using career centers of selected organizations to search for openings; following the organization on social media)
- Job Sites (including general job sites and international job sites)
- Foreign Newspapers and Trade Journals
- Recruiters (both by discipline and by geographic location)
- Government Sources (including governmental agencies, embassies, trade offices)
- International Job Fairs and Events

It is also important to take the opportunity to talk to others (contacts, alumni, colleagues, tutors, supervisors)—who are already working in a field within which you might want to specialize, or who may know people who are in that field. Take advantage of all networking sources, especially college alumni and professional organizations. People in your network can not only help you by alerting you to job leads, but can also help you with developing additional contacts, understanding the economics and culture of the country where they reside, and other key background information that may be helpful in your job-search.

1.3.2 Research Potential Jobs

In this step, consider building a spreadsheet that contains all the information you need to know, including job titles, skills and experience required, organization name and location, and citizenship or work eligibility requirements. If you have no real sense of what jobs you are best suited to, beginning to explore who you are as a job seeker can be the first step. This step is important because it is a journey of self-exploration.

a. First, go back and examine *what values are important to you in your ideal career? Why are you interested in making a career in international organizations?*

b. Search careers database and learn more about *what style of work environment you are looking for. What can you see yourself enjoy doing in that work environment? What kind of experience would you like to gain?*

c. Third, assess your accomplishments from previous work, internship, or volunteer experiences; develop a list of skills you've mastered; and determine *what are your unique skills, talents, values, and interests? What are your personal strengths and weakness?*

d. Fourth, analyze the results of the above steps and see if you can develop a profile of the types of jobs that interest you and that you are qualified for. Be specific.[1]

Studies show that the three key items global employers desire from job-seekers are: technical knowledge in your field, cross-cultural adaptability and language fluency skills, and prior work experience. If you feel you are weak or lacking in a certain area, now is the time to get the education/training you need.

1.3.3 Prepare Job-Search Correspondence

As with any kind of job search, your job-search correspondence is critically important; perhaps even more so because of the regional differences in resumes and curriculum vitae (CV).

First, your cover letter. Remember the key rules of any cover letter:

a. Address the letter to a named individual (the hiring manager ideally);

b. Write an enticing and attention-grabbing first paragraph explaining why you are writing;

c. Relate how your mix of skills, accomplishments, and education matches the employer's needs;

d. End the letter proactively by asking for an interview.

Second, your resume. More than likely, you will need to convert your resume to a CV. Most countries outside the U.S. favor the CV over the resume. Do your homework on the region of the world where you want to work and tailor your CV to fit.

---

1 Source from the website of CSUSB, "Home/Students/Alumni/Career Center/Job, Internship, and Volunteer Search", accessed on October 9th, 2021.

1.3.4　Prepare for the Job Interview

The majority of your initial job (screening) interviews will probably be conducted in a non-personal medium e.g., email, telephone, or video conferencing. You need to prepare not only for dealing with these specific types of interviewing methods, but also be confident in your language skills. As with any job interview, the key to your success is preparation and practice. Whatever the medium of the interview, you still need to articulate how your unique mix of accomplishments, skills, and education make you an ideal candidate for the position.

1.3.5　Follow-up All Job Leads

It's essential—for your job-search success—to make the effort to follow-up ALL job leads… don't let any potential jobs slip through your hands. Make phone calls and send e-mails to all your prospective employers and inquire about the status of the job openings. You have to be a bit more assertive in your follow-up, but be careful of sounding too aggressive. Again, know the culture of the country. And be sure to send thank-you notes after all interviews and other contacts.

Section 2

How to Set Foot into the UN System?

The United Nations, with offices in 193 countries and 44,000 employees, is the world's largest universal multilateral international organization. It inspires people from around the world to join its mission of maintaining peace, advancing human rights and promoting justice, equality and development.[1] Securing employment with the Organization can seem like a daunting task, but as the scope of its work is global and multidimensional, there are many different entry points for candidates of varied educational backgrounds and diverse professional experience.[2]

1　Source from the website of the United Nations Academic Impact, "#Work4UN Basic Facts about Working for the United Nations", accessed on July 10th, 2021.

2　Source from the website of the United Nations Academic Impact, "#Work4UN Young Professionals Programme", accessed on July 11th, 2021.

2.1　Job Opportunities

How then can one enter the UN career path? Neither the explanation nor the procedure is simple. In order to facilitate the understanding of these opportunities, the material has been divided according to the entry level of the candidate:

- a graduate school student
- a recent graduate
- a professional with experience

The UN categorizes their job postings based on the international nature of a position, the types and/or length of contracts, and the years of work experience required. The typical opportunity for the first category is an internship. Special entry programmes such as the Young Professionals Programme (YPP) and Junior Professional Officer Programme (JPO) are offered to those of the second category. And finally, once experience is accumulated, the doors open to those of the third category for professional staff, experts and consultants through external vacancy announcements.

2.1.1　Internship Programme

If you are thinking of entering the world of diplomacy and public policy, an internship at the United Nations could be the ideal start for you.

The objective of the internship programme is to provide a framework by which graduate and post-graduate students from diverse academic backgrounds may be attached to United Nations offices or departments; to give them a first-hand impression of the day-to-day working environment of the United Nations; and to provide departments at Headquarters with the assistance of students specialized in various professional fields relevant to their needs. As part of the team, working directly with outstanding and inspiring career professionals and senior management, you will be exposed to high-profile conferences, participate in meetings, and contribute to analytical work as well as organizational policy of the United Nations.

Keep in Mind[1]

- Duration: The internship programme lasts for at least two months and can be as long as six months. Once selected, you must begin your internship either prior to or within one year of graduation.

- Cost: United Nations interns are not paid. All costs related to travel, insurance, accommodation, and living expenses must be borne by either the interns or their sponsoring institutions.

- Visa: You will be responsible for obtaining and financing the necessary visas.

- Travel: You will arrange and finance your travel to the United Nations location where you will be an intern.

- Medical Insurance: You will be responsible for costs arising from accidents and/or illness incurred during the internship and must show proof of a valid major global medical insurance coverage.

- Confidentiality: You must be discreet and keep confidential any and all unpublished information obtained during the course of the internship and may not publish any documents based on such information.

- Academic Credit: You may get academic credit from your institution of higher education for the internship. Check with your university to confirm their academic credit policy for internships.

2.1.2 YPP and JPO

a. The UN Young Professionals Programme (YPP) is a recruitment initiative for talented, highly qualified professionals with little or no work experience to start a career as an international civil servant with the UN Secretariat. It consists of an entrance examination process and professional development once those successful start their career with the UN.

The YPP examination (formerly the National Competitive Recruitment Examination

---

1　Source from the website of the United Nations Careers, "Home/What are my career options/Internship programme".

[NCRE]) is held once a year in different subject areas, based on the requirements of the UN quota system of representation. YPP is open to nationals of countries that are un- or under-represented in the United Nations. The list of participating countries is published annually on the YPP home page of the UN Careers website and varies from year to year. This examination is also held for staff members of the United Nations Secretariat who work within the General Service and other related categories and aspire to a career within the Professional and higher categories.

Depending on the staffing needs of the United Nations, applicants are invited to apply for different exam subjects. Descriptions of responsibilities, expected competencies and education requirements differ depending on the area. However, to be eligible for the YPP, applicants must meet the basic application criteria:

- Have the nationality of a participating country;
- Hold at least a first-level university degree relevant for the exam (at least a relevant Bachelor's degree or a 3-year equivalent degree);
- Be 32 years old or younger in the year of the examination;
- Be fluent in either English or French.

b. The main goal of the Junior Professional Officer (JPO) Programme (formerly known as Associate Experts Programme) is to support *The 2030 Agenda for Sustainable Development* and to offer young professionals an opportunity to get hands-on experience in multilateral international cooperation at the United Nations. JPO positions are generally at the P1 or P2 level. Candidates are young professionals, usually with an advanced university degree and a minimum two years of professional experience.

JPOs are generally nationals of donor countries, and are recruited under bilateral agreements between the United Nations and donor countries.[1] The number of sponsored positions varies from year to year and by donor country. Initially JPOs are granted a one-year appointment which may be extended, with the agreement of the donor country, and

---

1   The following countries are currently participating in the UN JPO Programme: Australia, Austria, Belgium, China, Denmark, Egypt, Finland, France, Germany, Hungary, Israel, Italy, Japan, Kuwait, Luxembourg, Mongolia, Morocco, Netherlands, Norway, Republic of Korea, Saudi Arabia, Spain, Sweden, Switzerland, United Arab Emirates, United Kingdom, United States.

on the basis of good performance. There is no expectation of being selected for a regular staff position, but JPOs may apply for such positions as any other external candidate and go through the regular competitive selection process of the UN.[1]

Whilst a small number of JPOs do continue to serve within the UN system, the aim of the programme is not to provide long-term careers within the UN, but exposure to the co-operative work of the divisions. Typically, applicants should have a Masters (or equivalent) degree relevant to the work of the department, possess relevant work experience in a developing country (one to two years minimum), and be fluent in written and spoken English and at least one other UN language.[2]

Fact Sheet[3]

As of September 2021, the UN JPO Programme at the Department of Economic and Social Affairs (DESA) is managing and supporting the assignments of 287 Junior Professional Officers (JPOs) and Special Assistants to Resident Coordinators (SARCs) for the UN Secretariat (all UN departments and offices) and its entities:

- from 26 donor countries and from 36 different nationalities;
- 33% male and 67% female;
- assigned to more than 53 duty stations around the world;
- working for more than 42 different UN Departments/Offices including Regional Commissions, Peacekeeping Missions and Resident Coordinator Officers.

2.1.3 Consultants and Individual Contractors

The United Nations frequently engages experts under individual contracts to work on short-term projects either as a consultant or an individual contractor.

---

1 Source from the website of the United Nations Careers, "Home/What are my career options/Junior Professional Officer Programme", accessed on September 10th, 2021.

2 Source from the website of the Oxford University Careers Service, "Home/Explore Careers/Sectors and Occupations/International Organizations", accessed on June 6th, 2021.

3 Source from the website of the United Nations, Department of Economic and Social Affairs, "Junior Professional Officer Programme/Facts and Figures".

A consultant is a recognized authority or specialist in a specific field, engaged by the Organization in an advisory or consultative capacity. The functions of a consultant are results-oriented and normally involve analyzing problems, directing seminars or training courses, preparing documents for conferences and meetings, or writing reports on matters within their area of expertise.

An individual contractor is engaged by the Organization to provide expertise, skills or knowledge for the performance of a specific task or piece of work, which would be short-term by nature. The assignment may involve full-time or part-time functions similar to those of staff members.[1]

The competencies and qualifications required of the consultants and the experts are the most varied. In addition to a specialization in a specific area, language skills, interpersonal relations, and sensitivity towards cultures other than one's own are all important in the selection of an expert or a consultant. The combination of all these characteristics often makes it difficult to find the right candidate. It is not easy, for example, to find a specialist in irrigation systems that is specialized in a certain geographical area, and that speaks both Arabic and French very well. The combination of qualities complicates the research, especially when the time given is limited.

2.1.4   Language Careers

The United Nations is one of the world's largest employers of language professionals. Several hundred such staff work for the Department for General Assembly and Conference Management in New York, Geneva, Vienna and Nairobi, or at the United Nations regional commissions in Addis Ababa, Bangkok, Beirut, Geneva and Santiago.

At the United Nations, the term "language professional" covers a wide range of specialists, such as interpreters, translators, editors, verbatim reporters, terminologists, reference assistants and copy preparers/proofreaders/production editors.

United Nations language staff come from all over the globe and make up a uniquely diverse and multilingual community. What unites them is the pursuit of excellence in their respective areas, the excitement of being at the forefront of international affairs and the desire to contribute to the realization of the purposes of the United Nations, as

---

1   Source from the website of the United Nations Careers, "Home/What are my career options/Consultants", accessed on September 10th, 2021.

outlined in *The Charter*, by facilitating communication and decision-making.[1]

The main recruitment path for United Nations language professionals is through Competitive Examinations for Language Positions (CELPs), whereby successful examinees are placed on rosters for recruitment and are hired as and when job vacancies arise. CELPs are language- and function-specific examinations that comprise a series of skills tests conducted over a period of several months. Language professionals from all regions, who meet the eligibility requirements, are encouraged to apply. Candidates are judged solely on their academic and other qualifications and on their performance in the examination.

Language staff work mostly with the six official UN languages (Arabic, Chinese, English, French, Russian and Spanish). Applicants for language positions must have a perfect command of one official language and excellent knowledge of at least one other. The one exception is the small German Translation Section at UN Headquarters in New York, which requires a perfect command of German.

The distribution of positions varies by profession and language: for example, all the verbatim reporting positions are in New York, not every location has positions for interpreters, and the translation positions in Santiago are only for translators who translate into Spanish or English. The locations where positions might be available for those who succeed in a CELP are stated in the corresponding examination announcement.[2]

Do You Know?[3]

Finding the right profile of candidate for United Nations language positions is challenging, especially for certain language combinations. The United Nations is not the only international organization looking for skilled language professionals, and it deals with a wide variety of subjects, often politically sensitive. Its language staff

---

1   Source from the website of the United Nation, Department for General Assembly and Conference Management, "Home/Language careers", accessed on July 11th, 2021.

2   Source from the website of the United Nations Careers, "Home/What are my career options/Competitive examinations for language professionals", accessed on August 10th, 2021.

3   Source from the website of the United Nation, Department for General Assembly and Conference Management, "Home/Language careers".

must meet high quality and productivity standards. This is why the Department has had an outreach programme focusing on collaboration with universities since 2007. The Department hopes to build on existing partnerships, forge new partnerships, and attract the qualified staff it needs to continue providing high-quality conference services at the United Nations.

2.2   Job Information

You might have seen a job advertised online or in the paper. You might have heard about it from friends or family. But where did you go to find out about opportunities across the United Nations, its people, culture and values? Which areas interest you most? Are there areas you are already qualified for? Are there areas you would like to work in but for which you still need qualifications?

At the UN, there are 9 job networks and 45 job families.[1] Browse through the United Nations website to get a feel for the different types of work available at the UN:

- The first step is to research the various offices, programmes, and agencies by using the official United Nations employment website, and the International Civil Service Commission links to the job pages of UN agencies. Vacancies are constantly updated, so if you don't immediately see a position that fits your goals and qualifications, check back often.

Each individual UN agency also has its own job websites and, often, its own rosters, such as UNDP and United Nations Office for Project Services (UNOPS). Other UN agency website can be found at the UN System Chief Executives Board for Coordination.

---

1   Job networks have been established to promote greater career opportunities for staff members. Each network is a flexible grouping of job families with common, related and interrelated fields of work and functions. Job families in turn are occupations and sub-occupations grouped into a common field of work. As part of a network, United Nations employees can access multidisciplinary opportunities for developing new skills, and gain exposure to the different parts of the Organization. An eligible staff member can join one or more networks based on her or his background and career interests. For more information on each job network, see the website of the United Nations Careers, "Home/What can I do at the UN/Job Networks", accessed on October 5th, 2021.

The United Nations Careers Portal home page (herewith referred to as the "Careers Portal") offers a compendium of published job openings and a variety of useful information on pursuing career opportunities with the United Nations Secretariat. The Careers Portal provides information about what the United Nations does, where it operates and the organizational structure; career paths, career options and the recruitment process, as well as a showcase of United Nations staff members providing an insight to their experience working at the United Nations.

- Contacting Foreign Affairs Offices, Permanent Missions to the UN, and United Nations Information Centres (UNIC) Information on careers with the UN can also be obtained by contacting the Permanent Missions to the UN, or the Foreign Affairs Offices and the UN Information Centres of one's country directly.

The above list isn't intended as an exhaustive A-Z of international organizations and it is crucial that individuals who are serious about planning a career in this sector apply initiative and energetic networking skills in finding out about opportunities and gaining relevant experience to add to their CV.

2.3 Application Procedure[1]

Applying for a position is accomplished in several steps. The illustration below shows the high-level steps that are performed in the application process.

(1) Searching for Job Opening(s)

Look at the UN employment website to see current vacancies with organizations in the UN Secretariat. Most job openings are designed for a specific position in a particular office and duty station (job-specific openings). There are also generic job openings, which are used to create rosters, i.e., pools of candidates available for immediate selection across the Organization, and Recruit from Roster job openings which are only

---

1　Source from "Chapter 2 Overview of the Application Process", in *The Applicant's Manual: Manual for the Applicant on the Staff Selection System* (inspira), United Nations Careers, April 2012; see also the website of the United Nations Careers, "Home/How do I apply?/Application process".

open to candidates who have already been rostered. The application process is the same for all job opening types.

The United Nations publishes job opportunities in a compendium of job openings on a regular basis. You may actively search for job openings and apply to those for which you feel you are qualified. If you want to receive e-mails letting you know about newly posted jobs, you must first log into your account. You can then perform a Job Search that can be saved to create a Job Alert that matches your search criteria.

(2) Making Sure You Meet All the Requirements

UN careers are divided into different staff categories, each of which requires a specific educational background and area of expertise. The categories are further broken down into jobs at different levels that require varying amounts of work experience. Taking into account your skills, interest and experience, decide which category and level is appropriate for you. Here are the options:

a. Professional and higher categories (P and D)

b. General Service and related categories (G, TC, S, PIA, LT)

c. National Professional Officers (NO)

d. Field Service (FS)

e. Senior Appointments (SG, DSG, USG and ASG)

Before you apply for a job, be certain you meet all its requirements; if not, either have very good reasons for why the recruiter might overlook whatever is lacking, or don't apply. The UN website makes it clear that you can apply for as many vacancies as you like, but your credibility will be hurt if you apply for positions for which you are not qualified. Here are common requirements for many positions at the UN:

a. Fluency in English or French, the working languages of the Organization. Fluency in additional languages, particularly Arabic, Chinese, Spanish, or Russian, is helpful for most positions;

b. A bachelor's degree or higher. Some lower-level generalist positions (mostly clerical or secretarial jobs in the General Service category) require only a high school diploma and, usually, relevant work experience, but most positions in the UN require at least a bachelor's degree. Many specialist positions require advanced degrees in the area of specialty;

c. Work experience in a related field. Depending on the position for which you are applying, you might need anywhere from 1 to 7 years of work experience.

(3) Creating and Updating "My Profile"

Click on the "Login" option at the top of the UN employment website. Non-Staff Members must log into the inspira Careers Home page through the Careers Portal gateway. A one-time registration and creation of a login account is required to complete the registration process.

After you have registered you will be welcomed to your Applications Home page, which is where you will fill out and manage your profile, application form and all information relating to your application(s). This profile will be your confidential online resume, and includes important information, such as your name, nationality, contact information and marital status. It is the information that the United Nations will use to contact you during the application process. You will only need to complete this once, but you can edit it for different vacancies if you wish.

- You can complete the profile right away, or come back later. It will take between 30 minutes to one hour to complete, and you can save a partially completed profile at any time and return to finish it.

- Ensure that your profile is thorough, detailed, accurate, and picture perfect. When you apply for a position, the profile is the first (and, initially, only) thing the recruiter will see. If you don't do a good job of representing your qualifications, or if your profile is marred by spelling or grammar mistakes, your application will be passed over.

- You can continue to update your profile at any time, but make sure it is in perfect condition when you actually apply for a listed vacancy.

(4) Applying for the chosen vacancy

Completing the application involves four parts:

Part 1 - Create Your Application

Once your profile is saved, you can create one or several job applications. The application form is the part of your application that has information about your preferences, education and work experience, language skills, present and past jobs, etc. It is suggested that you start preparing an application form without immediately applying for a job by clicking *Create Draft Application*. After you have entered the data, you click *Save* to save the data without submitting. You can prepare, access, edit and save one or more fully, or partially completed application forms without applying for a job right away. It is recommended to click *Save* after each section before exiting the page. Also be aware that the session times out after 60 minutes of inactivity.

Part 2 - Write the Cover Letter

Part of the application includes the writing of a cover letter. The cover letter is the personal introduction that accompanies your application. A cover letter should be brief, three to four paragraphs, and as targeted as possible to the position.

A resume or CV is not accepted and is considered neither a substitute nor a complementary document to a duly completed online application. Any supplemental information or documentation that the Organization may require will be requested in the course of the application.

Part 3 - Update Your Draft Application

Once you have identified a job opening of interest, you should update the application to highlight important facts relevant to the job you are applying for, as well as to provide answers to the Job Requirements questions and to complete your motivation statement. It is important to accurately complete and update all the information as it serves as a basis for evaluating your eligibility and suitability for a job opening. It is also recommended that you update your application for every job opening you apply to so that it is targeted to the position.

Part 4 - Answer the Questions (as applicable)

If you want to apply for a specific job after you have filled out your application, click *Add Job to Application*. You will have to answer a set of questions (10 to 15) based on the job requirements which will give you the opportunity to demonstrate relevant experiences, highlight skills and knowledge, describe related published work, acquired licenses, certifications, and training.

After the job application is complete, you can submit your application by clicking Submit. Each application you have prepared and submitted, and the list of job openings to which you have applied, along with the application status (i.e., "Applied", "Under consideration", "Rostered" etc.), are displayed in the My Applications page.

(5) Evaluation of the Application

Your application is evaluated in terms of required and desirable evaluation criteria, e.g., experience, education, and languages. They can be identified in related parts of the job opening of the position you applied to as well as through the Job Requirements questions at the time of your application. You will be invited to participate in assessment exercises and/or a competency-based interview only if it is determined that you meet all the required evaluation criteria, and any additional desirable criteria that the hiring manager decides to apply for screening.

The assessment exercises might include a written exam, simulation exercise, case study, or other appropriate evaluation mechanism. You will be informed in advance of the time, type, and length of the assessment. If, based on the result of the assessment, you are short-listed for a competency-based interview, you will be informed accordingly. Please note, however, that the type and frequency of correspondence with individual candidates may vary throughout the application process.

(6) Waiting for Selection Notification

A pool of qualified candidates is recommended for selection following the outcome of the various assessment stages. Any recommendations are then evaluated by an independent review body, composed of staff and management representatives, to ensure that the applicable procedures were followed correctly. After the review body has endorsed the recommended candidates, a selection decision is made by the head of the department usually for one individual, or if several positions are available, for the corresponding number of vacancies.

You will be notified if you are the selected candidate for the job. If you were in the group of candidates recommended for the job opening but were not selected, you will be placed on the roster for similar functions at the level and category of the job opening for possible future selection. As a roster member, you will be notified when new job openings with the same job title, level, category and job family for which you have been rostered are advertised.

If you are not included in the pool of candidates recommended for selection, you will be notified at the appropriate time, that your application was unsuccessful for this job. In this case, you should not be discouraged but apply for other jobs for which you feel you are qualified.

Section 3

How to Prepare a Job Application Package?

An application portfolio is a set of application documents, and a typical layout of an application portfolio includes: an outer shell, a cover letter, a CV (curriculum vitae), certificates, work references (work samples) and other application-relevant documents.[1] Due to the large number of individuals attracted to this area of work, it is important to create a portfolio that stands out amongst the crowd. There are certain guidelines for the document preparation in a classic application portfolio:

3.1　Cover Letter

A cover letter represents your motivation for a position and contains an overview of your work experience most relevant to the job posting. Its purpose is to introduce yourself in a personal, compelling way so that the hiring manager wants to review your resume or CV. The length should not exceed two pages, ideally within one page, and answer the following questions:

Why do you apply for this position? (E.g., interesting tasks, career opportunities, new challenges, etc.)

Why do you choose this organization? (E.g., market positioning, industry, products, employer branding, etc.)

What professional qualifications do you bring? (E.g., further education, practical experience, intercultural competence, social engagement, etc.)

*What is your motivation for this job? (*E.g., visions of the organization, career opportunities, variety of tasks, chances for individual achievements, etc.)

Why should the organization hire you? (E.g., industry knowledge, practical experience, soft skills, negotiation abilities, specific focus (in professional life), *etc.)*

To really stand out, it's important to personalize your cover letter for each job

---

1　Lorenz Schneidmadel, "How to Prepare Your Job Application Folder", *EDUBAO,* March 18th, 2021.

application. You shouldn't use your cover letter as a chance to reiterate your whole resume. This is your chance to pick out a few keywords from the position description, and dive into examples showing how you've exhibited these skills. Make sure the cover letter does exactly what is asked for. Usually this means saying how your skills and experience match their requirements, and since each job has different requirements, it means EACH cover letter must be different.

(1) Formatting

There are different formats you can use when writing cover letters. Regardless of the format you choose to follow, it's critical you proofread, use formal terms such as "Dear" and "Sincerely," and lean towards a professional tone whenever possible.

Formatting Example

The basics first. The header of every professional cover letter for a job application should follow the rules of formal business letters and include the following:

1. Header—Input Contact Information

Your Name

Your Address

Your City, State, Zip Code

Cell: 555-555-5555

Email: name@email.com

Date

2. Greeting—The Hiring Manager/Department Information

Dear X, (try to find hiring manager's name… if you can't, you can put "Dear [Organization A] Hiring Committee")

3. Opening Paragraph

Make it personal and tailor it for each job application to grab the reader's attention.

4. Body Paragraphs

Describe what your major achievements are and how you will help them solve their current challenges. Mention why you are the right person for the job.

---

5. Closing Paragraph

6. Formal Salutation

Sincerely,

(*Leave four spaces for your signature, then type your name underneath the four spaces.)

Pro Tips

- Use an email address from a respected provider—that means either Gmail or your personal domain (if you have one).
- Your email address should only include your first and last name, which means names like *sexyvanessa@gmail.com* or *johnlikesgoats@hotmail.com* will be deal-breakers.
- Don't use your current work email. It's impolite to both your current and potential future employer.
- Make sure your contact information is consistent across your resume, cover letter, and social media profiles.
- Left justify all the details in the cover letter header.

(2) Paragraph One

In the first paragraph, explain how you heard about the organization or position, and if you know anyone at the company, mention them here. Next, express your own interest in the company or position and explain briefly how it relates to your own passions. Introduce yourself in this paragraph, writing your name, your education level, your major, and your interests.

Here's the brutal truth: *the opening line of your cover letter will determine whether the hiring manager will read on.* You need to make your cover letter introduction attract and hold the hiring manager's interest.

There are a few different, effective strategies for your cover letter opening. You can highlight your achievements, show how well you know your prospective employer's needs, or base the intro. on your enthusiasm. Now, see a properly written cover letter opening example:

> *As a lifelong enthusiast of XYZ's marketing initiatives, I was thrilled to see your posting for the position of Digital Marketing Manager. I am positive I can help with XYZ's upcoming challenges. I have experience of leading successful national online campaigns with budgets over $300,000. What is more, I have succeeded at expanding ABC's client base by 19% since 2011.*

(3) Paragraph Two and Three

What to write in a cover letter's second paragraph?

You need to get the hiring manager exactly what she's looking for. You have to show that you're going to satisfy most of the job requirements—the organization's specific needs. So, scan the position description and pick out a few qualities you think apply to you—just don't choose all the descriptors mentioned (it will appear disingenuous and make your cover letter too long).

Mentioning the traits directly in your cover letter shows you've read the position description, and makes your cover letter more scannable. If the hiring manager is looking for someone with content skills, she might scan your cover letter looking for the words that indicate experience with content.

Finally, brainstorm a few compelling examples to show how you embody the most important characteristics. Don't just write, "I have excellent customer service skills." You need to prove it. Support your claim by writing, "Last summer, I worked as an orientation leader at my college, serving as a resource for incoming students and their parents. This experience strengthened my customer service skills."

Even if you don't have a lot of (or any) job experience, think about highlighting skills you've gained from extracurricular, volunteer experience, or even passion projects (e.g. "my passion for dance led me to become a volunteer dance teacher, which helped me develop as a leader").

The future employers have needs. If they're willing to hire you, it's because they think you'll satisfy those needs. But what they also want is for you to actually enjoy working with them. They want your future job to feel rewarding to you—that way, they know you're more likely to stay with them for a longer period of time.

The key to writing a perfect cover letter in the third paragraph is showing the hiring manager why you want this job, not just any job.

Here's the easiest way to do it:

- Start with an organization fact—for instance, an upcoming project (1);
- Say why you find it interesting (2);
- Reiterate that your experience and knowledge will let you succeed with the project (3).

Have a look at this cover letter example (third paragraph):

I know that XYZ's current plans involve developing a comprehensive online portal focused on healthcare-related issues. This project is a perfect match for my personal and professional interests and an exciting opportunity to create a unique online base of knowledge for patients and healthcare professionals. I would love to leverage my knowledge of SEO marketing and online growth marketing to achieve groundbreaking results with this initiative.

(4) Closing

How to make the best cover letter ending? Long story short: *by providing value*. Tell the hiring manager that you're looking forward to meeting in person and discussing how your experience and knowledge can help your future employer in fulfilling their goals.

Two worst cover letter mistakes you can make in the final paragraph are:

- Coming off needy—focusing on how much you want the job, not on what you have to offer.
- Repeating the cliched phrase "Thank you for your consideration and your time."

If the internship application does not specify "please do not contact," you might choose to conclude by specifying how you will follow up, such as, "I will call next week to see if my qualifications are a match," or, "I am eager to meet with you to discuss this opportunity, and am available for an interview at a mutually convenient time." Conclude by thanking the hiring manager for taking the time to consider you, and end on a positive, confident note, such as, "I look forward to speaking with you soon." Like in the cover letter sample.

I would welcome the chance to discuss your digital marketing objectives and show you how my success at ABC can translate into digital and online marketing growth for XYZ.

Writing Sample

Cover Letter for Full Time Position at United Nations Children's Fund

POSITION: Communications Job

Mercy the Job Seeker

P. O. Box 1900-00100

Nairobi, Kenya

13th April 2015

The Human Resource Manager

UNICEF Kenya Country Office

P.O. Box 44145-00100

Nairobi, Kenya

Dear Sir/ Madam

RE: APPLICATION FOR A COMMUNICATIONS JOB AT UNICEF

I am writing to express my interest in the recently advertised Communication Specialist Job at UNICEF's Nairobi Office. Based on my education, skills and current NGO experience, I believe that I would be an outstanding candidate for this position.

Along with an advanced university degree in the social/behavioral sciences with emphasis on strategic communication planning for behavior development and research, I am fluent in Portuguese as per your job description and have the enthusiasm and determination for the challenging communication opportunity. As an accomplished Communications Officer currently working at GHUY, I possess broad knowledge of managing internal communication programs for staff and providing leadership and coordination for all communication activities of the NGO. Furthermore, I am accountable for all communication activities including liaison activities with organizations with similar interests locally and internationally.

My attached CV gives more details about my specific skills and qualifications significant to UN job requirements. I look forward to hearing from you soon. Thank you for your time and consideration.

Sincerely Yours,
(*hand-written signature*)

Attached: Resume and Reference Letters

3.2   CV

Unlike the resume, which is rarely longer than a one-sided single page, the CV is a far more comprehensive document. It goes above and beyond a mention of education and work experience and often lists—in thoughtful detail—your achievements, awards, honors, and publications. According to UNC Writing Center, the CV is a "fairly detailed overview of your life's accomplishments, especially those most relevant to the realm of academia," hence the variance in length; an early-stage grad student's CV is going to be a lot shorter than a sixth-year student preparing to write a dissertation.[1]

(1) Necessity of CV Tailoring

Your CV will be shaped by your personal experience, qualifications and skills, and it will grow and change with you. You also need to tailor it for each job application so that it tells a compelling story about your motivation to succeed in that particular job or career sector.[2] Potential employers need to see that you have an understanding of, passion for and ability to thrive in their organization and in the role advertised, or that you are applying for speculatively.

Highlight the skills that you have already gained in your degree—what are the most

---

1   Stacey Lastoe, "CV vs. Resume—Here Are the Differences", *The Muse*, accessed on September 18th, 2021.

2   Your CV needs to be explicit about your experience. Just because you worked at an immigration support center, for instance, don't assume multicultural experience is implied; spell it out! Just because you have worked as a firefighter, don't assume emergency response experience is assumed; say it!

relevant modules you have taken or transferable skills you have built? How have these skills been further developed outside of your degree, through roles in societies, student editorial work, freelance consultancy, travel, previous work experience and internships, etc.? Are you doing all you can in the way you phrase the bullet points in your CV to convey the research, communication, team-work, problem-solving, numerical, regional, thematic or other interests you know that organization values?

Here are three TIPs to help you write your CV in a way that showcases your skills:

- When you are giving details of the skills you developed in a job, internship or work experience placement, reflect the competencies listed in the job description and give examples of the most relevant skills first.
- Use confident language to describe your skills, for example, by drawing attention to awards or praise employers have given you.
- If you're struggling to find a way to write about your holiday or part-time jobs on your CV, remember that it's better to focus on transferable skills than routine tasks.

(2) Skills to Include in a CV[1]

While the knowledge and skills required may vary from job to job, it's imperative that in your application forms, you convey how you've gained the core attributes that you think would make you a worthwhile addition to the organization. Here are some of the key employability skills that graduate employers will expect you to demonstrate. They are sometimes known as transferable skills because you develop them over time and take them with you as your career develops. Think of them as your passport to career success. It's vital that you understand these skills, and how you can show that you've developed them, in order to write a successful job application.

A. Emotional Intelligence

"Emotional intelligence refers to the ability to identify and manage one's own emotions, as well as the emotions of others".[2] In the workplace, this means you're

---

1　Source from Rachel Swain, "What Skills do Employers Want', *Prospects*, April, 2021.

2　Rachel Jay, "Top 20 Must-have Skills to Put on Your Resume", *Flexjobs*, accessed on October 9th, 2021.

rational and even-keeled. It is important for everybody, and is something that graduate employers have increasingly started to consider. How well do you cope with stressful situations or when something goes wrong? How do you react to unexpected changes or problems that occur during a project? You aren't expected to be unaffected by these events, but you need to be able to show that you have a bit of get-up-and-go and are able to handle ups and downs without losing control.

B. Good Communication Skills

This covers verbal and written communication, and listening. It's about being clear, concise and focused; being able to tailor your message for the audience and listening to the views of others. Employers will be keen to see how you build rapport, persuade and negotiate with people. Use your CV or application form to outline specific written and verbal examples of when you've put these skills into practice. This might be any public speaking you've done, or writing for a student newspaper, for example. Show how you tailored your message to the target audience.

C. Effective Leadership and Management

Even if you're not applying for a management position, you'll still need to demonstrate to employers that you have the potential to motivate and lead others in order to achieve common objectives. On application forms, detail situations where you've had the opportunity to plan and coordinate tasks during your degree or in extra-curricular activities such as university clubs and societies. The ability to solve problems and conflicts is always highly-valued by recruiters.

D. Planning and Organizing Skills

To accomplish certain work tasks, you may need to come up with a suitable strategy and plan of action. This could involve seeking out relevant information from various sources. How you analyse, interpret and report these findings is what's important here. Highlight the relevant skills that you've developed during your degree course—reading around a subject and analysing that information before writing an essay, for instance, or interpreting the results of a scientific experiment.

E. Self-management and Responsibility

The specific activities of your job will always be viewed in the context of the business's goals and what it's trying to achieve. By successfully directing your work towards these objectives- prioritising your duties, working well under pressure and managing your time effectively-you can demonstrate that you're flexible and can be trusted. You could give examples of times when you've had to balance your university work with other commitments in order to meet multiple deadlines.

F. Teamwork and Interpersonal Skills

Most jobs will sometimes require you to work with other people at some point, and employers want to know that you can succeed in a team environment. Some jobs will prize this skill more than others. Usually, employers will be looking at your individual contribution towards achieving common goals. This isn't just about times when you've led a team successfully, but also when you've been an effective team member taking instructions and direction from somebody else.

(3) Steps to an Excellent CV

Studies have shown that on average recruiters spend just seven seconds looking at a CV before deciding whether a candidate is suitable for the role.[1] First impressions are therefore critical to success. Here are several simple but effective ways to write the right CV.

Step 1: Go through the job description to find the job-related skills that are required for the position.

> **Identify what the employer wants from a candidate:**
>
> Here look for the precise skill sets that the employer is asking for. They could be given as a short sentence or simply a keyword.
>
> **Sentence examples:**
> - Candidate must have 2 years Project Management experience.
> - Experience of working in a clothes retail shop.

---

1 Sophie-Anne Bradley, "7 Simple but Effective Ways to Make Your CV Stand Out", *QS Top Universities*, October 3rd, 2021.

Keywords examples:

- Customer service

- Insurance sales

- JavaScript

It's vital you make an accurate and precise list of these. Go through the list of required skills and make sure you have those. If you do, great, if you don't then move on, as there's no point applying for jobs you are not qualified for.

Step 2: These job-related skills should go in your resume skills section and possibly in your resume objective or summary so an employer will see them right away. There should be evidence (work experience, education, training) that proves your ability to demonstrate these key skills on a resume.

Step 3: Next, look for all of the adaptive and transferable skills that the employer wants on top of the regular job-related skills.

Step 4: Sprinkle proof that you have these types of skills throughout your resume. Now start putting together a CV that includes all of the keywords and phrases you saw in the job advert. If you have the expertise asked for in a job posting, make sure it is detailed in your CV.

Working from this general outline, it's also recommended to then break down the overall content into smaller bits and pieces, which are easily digestible by readers, including the use of bullet points and smaller boxes of facts and figures. These can then fit into the various boxes and subheadings of the newsletter templates, for an attractive visual layout. These are just a few of the ways to show your message in an appealing way.

3.3   Job Interview

The United Nations' greatest asset is the quality of its staff. To ensure that the very best people join the UN team, they use a competency-based interview process. Competency-based interviews are also called "behavioral interviews" or "criterion-based interviews". Such interviews are based on the concept that past behavior and experience are the best indicators of future performance. In other words, your history tells a story about you: your talents, skills, abilities, knowledge and actual experience in handling a variety of situations.

(1) Competency Interviewing Questions

- *Tell us about a situation when you went above and beyond your manager's expectations.*
- *Give an example of a time when you used your problem-solving abilities to resolve an issue?*
- *Tell us about a time where you had a number of demands being made on you at the same time? How did you handle it?*

(2) Useful Tips for Your Interview

- Prepare a wide range of brief real-life stories about your accomplishments. Be aware of the specific skills each story illustrates and remember to include the positive outcome or lesson learned from each experience;
- Be ready to discuss your strengths and your ability to learn from past experiences. Also think about how you could contribute to the work of the United Nations and to the specific position you are applying for;
- Review the competencies mentioned in the job opening. These will be probed in your interview, so your stories should show your skill in these competency areas;
- You should be prepared to address positive results and achievements using these competencies and also challenges you have had in each of these areas;
- The structure of your answer should be: Situation, Action, Result;
- Share information you feel is appropriate and relevant;
- Listen to the question carefully. Keep to the point. Be as specific as possible;
- Do some research on competency, or behavior-based interviews. There is a lot of material available about preparing for such an interview structure;
- Learn as much as you can about the Department and Office you are applying to and the work it does;
- Practice, practice, practice.

(3) Interview Etiquette

Interview etiquette is all about being professional, respectful and dignified throughout the interview. Doing so can actually have a bigger impact on the interviewer and could possibly improve your chances and reap the benefits in many situations.

A. What to Wear

- Always dress to impress for an interview, even if it is for a rather informal office or behind the counter in a fast-food restaurant. Dressing well not only shows respect but will also impress.

    —Men the traditional suit and tie.

    —Women can be the pants suit, tasteful dress or skirt and blazer combo.

- Hair should be neat or tied back.
- No nail polish, clear is OK.
- Recommend removing any and all facial piercings.

B. When to Leave

After doing your practise run[1] before the interview, you should now know how long it takes to get there—so after factoring in how long it will take for you to get ready, you should always be at least 10—15 minutes early for an interview. This shows you are well prepared and you get to show off some time-management skills before they even meet you. Plus, it is just good etiquette.

C. Before

You have approximately 30 seconds to make a first impression at an interview, so make it count.

- Turn off your phone; don't be fussing with any technology waiting for the interviewer.
- Sit straight and wait patiently. Try running over possible answers in your head while you wait.

D. During

- When you are called, shake hands and introduce yourself. Thank them twice, before and after; it's just good etiquette and they cost nothing but are remembered.
- After you've exchanged pleasantries, wait to be offered a seat: it's bad etiquette to take a seat before being asked. When seated, put anything you have brought with you, like handbags/briefcases, under your chair or just next to you.

---

1   A practice run indicates a trial or practice before a real-world deployment or occurrence. So it means a "rehearsal", or a "run-through".

- Be careful with your body language, slouching comes across as too casual and uninterested. Sit up straight with both feet on the floor.

- It's only polite to let people finish their sentences, don't cut them off, you will get your turn to talk. Interviewers usually allot a few minutes at the end for you to ask any questions.

- Don't be afraid to ask questions. The interview is not just for them to get to know about you, but also for you about them. While they're learning about you, you can find out what sort of management style they have, the working atmosphere and whether or not they promote you internally. We would recommend asking at least 2—3 questions, if you don't have any, they may think you are not interested in the position.

E. Leaving

- Say again how interested you are in the position, thank them and shake their hands once more before you leave, still smiling.

- Do not turn your phone back on until you have left the building.

Tasks

Activity 1 Team-Building Activity

Code of Conduct

1. Description: A simple but meaningful activity that sets the tone for an event and builds consensus on shared values. Teams list what matters to them on a whiteboard.

2. Objective: Build mutual trust, establish group values.

3. Duration: 15+ mins

4. Number of Participants: 10—30

5. How to Play:

   a. On a whiteboard, write down the words "Meaningful" and "Pleasant".

   b. Ask everyone in the group to shout out what will make this workshop meaningful and pleasant. Alternatively, ask them to write their ideas on sticky notes.

   c. Record each participant's suggestion in the form of a mind map.

   d. For each suggestion, ensure that all participants have the same understanding of the idea. If not, change the suggestion until it has consensus from all participants.

e. Go through each suggested item and ask participants how they would ensure that the idea is carried out during the workshop. Record these on the whiteboard in sticky notes.

f. All ideas mutually agreed on as being "Pleasant" and "Meaningful" make up the *Code of Conduct* for the group. The group has the responsibility to uphold this code through the remainder of the workshop.

6. Strategy: For any team-building activity to be successful, the team has to have a few common values and beliefs about what makes a successful team meeting. Establishing these values early in the workshop/team meeting can make the rest of the workshop run much smoother.

Activity 2 | Multiple Choice

Inter-governmental cooperation is essential to resolve issues of global importance. That cooperation is often made possible by organizations and events dedicated to global governance. Test what you know about past and present efforts to make the world a better (or, at least, different) place.

1. Which international alliance's self-defense clause was first invoked in 2001, following terrorist attacks on the World Trade Center and Pentagon?

 A. NATO.   B. European Union.

 C. Warsaw Pact.   D. SEATO.

2. Which organization, established as a military counterweight to the Soviet military presence in eastern Europe during the Cold War, formed a cooperative bond with Russia in 2001 to address arms control and terrorism?

 A. NATO.   B. League of Nations.

 C. United Nations.   D. Non-aligned Movement.

3. The World Bank was set up following which event?

 A. Bretton Woods Conference. B. Casablanca Conference.

 C. Cairo Conference.   D. Yalta Conference.

4. Which organization was established at the initiative of the victorious Allied Powers at the end of World War I?

 A. World Trade Organization. B. Asia Pacific Economic Council.

C. League of Nations.   D. United Nations.

5. What organization was established in the 20th century to stabilize currency exchange and eliminate destructive trade policies?

   A. World Trade Organization.   B. Association of South Eastern Asian Nations.

   C. World Bank.   D. International Monetary Fund.

6. Which group is sometimes called the "Blue Helmets"?

   A. British Army.   B. United Nations peacekeeping troops.

   C. United States Air Force.   D. United States Army.

7. Where was the first United Nations conference on environmental issues held, in 1972?

   A. In New York.   B. In Stockholm.   C. In London.   D. In Paris.

8. Who was the first Secretary-General of the United Nations?

   A. Kofi Annan.   B. Dag Hammarskjöld.

   C. Ban Ki-moon.   D. Trygve Lie.

Activity 3 Quick Quiz

Will you ace the job interview?

1. When preparing for the interview, how many questions should you plan to ask the person interviewing you?

   A. None. The focus of the interview is on you answering questions, not asking them.

   B. At least a few. Show you are interested and knowledgeable about the position and organization.

   C. Bring a list of 10 questions and don't leave until you get them all answered.

   D. Ask as many questions as you can, until you're sure you understand the full situation.

2. What is the best way to greet the person interviewing you?

   A. A hug and a kiss on the cheek, just as you would greet a close relative.

   B. A firm handshake.

   C. A bow.

   D. A hesitant wave from a distance of 15 feet.

3. Your job interview is scheduled for 9 a.m. What time should you arrive?

   A. 1 minute before the interview begins.

    B. 30 minutes before the interview begins.

    C. 45 minutes before the interview begins.

    D. 10 minutes before the interview begins.

4. What should you NOT wear to a job interview?

    A. Lots of perfume or aftershave.

    B. Clothing slightly dressier than what you'd wear on the job.

    C. A watch.

    D. Polished shoes.

5. Which is the best way to follow up with a prospective employer after an interview?

    A. Email.

    B. Handwritten note.

    C. Phone call.

    D. Video call.

6. If someone asks you why you're looking for work, what should you NOT say?

    A. "I'm looking for a new challenge."

    B. "My old boss was a complete idiot."

    C. "I think this job is right for me based on my experience."

    D. "My organization was forced to downsize, and I lost my job."

7. What is a good answer to this question: "How would you feel about working for someone younger than you?"

    A. "I can work well with people of any age."

    B. "I don't understand the question."

    C. "I don't see how that question is relevant."

    D. "In my experience, older workers are better colleagues."

8. What is NOT a good question to ask during the job interview?

    A. "Will this position require travel?"

    B. "When do you expect to fill this position?"

    C. "Can I have an office with a window?"

    D. "What will be my responsibilities in this job?"

Activity 4 Job-Interview Exercise

A successful job interview requires confidence, thinking on your feet and quickly finding the right words to impress your audience—the same qualities that improv comedy performers need to demonstrate on stage. Try these 5 exercises from improv coaches to limber up physically and mentally for your future job interview.

(1) Flex Your Imagination

Take any object—a belt, a pen, a piece of paper, an eraser, etc.—and use it in any way, other than the way it was originally intended. For example, instead of only holding up pants, a belt can be a dog leash, a snake on the ground or a jump rope; a pen can be a dart, a syringe or a lightsaber; and a piece of paper can be an airplane, a telescope or a ball.

"This exercise gives you practice using your imagination, and is one that is often used in actual interviews to test creativity and flexibility."

—Bob Kulhan, Founder and CEO of Business Improv in the New York City Area

(2) Put Your Ears to Work

With a partner, pretend you're in a scenario, such as two business partners on a plane. Each person must start their sentence with the last big idea of their partner's sentence. For example, Partner 1 says, "I am so excited to go to Florida for vacation. I haven't been since I started my own cupcake company." Partner 2 replies, "Yeah, starting your own company is a time-consuming thing..." This enforces listening and promotes not having an agenda when you speak. You must listen to the end, and although you may have ideas or "comebacks," you listen to everything before you speak.

(3) Harness the Power of Pretend

"Practice the art of 'if you don't know it, pretend you do,' either with friends or by recording yourself. Launch yourself into a seminar about a topic that you know nothing about. The point is not to be correct; it's to practice speaking authoritatively. That way, when you speak about something you do know about, you'll realize you know more than you give yourself credit for and be comfortable with your authoritative tone."

—Holly Mandel, Founder of iMergence in Los Angeles

(4) Keep Talking

The main tenet of improv is "Yes, and...," which emphasizes taking what's introduced by others, accepting it and building upon it. Practicing this type of response can help someone who might feel self-conscious or doesn't know what to say next. Start with the question, "Why do you want this job?" and just start talking; do not stop, and don't judge in your head or think, "I need to start over." Practice going and going and thinking of more reasons, even if they sound crazy.

(5) Play Both Sides

With a partner, create a situation with a potential conflict, such as parents at a police station after their kids are picked up for underage drinking. One participant plays an uptight do-gooder; the other is laid-back and thinks laws are meant to be broken. Have a conversation where everyone takes turns expressing how they feel and responding. Once it feels complete, stop the scene and switch sides; then go through it again with the roles reversed.

"As improvisers, we want to be free from having to be 'correct'—instead, we want to be freed up and just do what our character would do. This breeds acceptance and teamwork in any situation because it forces you to 'defend' the other side."

—Rebecca Stuard, Creative Director of Improvolution in the New York City Area

---

Activity 5 | Reading Comprehension

A Model for Today's International Civil Servant[1]

Widely hailed, among his many accomplishments, as a great international civil servant, American and citizen of the world, Ralph Johnson Bunche's life story is one full of inspiration to all engaged in the pursuit of peace. As a year-long programme marking the 100th anniversary of his birth in Detroit, Michigan, commences to celebrate and build upon the legacy of this diplomat, scholar and internationalist, it is timely for the current staff of the United Nations, to which Ralph Bunche devoted 25 years of his spectacular career, to reflect on one of its most famous and optimistic alumni. A visible reminder of the esteem with which he is regarded within the United Nations and the City of New York is the Ralph Bunche Park located directly opposite the UN Secretariat building.

Many staff members who pass this memorial, however, may not be fully aware of his great legacy. Such reflection is timely because in 2003, when the Iraq crisis was added to the long list of conflicts with which the Organization has been confronted,

---

1   David K. J. Jeffrey, "A Model for Today's International Civil Servant—Perspective", Magazine Article, UN Chronicle.

the relevance and even future of the United Nations has again been scrutinized and questioned.

However, within the Organization, while the mood may have at times been troubled, the outlook was much more positive. An unofficial survey of stall members revealed that 80 per cent did not see the crisis as making the United Nations irrelevant. Further, 60 per cent felt optimistic about its future, while only 20 per cent were decidedly pessimistic. So, during these challenging times, what can be gleaned from Ralph Bunche's views on the meaning of being an international civil servant and how can they be pursued by his current successors?

Staff members today are required to make the same commitment to the United Nations, as did all their predecessors. As international civil servants, they are charged with translating into reality the ideals of the United Nations and its specialized agencies, as enshrined in *The UN Charter*. UN staff are part of the international civil service which "relies on the great traditions of public administration that have grown up in Member States: competence, integrity, impartiality, independence and discretion. But over and above this, international civil servants have a special calling: to serve the ideals of peace, of respect for fundamental rights, of economic and social progress, and of international cooperation".

It was this same calling to which Ralph Bunche responded in 1946 when he was asked by then UN Secretary-General Trygve Lie to leave his senior role at the United States State Department and join the fledgling United Nations, in charge of the Department of Trusteeship, where he would oversee post-war decolonization efforts.

"I am a professional optimist", Ralph Bunche told journalists at Nicosia International Airport at the conclusion of a visit in July 1966 to view the peacekeeping operations in Cyprus. "If I were not a professional optimist through 21 years in the United Nations service, mainly in conflict areas—Palestine, Congo, here and in Kashmir—I would be crazy. You have to be optimistic in this work or get out of it.... That is, optimistic in the sense of assuming that there is no problem—Cyprus or any other—which cannot be solved, and that, therefore, you have to keep at it persistently and you have to have confidence that it can be solved."

• Assignments

1. Read the article and summarize the general ideas of each paragraph.
2. Ralph Bunche was an academic, political scientist, activist, and diplomat who few likely know by now. While alive, he was celebrated for his peacekeeping efforts in the Middle

East, Africa and the Mediterranean, for helping form the United Nations, and for his work in the Civil Rights Movement. And, not only was he the first African American to be awarded the Nobel Peace Prize, he was the first person of color to receive the award. Please search online for more information on his personal stories, inspiring ideas, and simple wisdom that can be applied to our daily life.

Chapter 6
True Stories about the International Civil Service

As for Humanity: if you want to make a stand, help others make a stand, and if you want to reach your goal, help others reach their goal. Consider yourself and treat others accordingly: this is the method of Humanity.

—Confucius, a Chinese thinker of the Spring and Autumn Period [1]

---

1 Confucius (born 551, Qufu, state of Lu [now in Shandong province, China]—died 479 BCE, Lu) was China's most famous teacher, philosopher, and political theorist, whose ideas have profoundly influenced the civilizations of China and other East Asian countries. FYI, the original Chinese version of the quote is as follows: "夫仁者，己欲立而立人，己欲达而达人。能近取譬，可谓仁之方也已。"——《论语·雍也》

Overview

Learning Objectives

a. To continue with the topic of the last chapter by reading real-world work stories from individuals with having personal experiences in international civil service;

b. To have a basic knowledge of what it is like to work in a truly international organization, and how to pursue a career with the United Nations or any other international development agency;

c. To internalize new information, shape perception and vision, and foster the necessary knowledge, expertise, and experience required to work for an international organization.

Main Contents

There's no way to overestimate the importance of learning from others. When we're open to learning from the key stakeholders around, we receive several benefits that cannot be gained from learning alone: leveraging prosocial motivation, steering clear of common pitfalls, avoiding recreating the wheel, and identifying the right knowledge. To better process pertinent facts and information about international civil services, we list individual stories and in-depth interviews from several front-line civil servants around the world here. They work in large governmental international organizations, such as the United Nations and World Bank Group, as well as NGOs and volunteer programmes, including the Canadian Red Cross, the Peace Corps, and the United Nations Volunteer. They will share what it's really like working in a multicultural and multilingual environment; give a personal insight into the crucial role of international organizations in international affairs; and provide information and advice on internship opportunities and graduate careers that humanities and social sciences students could excel in.

Warm-up

100 years after the establishment of *The League of Nations*, the international civil service has thrived into an independent impartial body, which today provides a bond holding the multilateral system together. Through independent research outside of class, please share with your classmates your views on "multilateralism" as well as "international civil service". To give you some inspirations, here is a list of tasks you might choose to complete:

  a. What do you know about "multilateralism"? Name at least 5 living examples specific to multilateral cooperation.

  b. How does the international civil service promote and enhance the multilateralism?

  c. Throughout history, it is men who have made the biggest impact on the global integration. Try to illustrate with more examples, as you may think, of those who pushed the development of international convergence and benefited the maturity of the shared culture.

  d. Discuss briefly about the quote, "In an era of unprecedented opportunities and threats that transcend political borders, organizations and civil servants that serve the world as a whole are an indispensable source of support for necessary collective action"[1].

Section 1
Why to Choose a Job with an Inter-Governmental Organization?

Why work with an IGO? Experience daily challenges and achievements; constantly improve your qualifications; work in a multicultural environment with incredible people from around the globe; expand horizons by traveling to different places all over the world; make your curriculum stand out, with experience that is highly valued by the world of work...[2] What follows are insights from some of the professionals who have successfully made their way into these organizations.

1　Kemal Dervi, "The Case for International Civil Servants", *Brookings*, November 1st, 2019.

2　Source from the website of OpenIGO, "Home/About Us/Why work with an IGO", accessed on June 1st, 2022.

1.1   Reflections of Zhao Yao[1]

My career choice of working for International Organizations (IOs) stems from undergraduate studies in diplomacy and international studies. China Foreign Affairs University, my *alma mater*, is known as the "cradle of Chinese diplomats". Academic courses, lectures, extracurricular activities such as Model UN[2] were all geared toward foreign languages, current affairs and international relations, so I was exposed to global multilateralism early on, but I had no idea what I wanted to do as a career then. I didn't see myself join the Chinese foreign service as my parents desired or many of my classmates did. I was completely lost right after graduation.

Read This[3]

Since its founding in 1955, China Foreign Affairs University (CFAU) has been dedicated to grooming China's most promising young minds with global vision and great learning to work for China's foreign services and for world peace and prosperity. Directly affiliated with China's Ministry of Foreign Affairs and co-built by the Ministry of Education, CFAU offers a unique educational experience that prides itself in intellectual integrity and academic excellence.

Over the past 60 years, approximately 20,000 students have graduated. Amongst CFAU's alumni, more than 30 have been charged with official ministerial duties, about 500 have served as ambassadors to foreign countries, and more than 1,000 have served as counselors in Chinese embassies abroad, directors of governmental departments and agencies other than the Foreign Ministry, or professors and scholars with senior professional titles, making CFAU truly worthy of the name, "The Cradle of Chinese Diplomats".

---

1   Zhao Yao, Energy Professional at the World Bank Group, Washington D.C. (2014-). The essay was originally provided by Mr. Zhao at the invitation of the editor.

2   Model United Nations (MUN) simulations are popular exercises for those interested in learning more about how the UN operates. Hundreds of thousands of students worldwide participate every year in MUN at all educational levels—from primary school to university. Many of today's leaders in law, government, business and the arts participated in MUN as students. For more information, please check the homepage of the United Nations model UN Programme.

3   Source from the website of China Foreign Affairs University, "Home/About CFAU/Introduction".

Without knowing what the future would hold, I decided to follow my strong urge to see the world a bit more, so I embarked upon a backpacking trip on my own that eventually took me through Southeast Asia and across northern India. I fed baby tigers in Chiang Mai, watched sunrise on holy Ganges River, volunteered in Mother Teresa's Missionary Charity in Kolkata alongside religious workers from all over the world. Till this day, those few months on the road were still the happiest time of my life.

During the trip, I realized I wanted to work on a global stage, so I needed an international degree. I wrote my application for graduate study in the US and submitted it in an Indian village. I received an offer from Johns Hopkins University School of Advanced International Studies (SAIS)[1] in Washington D.C., one of the top programs in the field.

Washington D.C. is truly international, surrounded by world-class IOs such as the World Bank and the International Monetary Fund (IMF). While at SAIS, I focused on renewable energy and its application to deliver modern electricity service in rural areas. This line of work took me back to India and worked on small solar energy projects in Bihar, the poorest state in India. I wanted to continue working on clean energy deployment after receiving my master's degree. My professor, also a mentor, referred me to International Renewable Energy Agency (IRENA) in Abu Dhabi. That's how I officially started my career in IOs on a truly international stage.

This journey did involve some planning but most times I went where opportunities took me. I do have to admit that there is vanity in this career choice. The aura around an international diplomat is alluring. The layperson reputation of the UN or the World Bank is convenient when asked "What do you do", not to mention the benefits, travel opportunities and comfortable lifestyle.

I am often asked "How can I find a job in the IOs". My experience is that IOs care more about referrals and recommendations from current staff than other professions

---

1　The Johns Hopkins University's Paul H. Nitze School of Advanced International Studies (Johns Hopkins SAIS) is a premier graduate school devoted to the study of international relations. A division of the Johns Hopkins University since 1950, Johns Hopkins SAIS is a truly global institution with a permanent physical presence on three continents: North America, Europe and Asia, in Washington, D.C., Bologna, Italy, and Nanjing, China. Source from the website of Johns Hopkins University, "Home/Nitze School of Advanced International Studies/Overview", accessed on May 26th, 2021.

such as banking or consulting. Networking to know the right people is important for landing a position in IOs. Alumni are useful resources to put your feet at the door. That said, there are also formalized online recruiting programs such as the Junior Professional Association (JPA) and Young Professional Program (YPP) at the UN, the World Bank and most other IOs.

Now I have been working for IOs for seven years (as of writing this in 2019), I find the experience a double-edged sword. While it is truly a great experience working on impactful issues such as climate change and poverty alleviation with professionals from all over the world, the bureaucracy at most IOs is frustrating. One project can take years to come to fruition. Many reports are nothing more than reinventing the wheel. Compared to private sector, IOs often are not at the frontier in terms of knowledge and thought leadership. I would not recommend students fresh out of school to join IOs as the learning curve is not as great as private sector. At the beginning of one's career, it is most important to accumulate sector expertise, whether it's energy, public health or finance, which is always the most appreciated skills in IOs, replete with generalists and diplomats.

1.2   Reflections of Liu Yi[1]

"The best way to not feel hopeless is to get up and do something".

This short comment from Barack Obama sprang to my mind on the second day of Model United Nations (MUN) when the Human Rights Council witnessed a moment of silence and I was disappointed not to hear voices from developing countries. I made the decision to go above and beyond my chairing responsibilities and encourage delegates from developing countries to express their concerns. It ended up happening that, as soon as one of these delegates aired their concerns, the other countries with comparable stances followed suit and voiced their concerns as well. The ripple effect worked.

---

1   At the moment, Liu Yi works as a Monitoring and Evaluation Specialist with the United Nations Capital Development Fund (UNCDF) in Rwanda. Before joining the UNCDF, she spent three years as a research assistant for a think tank which is specialized in international relations. She built up development experience by working for an international NGO in Belgium, and got knowledge of market system development (MSD) while employed by a management consulting fi rm in Shanghai. Yi holds three master's degrees in International Relations (Tongji University, China), Public Policy (Vrije Universiteit Brussel, Belgium) and International Law (University for Peace, Costa Rica).

Consequently, the pursuits of developing countries were included in the final draft UN resolution, which contrasted sharply with agendas that developed countries were pushing.

Where else can developing countries express their voices to the international community, if the UN, the largest multilateral forum in the world, is unable to do so? My interest in the unheard voices of technology development from Global South countries and how the UN may bridge that gap was sparked by my involvement in the Model UN, which inspired me to work for one of the UN's development agencies in an African least developed country.

How does it feel to work for an UN agency?

To generalize, I'd use the terms: "fulfilling", "result-oriented", and "dignity".

First, our work at the UN's development department requires that we frequently visit the communities of marginalized people, analyze the problems that prevent projects from being implemented, and create workable solutions in order to better assist those who are in dire need of a means of subsistence. The field trips, analytical works, market scoping and donor prospecting, workshops and conferences, all give us the opportunity to engage with real people, real problems, and they also equip us with transferable skills that will enable us to adapt to a variety of work environments;

Second, the majority of work done at the UN's country office involves implementing specific projects rather than developing long-term strategies. I use a strict result-oriented approach in my daily work to deliver projects on time and within budget, which serves as a reminder that a career in international development is not a charity job, but requires professionalism in development practices;

Third, the working culture of the UN encourages staff to have a work-life balance so they have time and space to reflect and think outside the box. The UN agencies also have a custom of organizing retreat trips for executives and workers to exchange views on work openly in a relaxing environment. It is fair to say that the UN agencies ensure their employees work with dignity rather than cramming their workdays full-speed ahead with no time for breaks or internal needs.

What are the key competencies for international civil servants or development practitioners?

According to my practical experience, having an edge in problem-solving, communication and coordination skills is necessary to be qualified for the employment at the UN's country office. Addressing practical problems in underdeveloped communities makes up a significant portion of development work at the country level, necessitating the development of individuals with strong problem-solving skills. Since development projects often involve many different stakeholders, such as partner institutions, donor institutions, governmental agencies, civil societies and so on, the candidates must also possess good communication and coordination abilities to support the delivery of projects.

This is my personal account and some useful insights about my time working for the UN. The textbook will give you more details on international organizations in this manner—allowing you to develop a comprehensive understanding of them from all angles, such as geopolitics, institutions, career planning, and so forth.

"What destroys a man more quickly than to work, think and feel without inner necessity", as Nietzsche once put it. There are many ways to comprehend this world, but in my view, understanding it via the lens of the international political economy makes the greatest sense. Because we live in a new era with an open future of world order, our generation has the privilege of rising up and taking action in answer to the national call for "community with a shared future for mankind" (*renlei mingyun gongtongti*).

1.3　Reflections of Munyaradzi Chenje[1]

Working for the UN is like being at the university of life—every day is a learning experience—learning-by-doing, new concepts, and adapting to new situations, and interests. Working for the UN is not just a job—it's service.

I have learnt from brilliant scientists and professionals. I have also acquired invaluable knowledge from many at the community and grassroots levels. The unbridled enthusiasm of many interns with whom I have worked has been rewarding.

1　In 2019, Munyaradzi Chenje was appointed the Regional Director for the UN Development Coordination Office (DCO) Regional Office for Africa based in Addis Ababa, Ethiopia. This passage was written just before his retirement in July 2021. Source: Munyaradzi Chenje, "Reflections on My Career with the UN", *Africa Renewal*, July 30th, 2021.

(1) Dull Moments Are Few and Far-Between

Being paid to do what I enjoy—making a difference—is priceless. Supporting UN member states in their efforts for collective action to global challenges with massive national impacts is rewarding. Negotiations may be long, arduous, fractious, and frustrating, but it was well worth it to be in the room and be witness to historic and landmark decisions such as the "Future We Want" and the "2030 Agenda".

Frustrations of divergent views and special interests are overshadowed when the outcomes—*The 2030 Agenda, Paris Climate Change Agreement*, and many others—redefine how we should contribute to changing the trajectory of the world in which we all live.

Working for the UN is a privilege, and my greatest honour was being appointed by the Secretary-General as the founding Africa Regional Director of the UN Development Coordination Office (UNDCO). It's an honour that I share with just but a few because it's not every day or every year that the UN establishes a new office!

The work of the UN sustainable development system is to provide the whole-of-UN-system action in engaging with the whole-of-Government and with partners and stakeholders in implementing *The 2030 Agenda* and *The Sustainable Development Goals (SDGs)*[1]; and also, the African Union vision—*Agenda 2063*. The commitment at all levels is to leave no one behind in such transformation, taking integrated action on social, economic, and environmental issues and opportunities.

My team's work involved visiting RCs and UNCTs across Africa to better understand the environment in which they work, the support they need to effectively respond to the expectations of governments and their people. However, the COVID-19 pandemic upended our business model over the past year-and-half, forcing us to conduct most of our engagement on online platforms such as Teams and Zoom.

Despite the challenging impacts of COVID-19 on lives and livelihoods; and how we work at regional level, RCs and UNCTs across Africa have made tremendous progress

---

1   Adopted unanimously in 2015 by all UN Member States, the 2030 Agenda for Sustainable Development (2030 Agenda) with its 17 Sustainable Development Goals (SDGs), 169 targets, and 231 unique indicators shapes the direction of global and national development policies, and offers new entry points and opportunities for bridging the divide between human rights and development. It serves as the overall framework to guide global and national development action.

in translating UN resolutions; and the Secretary-General's vision of a 21st Century UN sustainable development system that is "focused more on people and less on processes, more on results for the most poor and excluded, and less on bureaucracy, more on integrated support to *The 2030 Agenda* and less on 'business-as-usual.'"

I was privileged to have been in such outstanding company, not only in the context of DCO, but all members of the UN family across the world who—individually and collectively—are responding to making a difference at country, regional and international levels.

(2) Focusing on Integration

As I reflect on my two decades in UN service, I realize that the main thread of my work has been on integration—tackling the interlinkages of social, economic, and environmental issues central to human well-being today and across generations.

In the 18 years that I was with the UN Environment Programme, I coordinated both regional and global environmental assessment and reporting work; supported the General Assembly's Second Committee consultations on sustainable development issues; and directed its regional presence work, supporting the integrated implementation of *The 2030 Agenda* and *SDGs* through its regional offices.

Working on four global and about 10 regional environmental assessments, I was exposed to diverse views and interests. I got to understand and acknowledge that science and policy are interdependent; and that science can be negotiated when it comes to policy decisions and action. Climate change and policy making are a good example.

Consensus evolves, and can be frustratingly glacial until competing interests are accommodated or not at all. For example, it took almost three decades for sustainable development to be universally embraced. With its roots in environmental discourse, sustainable development was often perceived as an environmental agenda to limit economic development. The world has since accepted that integrating the three dimensions of sustainable development—social, economic and environmental—is central to transformation, leaving no one behind.

(3) Lesson from the Field

Hard data and information tell a story, but cannot beat a human story. And people like stories to which they can relate.

In January 2020, for example, I visited the community in Fabidji in Niger, which is involved in strengthening social cohesion among farmers and herders in the Dosso and Maradi regions. The women, participating in this Peacebuilding Fund-supported project being implemented by UN Women and FAO, were excited to talk about their experience and how they were resolving tensions and conflicts.

The project helped train women as conflict mediators; and created 346 Dimitra clubs (men and women dialogue groups), providing for the effective participation of women, including Fulani women, in village assemblies (such participation is not culturally tolerated). The role of 600 women mediators in conflict prevention and management, and in land commissions is now increasingly accepted. Women's inheritance rights are also increasingly recognized in communities.

During the January 2020 field visit, some of the women conflict mediators excitedly spoke to us about their success, the positive impacts among communities, and the need for ongoing UN support. Their focus was on successful delivery and impact on their lives. They never spoke about quality planning and project documents. These are internal workings of the UN system, and of no interest in their lives.

I believe that their expectation is for the UN to deliver and to get them to their destination—a better life.

(4) Reflections on the Work Ahead

Beyond the health and socio-economic responses to the impacts of the COVID-19 pandemic on lives and livelihoods, I believe that it's important not to lose the pandemic's lessons—that we are in one world; that we are all in this together; and that neighbour now not only means next door and shared national boundaries, but also manifests across regions.

Sustainable development is today's human story. It's no less compelling than emergencies and disasters whose images always convey urgency and galvanize action.

I believe that a compelling human story about sustainable development should always convey urgency and galvanize action, including massive financing, which is currently limited.

Telling that compelling story is one of the major challenges that we face in our collective efforts to deliver on *The 2030 Agenda* and *SDGs*.

The SDGs have to be delivered daily in order to achieve transformation.

People want their daily bread today—not tomorrow, not next year, and certainly not in 2030 or 2063!

The 2030 Agenda and *SDGs* are best before 2030.

Yes, planning is critical for success; and quality plans and frameworks are just as important. I believe, howesver, that quality documents do not change people's lives—action does.

While financing sustainable development is a huge challenge; and delivery on the ground and transforming lives, leaving no one behind seem onerous, I believe that challenges galvanize action, and that the RCs and UNCTs in Africa and across the world are up to the challenge.

Section 2

What Is It Like to Work for a Non-Governmental Organization?

Even if working for a non-profit organization could be seen as a really challenging thing to engage in, it is, however, one of the most satisfying jobs for anyone that wants to affect society and grow. If you are contemplating whether or not to work for a non-profit organization, then continue reading to find out what a non-profit organization is all about and what it is really like from people who've actually worked there.

2.1　Reflections of Bi Fei[1]

Working for a non-profit is one of the choices you could have to enter the public sector.

There are so many non-profits dedicating to fixing the problems that the big international organizations and governments are focusing on: environment, clean energy, poverty eradication, gender equality, civic education, etc. If you are interested in these areas and aiming to build your career path in the public sector, working for a non-profit might be a good starting point.

1　Bi Fei, former Project Director of Asia-Pacific Youth Foundation for Communication and Development, Beijing(2017-2018). The essay was originally provided by Miss. Bi at the invitation of the editor.

I have spent the last 10 months (as of writing this in 2019) working at Asia-Pacific Youth Foundation for Communication and Development as Project Director. The foundation conducts projects along with the UN, APEC and other private organizations to promote capacity building and youth internationalization. Basically, my work was about people, mostly young people. So here, based on my observation and personal experiences, I would like to share some of my thoughts with people who would like to take their first step working in a non-profit to enter the public sector.

First of all, non-profits are NOT profit-driven. The fund, including all the sponsorship and project fees can't be capitalized. In this case, a person working for a non-profit normally can't expect a high salary and a lavish package that a capitalist company would offer. So, when it comes to choosing to work for a non-profit, you have to really think about whether this job is in align with your value and needs. But for some people, the amount of pleasure they feel by exerting a direct impact on other people's lives and living environment could never be bought by money.

Secondly, most non-profits are kept small-scale. Due to the limited budget, most non-profits would only maintain a small but effective team to run their daily business. That means, if you work for a non-profit, your work scope could be quite wide. For example, you may need to be responsible for:

 a. writing every e-mail between your end and your partner's end;

 b. communicating with your partners/participants and reporting updates to the superior on a regular basis;

 c. drafting project plans, project proposals and contracts;

 d. making PPTs and Excel sheets;

 e. translating documents;

 f. writing publicity posts;

 g. making cold calls;

 h. meeting and pitching to perspective partners;

 i. giving public speeches;

 j. arranging business trips;

 k. dealing with reimbursement...

Other than that, you may also need to do some extra work to help other people's projects if they are short-handed. In a word, you need to be versatile and responsive to every change and need from the work. Honestly, you may overwork sometimes. But you will grow and learn rapidly in a way that you could not do when you go to work for a big organization as a freshman. You normally don't need to stay at an entry-level position for one or two years till you get promoted to take charge of something big. Instead, by dealing with various issues and working intensely you could be able to take charge of major projects, have the autonomy to make big decisions, represent your organization on important occasions and then find out more possibilities in a short period of time.

Thirdly, it would be a lot easier to make yourself heard. As aforementioned, because most of the non-profits are relatively small, so there is no too complex a hierarchy of authority. You probably could attend every internal meeting, speak out your own thoughts, contribute your innovative ideas and add your own values to the decision-making in a more profound way.

Now, if you find working for a non-profit an attractive and viable way to help you break into the public sector, you may also want to know what kind of skills and qualifications you need to have when you apply for a position in a non-profit.

I have interviewed hundreds of students who are applying for our capacity building programs, dozens of applicants looking for an internship or a full-time job in our organization. By reading their resumes, talking to them through interviews and working with some of them, I personally think that these are the BASIC things you should pay attention to and get prepared for:

   a. *English is a MUST, and Chinese IS A MUST TOO!* Yes, English proficiency is the most common job requirement from international organizations, but it doesn't mean that Chinese becomes less important than English. Actually, an increasing number of well-established non-profits are setting up their East-Asia offices in China to expand their business in Asia. Using Chinese globally as a working language is a future tendency. Keep honing your Chinese skill is necessary even if it's your native language.

   b. *Writing skill is so important that it outweighs speaking skill sometimes.* Writing is mostly the way that you first reach out to people at work and through which the people get the first impression on you/your organization. It is very important to put your thoughts into tidy and logical writing. Try to think about how you would you feel if you read an e-mail that has no punctuation marks, paragraphs and is hard for people to understand. In some worse cases, an e-mail that contains ambiguous meaning forwarded to other relevant people could cause a disaster. Other than that, excellent writing skill is most needed when it comes to drafting project proposals, contracts, publicity materials…these are the things that account for most of your work, and you definitely don't want to screw it!

    c. *Public speaking makes you stand out.* Speaking in front of a large group of people is challenging, but if you do it well, it would be a great opportunity for you to stand out in a very short amount of time. Imagine what would you do if you only had 5 minutes to let everybody know you on a special occasion? Or if you need to represent your organization to introduce your project and compete for a chance? That is when you need public speaking.

Once you have good writing and public speaking skills, I think you probably are eligible for an internship or entry-level position. When starting the application, you may need to know:

    a. Prepare your resume based on the job description. Employers want to know immediately whether you are an eligible candidate through your resume. So please list ONLY relevant skills and experiences on your resume and try to keep it no longer than two pages.

    b. Do some research on the organization before interview. Organizations want to know how much you know about the organization and what it does, it shows how much you are well-prepared and whether you really want to work for them.

    c. Try to convince the employer you can do what they need instead of saying "I want to learn…". It is understandable that you need a transition to get familiar with your work, employers know it too. Some of them would also offer training sessions to help you grow. The point is, you have to make them believe that you are worthy of the opportunity to grow. If you keep emphasizing on the learning part instead of the working part, employers might feel that they need to spend too much time and resources on teaching you new things and to them it will be a burden. After all, workplace isn't school, you can't expect to get paid to take classes.

d. Don't be afraid to ask questions and negotiate for good terms in your job interview. When an interview comes close to the end, normally the employer would ask "Is there any questions you want to ask?" At this time, you should seize the opportunity to figure out all the things you want to know once you are hired. (That's where the importance of research work shows.) For example, the salary, working hours, promotion mechanism, annual/ sick leave … If you feel there's room for negotiation, go for it! You are the one who has the absolute agency to look out for your interests.

Working for a non-profit is challenging. But at the same time, it's awarding. If you want to know what it's like to work in the public sector and are trying to accumulate experience to get to the next-level, again, working for a non-profit might be something worth trying.

2.2　Reflections Xu Zhengxue[1]

My aspiration to developmental practice was seeded in 2016. After earning my master's degree in Environmental Engineering, I applied for a one-year traineeship at the International Hydro-logical Programme (IHP), which is co-administered by UNESCO and China government.

As something you can imagine, I yearned to put my academic background to use on international development projects while working out of the Montevideo Office in Uruguay. Nevertheless, my way of thinking about developmental issues has been permanently altered by my year there, which implanted questions in my head. *What are the relationships among individual, community and the planet? How might we attain well-being*? It also taught me that, in order to understand the world and its needs, I needed to return to my normal life: to interact with people around me, to confront

---

1　Xu Zhengxue was a graduate student at the United Nations University for Peace in Costa Rica, specializing in responsible management and sustainable economic development. She holds master's and bachelor's degrees in Environmental Engineering from Jilin University and was among the first batch of Chinese facilitators for UNDP's 2020 Movers Project. Since 2018, Xu has been dedicated to promoting cultural preservation and community development in Huanggang Dong Village, Guizhou Province. Her initiatives include founding the folk organization Yueye Academy and the Yueye Dong Orchestra. Throughout her career, Xu has held significant roles at UNESCO, the Regional Office of Latin America and the Caribbean, the Environment Unit of the Delegation of European Union in Beijing, and the Research Institute for Ecological Civilization at the Chinese Academy of Social Sciences.

difficulties, and to learn about social needs.

After returning from Uruguay, I decided to devote myself to an SDGs pilot project in a reserve village for ethnic minorities. I paid a personal visit to the village, before formally beginning my daily life construction there. When I first arrived, I was drawn to the village's rich ethnic cultures. There were rows of ethnic houses held up by wooden pillars. One of them occasionally released cooking smoke. Women dressed in traditional attire swept the courtyard in front of the house, while the men worked in groups. Some were carrying lumber while others were repairing the house. On the ground, children were singing and having a good time.

The picture was delicate, like a peaceful fantasy land. I had a strong urge to visit this place right away in order to contribute to the preservation and promotion of their fascinating yet ancient cultural heritage. I went back to the village a month later, when UNESCO announced that it had begun accepting 2018's applications for Asia-Pacific Awards for Cultural Heritage Conservation. I wanted to assist with the award application by collecting evidence of its cultural heritage. That was all I was capable of doing, and it also marked the beginning of my very first self-funded pilot project.

But as I became more accustomed to local life, I gradually found some of the struggles that the villagers had to endure despite their idyllic lifestyle and rich culture. Due to its isolation from modern, outside worlds, the village was in severe shortage of medical service and educational resources. Folk tales and music are just two examples of the many local cultural practices that can only be inherited by word of mouth.

Moreover, I actually saw conflicts arise between cultural reservations and economic needs. On the one hand, the local environment was being threatened by some village practices pursued for economic gain. On the other hand, because the village also enjoys a Globally Important Agricultural Heritage System, many young villagers chose to leave this land for better job opportunities in cities rather than relying on seasonal labor on terrace to maintain the system. As a result, the village was facing a loss of its cultural inheritors, a problem with waste treatment, and an increasing number of leftover children.

What can be done? This was the first and foremost question that kept popping up in my head. I tried to find an answer.

I established an Academy in the village and invited local folk musicians and ethnic instrument players to teach younger generation traditional music—as my first non-profit educational program. Additionally, I put together a 33-person orchestra for public performance and to promote the legacy of traditional music. Over 3 years, the program had been running well. With a work force of 6 people, we have successfully established courses more than folk music. By adding environmental science, historic research and sex education, we are able to introduce part of Academy's course catalog into the local primary school and strengthen course offerings there. More importantly, through the platform of Academy, we mobilized external resources for value co-creation within sustainable community building in village for common good.

I was overjoyed that this invest-in-myself project had given me a fresh perspective on village development. I was also thrilled to have seen what happened in a reserve village in the context of a-towering-change modern world. Thanks to my expanded practice, I have come to the profound realization that I need to devise strategies for substantiating meaningful changes in a systemic, sustainable and scalable manner. The new drive brought me here today, where I can see clearly how big changes can actually be imbedded in the trifles in one's life. If you are standing on the earth, the world is not far.

It has been over 6 years since I took my first step into International Organizations. It is a transformational choice. I am more assured than I was when I first started listening to my inner voice.

International Organization is not only global version of an organization. It would be a journey you deserve, if you are curious about how inclusive and self-assured you will appear, if you want to gain a participatory perspective on human civilization, or if you simply feel a drive in your depth.

2.3 Interviews with Tom Bamforth[1]

Tom Bamforth was in Pakistan on an archaeological tour when he first started

---

1 Tom Bamforth is an author and aid worker. He has worked Pakistan, Sudan, Philippines and the Pacific in emergency relief and longer-term disaster risk education programs. His writing has appeared in *Granta, Griffith Review and The Age*. He is the author of *Deep Field: Dispatches from the Frontlines of Aid Relief*. This interview below is excerpted from "Reflections of a Humanitarian Aid Worker: An Interview with om Bamforth", Devpolicy Blog, July 30th, 2014.

to work in natural disaster and conflict areas. From Pakistan he went to Darfur, then Mindanao and the Pacific Islands. His book of reflections on humanitarian work, *Deep Field*, was published in 2014.[1] Tom now works as Program Coordinator for the Pacific Disaster Management Partnership at the Australian Red Cross. Development Policy Centre Visiting Fellow, Margaret Callan, met Tom at his Melbourne office to discuss some of the issues raised in the book.

Margaret: *Let's start with your experience of the response to the Pakistan earthquake.[2] I was struck by your description of the fairly chaotic situation when you arrived, then a period of transition after which "it all came together". How did that happen?*

Tom: When I arrived, it was about 3 weeks after the earthquake had hit. I was with IOM,[3] the organization designated to take on a shelter cluster coordination role. A number of NGOs had been there for a few weeks, and they felt very strongly that coordination was needed. Many were genuinely angry that the UN coordination mechanism hadn't been there right at the beginning. So, there was an uphill battle to gain credibility, legitimacy, and respect.

There were about 60 INGOs in a small town in the Northwest Frontier Province (now known as Khyber Pakhtunkhwa or KPK). At the start of the response, they had probably had some ad hoc meetings but then they just got on with providing an initial response. They were very concerned about the coming Himalayan winter—many people had lost their houses—and they feared an ongoing humanitarian emergency if steps weren't taken quickly to start the recovery phase.

1　"Deep Field" is a UN term for humanitarian operations that take place in extremis—amid the destruction caused by war and natural disaster. In *Deep Field: Dispatches from the Frontlines of Aid Relief*, Australian aid worker Tom Bamforth takes you with him as he responds to the challenges of delivering humanitarian aid under extreme circumstances travelling to some of the most dangerous and difficult regions of the world. "It reads as if Don Delillo had been sent to Darfur," John Freeman commented.

2　Tom Bamforth experienced the 2005 Pakistan earthquake first hand while on an archaeological tour and has subsequently worked in natural disaster and conflict areas in Pakistan's North West Frontier Province and Kashmir, Sudan's Dafur states, the Philippines' Mindanao region and across the Pacific Islands.

3　Established in 1951, IOM is the leading Inter-Governmental Organization in the field of migration and works closely with governmental, inter-governmental and non-governmental partners. IOM works to help ensure the orderly and humane management of migration to promote international cooperation on migration issues, and to provide humanitarian assistance to migrants in need, including refugees and internally displaced people. Source from the website of IOM, "Home/Who We Are", accessed on June 10th, 2022.

We were able to bring everyone together once we established a presence, and we brought people in from Islamabad, so we looked more like a sizable team. That was a turning point. There was a real appetite for coordination, sharing assessments and resources, developing a multi-agency response strategy, advocating for appropriate technical shelter standards, and linking with other areas of the response such as camp management, protection, education, water and sanitation, and donors.

Margaret: *Ideally it is the local authorities who should coordinate the response after a disaster. Why didn't that happen in Pakistan?*

Tom: Firstly, the local authorities have been affected by the earthquake very significantly and there was a lot of damage to civilian infrastructure. Moreover, Pakistan had a military government, and the capacity of the local government was very low, certainly much lower than the capacity of the military to respond. But this raised political questions for the humanitarian response.

Margaret: *That brings me to my next question. In such a situation, how do humanitarian organizations develop a shared understanding of the local context, in this case: political, military, and civilian?*

Tom: In the Pakistan context, long-term development agencies have a sophisticated understanding of the context. Also, institutions like the International Crisis Group[1] did a lot of advocacies to build understanding about the possible long-term political consequences of humanitarian work there.

However, after the earthquake struck, there was an influx of people from pretty much every UN agency and NGO. A lot of these people bring sectoral and technical expertise, for example in water supply, health, shelter and community mobilization, and they know how the humanitarian system works. But many knew little about the local context and politics, so they risked playing into the political objectives of the military government through working with its representatives and not local civilian counterparts.

A very important issue in Pakistan was the targeting of beneficiaries and the extent to which the military directed this targeting. This was very complex because

---

1   The International Crisis Group is an independent organization working to prevent wars and shape policies that will build a more peaceful world. In this more polarized, fragmented and dangerous world, Crisis Group sounds the alarm to prevent deadly conflict. Sources from the website of International Crisis Group, "Home/Who We Are/ Preventing War. Shaping Peace.", accessed on June 10th, 2022.

hurdle.[1] Here are some real tips for seeking out internship and volunteering experience in this sector.

3.1   *Reflections of Christopher Crachiola*[2]

So, you are looking for an internship.

What kind of internship are you looking for? Why are you seeking this kind of internship? What skills do you want to gain from the experience? These may be questions that you are asking yourself, and this is a great first step.

In fact, I will argue that this personal inquiry is what makes internships so important. Sure, internships provide concrete experience that cannot be learned through any textbook or how-to book at a store. But even more practical may be what we can learn about ourselves through self-reflection.

First and foremost, there is no perfect internship. Getting an internship at a big, well-known international organization or company is not the sole path to getting quality experience. In fact, internships that are not in your field of expertise, or even those in a field you know nothing about, may be the most ideal.

My first time coming to China was actually through an internship, and the focus was something I knew nothing about: batteries. On the fourteenth floor in a converted residential apartment in Beijing, modified with cubicle dividers and tables, I joined ten other diligent public servants reviewing the latest in international policy efforts related to "energy storage". It was not a big-name international organization, it was not glamorous, and it most certainly did not have me brushing shoulders with UN delegates or global CEO's. But this was not what I was looking for. Rather, I wanted to take my studies in Public Policy and see it in action, particularly before I was to continue my studies as a graduate student. By doing an internship with this research team, I was able to be a part of a group tapping into some big questions—namely, how do we promote reliable energy storage in our society?

So, like me, you may ask what "energy storage" even means? At first, I didn't

---

1   Emma Smith, "How to Find and Leverage Volunteer and Internship Opportunities", *Devex*, March 14th, 2019.

2   Christopher Crachiola, US Peace Corps Volunteer Instructor at Sichuan International Studies University, Chongqing (2017-2019). The essay was originally provided by Mr. Crachiola at the invitation of the editor.

even know myself! Green energy is certainly attractive in China and all over the world. Images of wind turbines and solar panels entice us with visions of a cleaner, more efficient energy future. But what happens when it is overcast and there is no light, what happens when there is no wind? How can these promising renewable energy sources provide us with a consistent and reliable supply of energy? This was where batteries come in—finding novel ways to promote research and development of storage capacity to harness renewable energy for moments when we need it. Beyond just technology, however, there were many other complex factors in the industry. For example, assessing subsidies or incentives for these budding industries, or finding novel ways to offset the prohibitive costs of integrating new technologies into a competitive market. These were the issues I was able to closely analyze during my internship period.

The main point here is not that I learned a lot about batteries. Rather, it was less about what I was learning, and more about how I was learning. This was where my experiences became more practical and offered perspectives far beyond the classroom. First, I learned a lot about a topic I knew little about in a very short amount of time. I believe that this is a very important experience for anyone to have in an internship. Regardless of what you study, or what you think you may want to pursue in the future as a career, it is valuable to be in a situation to learn about something you know very little about. I probably left work each day with more questions than answers, and this was healthy. In fact, this kind of learning was very beneficial to me later as a graduate student where courses were focused more on complex challenges and no clear answers. I was taking notice of the connection of very big topics, including economics, policy, and technology and how the pieces fit together.

Naturally, the lessons were not all from learning new content about a new industry. I was in a new city, in a foreign country, working with people of various ages. Perhaps more than any other benefit of an internship is having experience of working in teams with different people. The obvious benefits include encountering new and diverse outlooks and perspectives, but perhaps more importantly you will be put in situations that will make you step back and reflect upon yourself.

I am a strong proponent of self-reflection and keeping journals. Reflecting on one's experience is a chance to ask many questions that can make us a more efficient worker in the next step in our lives. For example, what skills do I contribute to the team? What do I do when I have a question or idea, and how do I take initiative? How do I know that I am encountering stress, and how do I deal with it? An internship will likely provide many new challenges and learning opportunities that can prompt such self-reflections.

What kind of challenges, you may ask? Frankly, an internship will not be perfect. The work may be tedious. Sometimes it may be boring. You may find that you feel public sector work is inefficient, or on the other end, private sector work does not match with your core values. You may find that the working style is different than you are used to, or that teams are managed in a way that puts you out of your comfort zone. Any of these situations are plausible, and reflecting on what makes you feel this way, and how you deal with these situations may be more insightful than any other benefit of an internship. You may need to have a few jobs you do not like to find out what job path you will find fulfilling. Similarly, you need to be in uncomfortable situations that push your boundaries to know what the best working style and environment is for you. In this capacity, internships are the perfect trial periods to figure this out.

This leads to one key reason why self-reflection is so useful—we learn about ourselves. What we like, what we don't like. What we are skilled at, and where we can improve. The answers you begin to uncover from an internship experience can be very useful as you embark on further education or employment.

We all will inevitably need to put our experiences into the form of a resume or job interview response. By reflecting on our experiences and putting them down on paper, we are already many steps ahead at one of the greatest challenges of entering the job market: how to describe our experiences. For example, I do not think that the key skill that I learned at my internship in China was that I knew more about massive batteries. Rather, I learned about differences in Chinese, European, and American policies related to energy. Even more importantly, I proved that I can learn about unfamiliar industries in a short time. I learned conversational language skills rapidly in a language I never previously studied. I worked independently and in teams, sometimes with people of different generations, or in bilingual meetings. All of these are perhaps more important skills that helped me in the next steps of my academic career or entering the job market.

The value of self-reflection is that you do not need to land an internship at a glossy well-known organization to develop these skills. You can go to a country you have never thought of much before. You can try to do work in an industry that you may not know much about. You do not even need to go abroad, as sometimes the most eye-opening life experiences can be in communities in small towns or nearby cities that we otherwise have not paid attention to before.

The bottom-line is that when it comes to internship experience, it is far more valuable to demonstrate what you personally gained through self-reflection. As you continue on to further education or an entry-level job, it will be your personal values of teamwork and work ethic as well as your demonstrated inquisitiveness and willingness to learn in challenging situations that will be some of the most important factors in your success. And they will also make your experiences more enriching as well.

So, as you continue your search for internships, I encourage you to start self-reflecting right away and also be open to opportunities you may not have considered before. The lessons you learn through unfamiliar and challenging situations may turn out to be the most valuable.

3.2　Reflections of Wang Ling[1]

Why Do You Want to Apply for This Internship?

On my very first day as an intern at the United Nations Headquarters, I was confronted with the question during my introduction to the department: "*Why do you want this internship?*" Sounds simple, right? But trust me, it's far more than just an icebreaker—it's the kind of question that demands deep reflection. If you're planning to apply for an internship at an international organization, you should ponder this questions yourself. Why? Because knowing your "why" will guide you in making better decisions, and those decisions will significantly shape your subsequent experience.

A Universe of Opportunities

The world offers a plethora of international organizations that provide internship opportunities specifically tailored to university students. These programs span a wide

---

1　Wang Ling (Elly), marketing professional at a renowned multinational company, previously interned at the United Nations Headquarter in New York City. This essay was provided by the author in response to an invitation from the editor.

array of fields, including international relations, environmental protection, public health, technological innovation, and human rights, to name just a few. Prominent organizations such as UNESCO, the World Bank, the International Red Cross (ICRC), and the World Wildlife Fund (WWF) are just a few examples.

If you're deeply passionate about a particular field or organization, take the time to explore their internship programs, understand their requirements, and strategically prepare your application. For instance, if you're a physics student, CERN (the European Organization for Nuclear Research) might be an ideal fit. If you're more broadly curious about how international organizations function, you might opt for a comprehensive experience within the UN management sector.

The first step? Clarify your purpose. Once you're clear on why you want this internship, select an organization that aligns with your goals. Then, gather necessary information, meet the application requirements, and plan your approach meticulously.

The Big Question: "What If I'm Not Good Enough?"

A frequent worry among students is, "What if I don't have enough experience? What if the competition is too fierce? Or what if I'm not good enough?" These concerns often prevent many from even starting their applications. Here's my advice: Don't be afraid—if you truly want it, go for it. The worst that can happen is rejection, and that costs you nothing. But if you don't try, you lose your chance completely.

Many students erect mental barriers, believing that international organizations are too exclusive or that they lack the necessary qualifications. Instead of dwelling on what might go wrong, revisit the fundamental question: "Why do you want this opportunity? Do you genuinely want to seize it?" If your answer is an emphatic "yes", then nothing else should deter you.

Naturally, your qualifications must align with the program's basic requirements. For example, if a program explicitly requires a master's degree, it's not advisable to apply as an undergraduate. However, if you meet the criteria, don't hesitate to take the leap. Prepare thoroughly, give it your best shot, and don't disqualify yourself before anyone else does. Even if your application doesn't ultimately succeed, the preparation process itself will undoubtedly sharpen your skills and boost your confidence for future opportunities.

Dream Job or Desk Job? When You Are on Aboard of Interning at International Organizations

Congratulations! Securing an internship at an international organization is an incredible achievement. However, I'd like to sprinkle a touch of realism here: while the prestige and excitement are undoubtedly alluring, keep in mind that work is still work, regardless of the setting.

Even at prestigious international organizations, a significant portion of your day might involve administrative tasks—think paperwork, creating PowerPoint presentations, and drafting internal reports. You might also encounter similar workplace challenges, such as bureaucratic inefficiencies or slow processes. For example, when I started my UN internship, I applied for my official email account on day one, but it was approved until a month later.

Managing your expectations is the key. If your experience doesn't match your initial vision, it is important to communicate openly with your mentor or colleagues. Adjusting your mindset and understanding the practical aspects of the workplace will help you navigate any disillusionment and maximize the value of your internship.

Why Interning at an International Organization Is Worth It

Despite the challenges, I wholeheartedly encourage students to pursue internships at international organizations. These institutions offer unparalleled opportunities for personal and professional growth, offering a rich tapestry of diversity, and global exposure.

Here, you'll gain firsthand insights into how international organizations function. You'll gain access to cutting-edge information, connect with brilliant peers, and work alongside with seasoned professionals from various industries. But perhaps most importantly, you'll gain a clearer understanding of your own career aspirations.

Many university students struggle with uncertainty about their future, often feeling anxious about what lies ahead. An internship at such an organization is not just a resume booster—it's a unique chance to engage with the real world, test your interests, and refine your goals through hands-on experience.

Remember, university is the ideal time for experimentation because the cost of failure is relatively low. Embrace risks and apply for opportunities even if you're unsure of the outcome. International organizations, too, are not immune to mistakes—official meetings sometimes feature typos in their PowerPoint slides! So, why stress about perfection in every trial?

If you're even remotely interested in interning at an international organization, my advice is straightforward: go for it. Research thoroughly, prepare diligently, and apply with confidence. Even if you encounter setbacks, you'll learn and grow from the experience. After all, some of the best discoveries happen when you venture beyond your comfort zone.

So, take the first step today—your global adventure awaits!

3.3   Interview with Vojtech Hledik[1]

So, you want to work for the United Nations—great! That decision was the easy part. The UN is a massive organization and the opportunities for working at the UN are incredibly diverse. To kick things off, we spoke with Vojtech Hledik, the UN Volunteer Programme Officer in Ukraine. In this interview, he gives us a closer look at the UN Volunteer Programme and shares his advice for those considering a UN career.

Nicole Winchell: *Tell us about yourself.*

Vojtech Hledik: When I was five years old, I wanted to be the Pope. Later on, a doctor. In high school I was almost sure I would be a biologist but then I got involved in Model UN, and various organizations promoting European integration, which shifted my interest towards politics.

I studied international politics and European studies at the University of Economics in Prague. During my studies I worked for a youth organization, was active in a small political party, and worked for the Czech government in the area of EU affairs.

One day a friend of mine sent me a link that the Czech Republic funds several UN Volunteer assignments a year. I always wanted to work for the UN so I applied and was accepted. I worked for a year for UNAIDS in Uzbekistan in the area of advocacy and communication. Then I became the UNV Programme Officer (country level representative of UNV) in Uzbekistan, and after two years I moved to Ukraine.

---

1   The interview below is from: Nicole Winchell, "A Day in the Job of a United Nations Volunteer Programme Officer", *tbd* Newsletter*, January 20th, 2018.

Nicole Winchell: *The UN is a massive organization, and the UN Volunteer Programme is one opportunity within the UN system. Can you break down your department/its mission, as well as your specific role as a UN Volunteer?*

Vojtech Hledik: Massive indeed. UN Volunteers programme is administered by United Nations Development Programme (UNDP) but UN Volunteers work across the whole UN system. To illustrate, in 2015, UNV deployed 6,796 UN Volunteers to 122 countries. Largest number of UN Volunteers was hosted by UNDPKO (UN Peacekeeping Operations), UNDPA (UN Department of Political Affairs), second place belongs to UNDP, third to UNHCR (UN Refugee Agency).[1] Overall UN Volunteers were deployed to 38 different UN entities.

The professional backgrounds of UN Volunteers are equally diverse ranging from doctors, midwives, human rights officers, and vehicle mechanics to social media specialists, election observers or lawyers, there are more than 100 job profiles we look for. In 1970, UNV was primarily created to deploy volunteers within the UN System. That is still our main role, but since then our mandate has expanded to promote volunteerism for peace and development. We also have our own programme initiatives and priority areas: basic social services, peace-building, disaster risk reduction, youth and volunteer infrastructure. Our mandate is therefore very relevant to the new global agenda—*The Sustainable Development Goals*. The UNV HQ is in Bonn, Germany.

I am the UNV Programme Officer. I coordinate the UNV programme in Ukraine while still being a UN Volunteer myself. I am responsible for administering and supporting the serving UN Volunteers, hiring new ones, representing the programme in the country, building partnerships with the host government, civil society, other UN agencies and international organizations.

Nicole Winchell: *How is being a UN Volunteer different from being an intern or JPO at the UN?*

Vojtech Hledik: Inclusiveness. I would say that being a UNV is the most accessible

---

1　The United Nations Volunteers (UNV) programme contributes to peace and development through volunteerism worldwide. UNV is administered by the United Nations Development Programme (UNDP) and reports to the UNDP/ UNFPA/UNOPS Executive Board. In 2020, UNV has around 150 staff members at headquarters, and over 9400 volunteers deployed in the field. More information is available at: the website of the UN Volunteers, "Home/About UNV/Who we are", accessed on June 13th, 2022.

option for everyone. Internships are for those who can afford to live in sometimes quite expensive UN HQ locations, and are by default short term and seen as something to kick start your career.

JPOs are sponsored by UN member states so it is opened to you only if you are a citizen of a country that provides that. They are also designed as a first step in a UN career.

UNV positions are open to everyone (there are also assignments funded by some member states though but that is a small portion in the overall total number). UN Volunteers receive a living allowance so they can cover their expenses while serving so it doesn't matter from where you come. We don't care if you are rich or poor, we are interested in your skills.

UNV was initially designed for professionals in their respective fields who wanted to contribute using their skills to the work of United Nations by dedicating a couple of months or years to this service. It is not meant to be a gateway in to the UN. However, recently UNV launched a Youth UN Volunteer modality for young people from the ages of 18 to 29 who do not have significant work experience in order to open the organization to more young people to contribute and have their voices heard. Inclusiveness is our key principle.

The fact that some people stay with the UN after their assignment is proof that UN Volunteers are high quality professionals.

Nicole Winchell: *What does a "normal" day at work look like for you?*

Vojtech Hledik: It is more of a desk job than people might imagine. Most of the time is filled with writing emails, drafting reports and concept notes, and sitting in meetings pretending to look smart. There is also a lot of stuff to read. I wish I had the time and capacity to read everything I receive or find. In this information age there is too much exciting and important information, so, prioritizing and continuous learning is a big part of the job.

My favorite activity is meeting young and motivated people from various civil society organizations. Sometimes I get invited to speak at an event because those who invite me to presume, I will say something wise or give valuable advice, so I try not to disappoint them. Also, meeting government officials who want to promote volunteerism values in their country is very rewarding. In Ukraine, I have met quite a few.

The most important part of my job is to make sure that the serving UN Volunteers in my country are well supported and have proper conditions to do their job. The hardest part of my work is persuading the other UN agencies that they need much more UN Volunteers in their offices.

Nicole Winchell: *You and your UN Volunteer colleagues all have very diverse backgrounds—are there any common traits that unite you?*

Vojtech Hledik: That is the best part about UNV. We all work in different agencies, but we have in common the fact that we are UN Volunteers. There is always someone to support you, and you have a broader view of the UN's work in the country thanks to this "second hat" of a UNV. UN agencies are very autonomous entities and sometimes people get so consumed with their agency's particular work that they don't have the time to follow what others are doing.

Also, we all joined the UN because we wanted to work for a good cause and see the huge value of volunteerism.[1] We don't do it for money or prestige.

Nicole Winchell: *What three pieces of advice would you give to people considering a similar career path?*

Vojtech Hledik: As a first step I would go to UNV website and read all of the necessary qualifications and information about what we do and who we are hiring and what skills we need. For international assignments UNV uses a roster of candidates. Those interested can go to create their profile there. National UNV positions are advertised on the local UN websites. Make sure you have experience in or knowledge of a field we are looking for. Motivation is a big part of UNV assignments, but it is not enough. UN agencies are looking for skilled professionals. Previous volunteer experience is also a big plus.

Knowledge of languages is very important. English is a minimum, French and Spanish are a must for working in some regions, and knowing Arabic or Russian is a

---

1　Volunteerism is an opportunity for everyone, including marginalized groups, women, and youth, to have their voice heard and their actions recognized. UNV recognizes the shard universal values underpinning volunteerism—free will, commitment, equity, engagement, solidarity, compassion, empathy and respect for others. Source from: the website of UN Volunteers, "Home/Added value of UNV, UN Volunteers and volunteerism/What is volunteerism", accessed on June 8th, 2022.

great advantage. Interested people need to be prepared to serve in often challenging environments. By the way, we are now establishing a UNV Programme Officer Pool. Anyone who fits the criteria can apply. Detailed information is on the website under Special Recruitment.

Nicole Winchell: *Where do you see yourself in five years' time?*

Vojtech Hledik: A question hated by everyone. I hope I will be fortunate enough to still be working for the United Nations. Despite its many shortcomings, the UN is a crucial place for dialogue among nations, an organization giving voice to the voiceless, protecting the most vulnerable, raising issues that some would like to see to be ignored.

Nicole Winchell: *What makes you stay determined?*

Vojtech Hledik: I think that first of all, the work changed me. I see firsthand that complex issues have no simple and fast solutions. I see that some things are very different from what one might think sitting in his comfortable living room watching TV. I see that people from various countries can come together to fight for values that we all declared to be universal. I try to be more empathetic, try to fight my prejudices, and always keep the initial humanitarian ideals that made me choose this work.

Changing just one life is worth it. Very often, not much is needed. Providing some simple diagnostic machine to a rural hospital can save a life. Sharing to someone about a good idea or learning opportunity might help a young student start a company or get into a university.

It was important for me to accept that the UN will not change or save the world alone. The change always has to come from within. We are there to help create conditions for change, perhaps to motivate and show the way but for it to happen there has to be the willingness in an individual person, community, nation or state.

█ Tasks

Activity 1 │ Intercultural Quiz

Have a discussion with your partner and define what cultural values are reflected in each of the following proverbs. You might further explain the similarities and/or differences that can be noted for the most part in Eastern and Western culture.

a. The squeaky wheel gets the grease. (America)

b. The cricket bat is mightier than the pen and the sword combined. (Australia)

c. Think three times. Act after. (China)

d. By living a life based on wisdom and truth, one can discover the divinity of the soul, its union to the universe, the supreme peace and contentment which comes from satisfying the inner drive for self-discovery. (Egypt)

e. Too many cooks spoil the broth. (England)

f. If you pick up one end of the stick, you also pick up the other. (Ethiopia)

g. A society grows great when old men plant trees whose shade they know they shall never sit in. (Greece)

h. The three great mysteries: air to a bird, water to a fish, humankind to himself. (India)

i. Not knowing is Buddha. (Japan)

j. Fine feathers make fine birds. (Korea)

k. When the roots of a tree begin to decay, it spreads death to the branches. (Nigeria)

l. When you look at an elephant, look at its tail. When you look at a girl, look at her mother. (Thailand)

Activity 2 | Team-Building Activity

Whether it's in person or remotely, communication is crucial to the survival of a team/group/organization. Without communication, nothing can be managed, reported, brainstormed, tracked, or improved.

Campfire Stories

- Description: A classic activity that inspires storytelling and improves team bonding. Teams gather in a circle and share their experiences. Along the way, they learn things about each other and relive old memories.

- Objective: Encourage participants to share, and establish common experiences.

- Duration: 10+ mins

- Number of Participants: 5-15

- How to Play:

    a. Create a set of trigger words that can kickstart a storytelling session. Think of words like "first day at the school", "work or part-time experience", "summer vacation", "extra-curricular project", etc. Add them to sticky notes;

b. Divide a whiteboard into two sections. Post all the sticky notes from above on one section of the whiteboard;

c. Ask a participant to pick out one trigger word from the sticky notes and use it to share an experience (say, about his/her first day at the school/group/ organization). Shift the chosen sticky note to the other side of the whiteboard;

d. As the participant is relating his/her experience, ask others to jot down words that remind them of similar work-related stories. Add these words to sticky notes and paste them on the whiteboard;

e. Repeat this process until you have a "wall of words" with interconnected stories.

● Strategy: Storytelling is at the heart of the community experience. It is also how information gets passed on informally. A storytelling session focused on work-related stories can get a large group to loosen up and share their experiences.

(Activity 3) Reading Comprehension [1]

The World of NGOs represents a tradition of pioneering spirit and innovative thought, of unselfish devotion and dogged perseverance, to raise social awareness and voice sincerely-felt concern. It is a tradition which, in the hectic of daily life, is perhaps not quite appreciated to the full. When reference is made to the Hague as an international center for peace and justice, quite naturally, it is the Courts and Tribunals and organizations like OPCW or Europol and Eurojust that first come to mind.

Less prominent and less generally known perhaps, inasmuch as they do not often capture the limelight on a daily basis, are the scores of organizations of widely-varying size, nature, structure and aims that make up an equally important segment of the city's endeavors. They are best called by their generic name of NGOs. They have often been launched against all odds, by inspired individuals—visionaries and idealists most of them—later on to be elaborated by hosts of dedicated followers.

In historic perspective these organizations have played a decisive role in the genesis of the Hague Tradition. Thus, little known today, the very initiative to the 1907 Conference—the paramount gathering to find the Hague-based International Judiciary—

---

1 Excerpts from: *Guide to International Organizations in the Hague*, initiated by the City of The Hague, April, 2000, p. 67.

was taken, not by any Government or from within official circles of diplomacy or law, but by the Inter-Parliamentary Union (IPU) and the American Peace Society in a joint effort in 1904 on the occasion of their meeting at the St. Louise World Fair.

As so often with humanitarian endeavors, it was private initiative that triggered public response, private concern that exacted governmental action—as was the case in 1904 with President Theodore Roosevelt. If Henry Dunant stood at the base of the ICRC, it was the beneficial exchange of views among the members of the Institute de driot international, an informal body of legal scholars, from which emanated the texts that were to be enshrined in the "Hague Conventions", which today pose as the just pride of our city.

Unaware perhaps, in the Hague we are living, on a daily basis, in the midst of a never-ending cavalcade of initiatives, at the heart of developing ideas, and of projects and networks under construction that will help mould a future world and the living conditions of our grandchildren. Their aspirations cover virtually all the essentially trans-boundary issue, from climate to environment, from education to the law, that keep our endangered planet enthralled, and trifle at meeting the many challenges posed by global society. The growing stream of NGOs that seek shelter in our city, from there to monitor the world, is a promising sign that, as the staunch advocates of L'Oeuvre de la Haye had aspired in 1907, the Hague is, also among these critical and discerning bodies, increasingly being seen as a Smithy of Society-in-the-Making.

◀ Questions

1. What did you find interesting in this passage? And why?

2. How do you think of the practice of NGOs is useful for the international community?

3. Are there any real-world experiences in your communities that reflect the effectiveness of NGOs to implement certain social actions?

Activity 4 | Quick-Quiz Questions

Do you love to learn about cultures? Do you often connect with people of different backgrounds? Assess your cross-cultural openness with this quiz.

1. How diverse is your social circle?

Do you have social relationships with people from different religions, cultures, ethnicities and/or sexual orientations?

A. No, I don't. I prefer to socialize with people I can relate to.

B. Sort of. I talk to people from different backgrounds in school-related situations, but I usually find it difficult to become good friends with them.

C. I have one or two friends from different backgrounds. I don't go out of my way to make friends with people who have different perspectives or beliefs.

D. Yes, my social circle reflects the diversity around me. I think a diverse group of friends can really enrich your life.

2. Are you curious about international issues?

Do you inform yourself about key issues in the international news?

A. Not really. I generally just pay attention to local news.

B. Sort of. I follow major international news stories that are reported on national stations.

C. Yes, I seek out any international news stories reported through sources in my home country. (Chinese sources: *China Daily*)

D. Yes, I follow the media and regularly consult Websites or publications from outside North America. (International sources: *The Economist*, *The Guardian Weekly*, *Al Jazeera*, etc.)

3. Are you an adventurous eater?

What would you do if a foreign student prepared you an elaborate, spicy meal with ingredients you'd never even heard of?

A. Yikes! I'd probably thank them but wouldn't try it. I don't like eating strange foods.

B. I'd be uneasy, but would try a few bites in order not to hurt her feelings. I'm sure I wouldn't really like it.

C. I would eat what the student made. Even if I didn't like it, I would try to think of it as a learning experience!

D. I would eat it, of course! If you don't try new things, you'll never know if you like them. Whether I liked it or not I'd be sure to ask about the ingredients and other food customs from the student's home country.

4. Could you share living space with an international student or host family abroad?

How would you adjust to living with an international student or local family while abroad?

   A. I don't think I would deal with it particularly well. My personal space is very important to me.

   B. It would be fine as long as we had some rules in place about personal space, kitchen usage and other parts of home life.

   C. I think I'd be good at compromising. It might even be interesting to see how other cultures do things at home.

   D. I'd love to live with someone from another background. What better way to learn about the intricacies of their culture and understand, for example, how others define the concepts of personal space?

5. What experience do you have of living abroad?

Have you been abroad to volunteer, intern, study, work or for cross-cultural travel?

   A. No, I have done none of the above.

   B. No, but I am considering going abroad to volunteer, intern, study, work or travel.

   C. Yes. I have spent time in another country for up to three months.

   D. Yes. I have spent time in another country for more than three months.

6. Can you travel independently?

How would you deal with traveling alone in a foreign country?

   A. I'd be very anxious, especially if I didn't speak the language. I'd rather stay home than go alone.

   B. I would be nervous. I'd want to plan all the details of my journey before leaving and would try to make sure local people show me around.

   C. I might find some parts of it challenging, but I think I could rise to the occasion if I pushed myself.

   D. Traveling alone is the best way to experience a foreign culture. I'd be confident and open to any unexpected opportunity that presented itself.

7. Can you travel in a way that is "street smart?"

If you were traveling alone in a foreign city, and weren't sure which areas were safe, what would you do?

   A. I'd probably just go wherever I wanted, no matter the time of day. Worrying about safety would ruin my trip.

B. I would go wherever I wanted, but I'd make sure I always knew my location and had a sense of my surroundings.

C. I would consult my guidebook to see if there were any areas to avoid and I'd steer clear of those areas. If I got lost, I'd approach local merchants for directions.

D. I'd talk to local people about safety before exploring the town. I'd try to make my dress and body language blend in to avoid drawing attention to myself and hire a guide if necessary.

8. Do you consider yourself to be self-aware?

If you were traveling in a foreign country where you got the impression that everyone was staring at you, what would you do?

A. I would get angry and make it clear that I didn't want to be looked at. Tourists should be allowed to go where they like without people making them feel uncomfortable.

B. I would leave the area fairly quickly. I don't like being looked at.

C. I would look to see what other people were doing and try to see whether I was in some way drawing attention to myself.

D. I would ask a local person to help me behave appropriately, and I'd have to accept that I might get attention simply because I'm a foreigner.

9. Are you resourceful in frustrating circumstances?

Imagine that you have twice submitted paperwork requesting an extension on your visa while interning abroad; now the government official says that you have to return with yet another document. What do you do?

A. I would storm out of the office. My time is too valuable to waste on bureaucratic procedures. I skip getting the visa extension and prepare to take my chances without it.

B. I would comment on how inefficient the place was and ask to speak to a supervisor.

C. My body language might show my disappointment, but I would comply with the request.

D. I would ask the official to write down what was needed and ask whether I could bring my documentation back to him directly. A personal touch might make the process run more smoothly!

10. Would you be respectful of other cultures' traditions abroad?

How would you feel in a country where you had to be very conscious of your clothing, gestures, etc.? (For example, in a country where traditional, modest dress is the custom.)

A. I would feel anxious. I'd only change how I dress and behave if I was forced to.

B. I would feel a little uncomfortable, but I could tolerate it, especially if it was only for a short period.

C. I might not feel like myself in the beginning, but I'd be aware that showing respect would help me become integrated into my host culture.

D. I understand the importance of being respectful and culturally sensitive about my appearance and gestures. I'd learn how to recognize my host country's cultural cues as quickly as I could and enjoy adapting to them as necessary.

Activity 5 Extended Reading [1]

What is the overview of what an ambassador to the UN does?

It's not just turning up there and reading out statements like, "We won't give an inch." If that were the case, we shouldn't be there to begin with. The whole thing is, you state your position and then try to find common ground. And you need a team of people to chaperone all of that. That's the basics of the job, essentially.

And out of it you have two primary organs: the General Assembly that produces resolutions that carry the weight of a recommendation and contribute to norm setting, and the Security Council, which produces binding law. What the Security Council decides in resolutions is law. But out of the General Assembly, you can also have law in the form of treaties being negotiated there, which subsequently become binding law. In sum, the decisions themselves may be recommendations, but the General Assembly is also the nursery for international law.

What you find yourself doing as a head of a diplomatic mission is both pursuing what you're paid to do and volunteering for extra duties—such as chairing conferences and meetings, facilitating discussions. The permanent members of the Security Council, U.S.,

---

1 Excerpt from: Zeid Ra'ad Al Hussein, "The Role of UN Ambassador, Explained: Political Science, International Relations, Perry World House, Q&A", *Penn Today*, July 11th, 2019.

China, UK, France, and Russia, normally don't do the volunteering because the work of the U.N. Security Council is so overwhelming that they spend most of their time there.

And in the case of the U.S., only in two other broad areas within the spectra of U.N. work do the U.S. ambassadors venture out of the U.N. Security Council. One of those is on candidatures—if the U.S. has a candidate running for the International Court of Justice, for example, you might find the U.S. ambassador is lobbying. Or, if there is a country the U.S. doesn't want to have as a candidate or member of the Security Council—for instance, Sudan many years ago, when the U.S. lobbied to have Sudan off the Council and did so successfully.

And the other area where the U.S. ambassador ventures out is on U.N. reform. If there's a series of reform initiatives, the U.S. ambassador is often willing to come out of that Security Council and deal with those issues. Basically, most of the work of the U.S. ambassador is within the U.N. Security Council. That's where they spend most of their time.

Acknowledgment

Compiling a book is harder than I thought, but also more fulfilling than I could have ever imagined. There were many people engaged in the process of turning this book from a concept in my head into a manuscript, and they all deserve to be acknowledged and thanked.

First and foremost, I want to thank my darling pals for their support and encouragement, which got me through the many writing stages. My special thanks go to Miss Bi Fei, Mr. Christopher Crachiola, Miss Liu Yi, Miss Xu Zhengxue, Miss Wang Ling, and Mr. Zhao Yao, six outstanding professionals in their respective industries, who graciously agreed to share their firsthand knowledge gained through working for international organizations. To Chen Jiadai, Li Boya, Ni Congcong, Ouyang Ruize, Qi Jiayu, Zhang Lei, and Zhang Zhiqi, for their willingness to assist me in locating sources of background information. Equally deserving of praise are Duan Jialiang, Wang Wei, Yang Xue, and Zhang Ranyan, who made suggestions on how to improve the book's overall quality while proofreading different sections of it.

I'd also like to thank all my mentors and instructors over the years. To the teachers at SISU (Sichuan International Studies University), whose guidance helped shape me into the person I am today and was driving force behind my decision to pursue an academic career. My heartfelt gratitude goes to Prof. Song Guohua, Dean of the School of International Relations (SIR), who provided me with much needed advice and the most valuable counsel during my time there. To my thesis advisors and career coaches from UPEACE (United Nations-mandated University for Peace), who taught me a lot and instilled in me sharper insights into the realities of international affairs. Prof. Mihir Kanade, Coordinator of Academics at UPEACE, in particular, has been a fantastic teacher and true inspiration to me. I developed a keen interest in globalization, human rights, and development as a result of him.

And I'm forever indebted to my publishing team for their editing assistance, astute judgment, and unwavering support in bringing this book to fruition. This book has significantly improved over its previous iterations thanks to their expert feedback and the extensive work they put into the editing process.

Last but not least, I wish to extend my sincere greetings, gratitude and love to many others whom I am not able to acknowledge. Thank you for making this book possible.